C000193697

The Cockermouth, Keswick & Penrith Railway

by
Robert Western

THE OAKWOOD PRESS

© Oakwood Press & Robert Western 2007

First Edition 2001
Revised Edition 2007

British Library Cataloguing in Publication Data
A Record for this book is available from the British Library
ISBN 978 0 85361 564 4

Typeset by Oakwood Graphics.
Repro by PKmediaworks, Cranborne, Dorset.
Printed by Cambrian Printers, Aberystwyth, Ceredigion.

All rights reserved. No part of this book may be reproduced or transmitted in any form or by any means, electronic or mechanical, including photocopying, recording or by any information storage and retrieval system, without permission from the Publisher in writing.

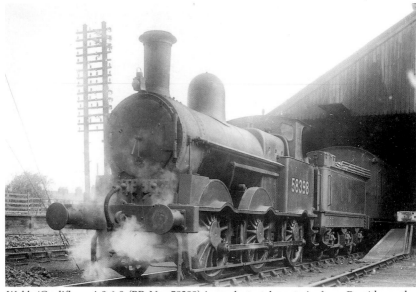

Webb 'Cauliflower' 0-6-0 (BR No. 58398) is ready to take a train from Penrith on the CK&PR in the late 1940s.   *R.S. Carpenter*

Title page: Freight and passenger trains at Keswick. Both are hauled by 'Cauliflowers', the mainstay as far as motive power was concerned.
P. Ransome Wallis/National Railway Museum

Published by The Oakwood Press (Usk), P.O. Box 13, Usk, Mon., NP15 1YS.
E-mail: sales@oakwoodpress.co.uk
Website: www.oakwoodpress.co.uk

Contents

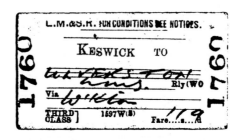

Preface

An Awakening

'Now it is high time to awake out of sleep . . . [Romans. 13 v. 11]

In *The Times* of 26th August, 1998 there was a news item headed 'Ministers pledge cash for revival of rail links'. Prominent against the text is a large photograph of Bassenthwaite Lake station, taken in 1959. Holidaymakers and local people are alighting from the two-coach diesel multiple unit which is standing at the platform. The train has 'Penrith' clearly visible on the destination board and the people in the photograph look happy. The station is well cared for with hedges neatly trimmed and flowers in the boarders. The hills, so impressive, make a superb back-drop to the scene. It is idyllic. Yet all is not well even though the people in the picture are smiling, possibly for the camera. The guard seems to look rather more concerned than happy; the railway system in this part of the country was coming under close scrutiny and, ultimately, a threat. In only a little more than a decade after the photograph was taken, the line would be closed.

In the accompanying article, Fraser Nelson, the writer, informed his readers about the recent moves by the Government to give the green light to a string of railway construction projects. Railtrack, it is reported, would be supporting proposals that it considered were strong, commercially viable, cases. These included a connection from Penrith to Keswick, in the Lake District. It is probably true to say that at that point in time only a small number of people even in their wildest dreams would have countenanced such a possibility. The Cockermouth Keswick & Penrith Railway (CK&PR) had been assigned to history. The story had ended. Nevertheless, the final decade of the 20th century witnessed a significant change in attitudes and it seemed, as a result, the railway may not have been lost for ever. However, Railtrack is no more and there seems to have been little movement in official circles to follow up the prospects of regeneration. Even so, there are those who have clung on to that hope of revival and still actively pursue not the establishment of a heritage line but a commercially viable working railway. In addition, further east, there is a group working to open a section of the former Eden Valley Railway (EVR). The track is still in place between Appleby and Warcop and already it is possible to run trains down a short section from Warcop. As well as these, a group based at Kirkby Stephen East station is developing the site in order to set up a railway heritage centre and also extend the EVR westwards. The overall scheme is ambitious, with the dream that one day the River Eden will once again be bridged near Musgrave and the EVR re-opened from Appleby down to Kirkby Stephen.

The CK&PR and the EVR were closely linked.

The change in attitude which has given rise to much of this thinking stems from money that is now available in the form of regeneration grants; money that was not there before. All may not be lost...........

5

'The Lakes Express' with '2MT' No. 46432 in charge is seen in the vicinity of Keswick.
E. Wilmshurst

The attractive station frontage of Keswick station in the Summer of 1999.   *Author*

Chapter One

East is East and West is West

'Opportunism', like so many other 'isms' of the late 20th century is a new word. The practice, however, is not. Opportunism, often seen in an unfavourable light, need not be something *infra dig*. It can reflect the imagination of an individual or individuals in recognising further potential in a particular situation, coupled with the vision to develop it in a way which results in benefit, albeit, usually, of a financial nature.

It appears Edward Waugh may well have been such an opportunist. As a Director of the Cockermouth and Workington Railway (C&WR), he had no doubt watched closely the developing situation in railway circles in the North East and the North West of England and taken careful stock of it.

In 1835, the Newcastle and Carlisle Railway had opened a line which would provide a link to bring coal from the North East over to Cumberland via the Maryport and Carlisle Railway (M&CR). The coalfields of South Durham, however, were not adequately served for the movement of coal from that region to the blast furnaces of West Cumberland.

The Darlington and Barnard Castle Railway opened in June 1856 and then a major step, or, perhaps more accurately, a leap, followed. The Pennines were crossed over Stainmore. There had been a number of proposals over a period of years involving two groups of people. In the East there was a group referred to as the Durham Party (or, sometimes, East County Group) and in the West, the Appleby Group (or Eden Valley Group). There had been much disagreement over schemes and the original plan which came from the Appleby Group to build a railway from just south of Penrith through Appleby, down to Kirkby Stephen and across to Barnard Castle foundered. The eventual outcome was a line from Barnard Castle to Tebay, where it joined the Lancaster and Carlisle Railway (L&CR), with what was, in effect, a branch line from Kirkby Stephen to a south-facing junction also on the Lancaster and Carlisle, just south of Penrith.

The Appleby Party had, to a large extent, been motivated by the desire (and, indeed, urgency) to maintain the importance of Appleby as the county town of Westmorland and so the members seemed little inclined, when the scheme was first mooted, to look beyond Penrith to any other possibilities there might be as far as through traffic was concerned. In any case, in the event, there was the Tebay connection and also the L&CR had insisted that the junction of the EVR with its line should be south facing only. There must be no challenges to the Scottish route by the inclusion of a north-facing junction. A repetition of what was happening at Lowgill, just to the South, could not be countenanced.

The Act for the South Durham and Lancashire Union Railway (SD&LUR), which would link the North East and, as the title suggests, South Durham in particular, to Tebay and beyond, is dated July 1857. Shortly afterwards, in May 1858, came an Act for the Eden Valley Railway.

The Engineer for both was Thomas Bouch (whose name will probably always be remembered in connection with the first Tay Bridge) and construction was put in hand. By 1860 the work was progressing well and in spite of problems with the weather, Bouch insisted the construction work was on schedule.

A cursory glance at the map was the only thing needed to realise that there was a gap in the scheme of things. The Workington to Cockermouth Railway had opened in 1847. In spite of the L&CR insistence on a south-facing junction for the EVR, there was potential for another line; a line which would connect Cockermouth to close proximity with the western end of the EVR; say Penrith.

It seems Edward Waugh had not only looked at the map but had decided to act on what he saw. He spoke with a group of friends who soon came to share his view and enthusiasm. A railway linking Cockermouth to Penrith, if built, seemed to offer the prospect of a good source of revenue and the opportunity should be seized.

Waugh carried out some preliminary negotiations and then put pen to paper to arrange a meeting. He sent out invitations to a number of people whom he felt could be influential and, further, let it be known there would be a meeting in the County Court Room in Keswick on 28th September (1860) to discuss the scheme.

Action had also been taken in other quarters. On 13th August, 1859 William Fletcher had written to Lord Lonsdale. It was felt important to enlist the support of such worthies as he, in order to give a scheme of this sort, credibility. The letter began

My Lord,
I think it is due to the interest you take in the things of Cumberland that you should have early information that the scheme for making a line from Cockermouth to Penrith via Keswick has been lately received. For some reason which I am sure your Lordship will not consider important I and others connected with the project feel very certain it will receive your co-operation . . .

He goes on to explain the Stockton & Darlington Railway (S&DR) objectives in wanting to have a direct railway to West Cumberland and the scheme for the South Durham & Lancashire Union Railway which had already been planned, together with the EVR. Fletcher expressed the view, shared by others, that the projected line to Cockermouth would be better under the control of West Cumberland shareholders rather than the S&DR . . . [unfortunately the last page of the letter is missing]. Lord Lonsdale's reply to this letter does not appear to have survived but it is not unreasonable to assume he supported the scheme in principle, even though he does not feature subsequently in the story. Such support can be deduced from a letter he wrote some 16 years previously. In 1843 Lonsdale received a letter from Lord Brougham (written on 4th February) about the projected Westmorland Railway. Brougham was always ill at ease with railway schemes (it was a remarkable achievement to get him to cut the first sod of the EVR) and in the letter he vowed to stand against it in order to defeat it. He had no time for those involved in the building of railways ('surveyors, navvies and the like') and went so far as to describe those who promoted such schemes as 'money robbers'. In his reply, Lonsdale pointed out that whilst he had no interest in the Westmorland Railway, 'I do not like to check the activity and enterprise of others who are quite satisfied that it would be a great benefit. If, however, there be any "foul deception" [Brougham's words] going on, let it be exposed by all means. If people concerned in the undertaking proceed honestly I do not like to interfere with them'.

William Fletcher wrote a further letter to Lord Lonsdale on 25th August. He apologises for not replying sooner to the letter he had received from his Lordship. Clearly there had been a request for further information and Fletcher pointed out that   Mr Harris of Darlington has just completed a preliminary survey of the route. Harris had suggested a cost of not more that £8,000 per mile and offered to get a 'capable and reliable contractor' who would do everything including acquiring the land. Fletcher is of the view that if the passengers were half those of the Windermere to Kendal line there would be a fair level of interest, taking into account the coal traffic as well. He also envisaged a large through traffic of Durham coke (something like 100,000 tons per annum). He discussed the possibility of other routes but remains convinced that the route they are planning is the best. Once again he emphasised the importance of local control (underlining this in the letter) and he went on to 'warn' that the Secretary of the S&DR had recently been sent into Cumberland to seek the support for a line from Clifton to Cockermouth to be made independently of the L&CR. He suggested such a scheme would be prejudicial to Lonsdale's interests in West Cumberland.

In spite of this, it would seem Lord Lonsdale did not become an active participant in the scheme - and Mr Harris was not heard of again, either!

'An Important Meeting'

By all accounts Waugh did an excellent job in arranging the meeting. A large number of people turned up at the County Court Room on 28th September. Included amongst those invited was Henry Howard of Greystoke Castle. H.C. Marshall was elected chairman of the meeting and others present   included Thomas Bouch and W.B.Gordon, the manager of the Cumberland Union Bank.

Not surprisingly, Waugh was called upon by the chairman to outline the objectives and give some details of the proposed railway. He was well received by 'an enthusiastic and crowded meeting'.

Waugh was quick to affirm that the key purpose of the railway would be to unite the railways of West Cumberland with the Eden Valley and the South Durham and Lancashire Union Railways. He pointed out that the proposed line would offer the shortest rail route between Durham and the iron furnaces of West Cumberland and, conversely, between the areas producing hematite ore in West Cumberland and the furnaces of Middlesborough and Durham. He reckoned that 130,000 tons of coke would be needed by the furnaces and argued that much of it would be brought over the line. To emphasise his points further, he listed the distances saved which would result if the line was built. These ranged from between 10 miles for Cockermouth and Lancaster, Liverpool and London to 30 miles for the blast furnaces at Norton and Stockton and the Whitehaven hematite ore mines. In his view it was the mineral traffic which would provide the main revenue but the advantages of having the line would not stop there. A considerable amount of additional revenue would be generated by the carriage of passengers to Keswick in the summer season. This observation was greeted by a round of applause. As to the cost of the line, Waugh quoted Thomas Bouch. The estimate was £186,000 and such an amount, in Waugh's opinion, was a small outlay for a line that could well yield 5¾ per cent. He then made a comparison with other railways. The Maryport and Carlisle at the time was making £42 per mile per week, the Whitehaven Junction £51, the Kendal and Windermere £24. The projected line, Waugh maintained, could easily realise £15 per mile per week and this 'modest figure would give rise to a dividend of 5¼ per cent'. There was applause, again, and those present became more and more enthusiastic when he announced with, we are told, great vigour, 'This line would, without doubt be successful and produce a reasonable return for the investors'. At this point Waugh sat down but he had clearly won over most of those present. Hopes were expressed that the Cockermouth and Workington would provide some capital because, it was noted, 'they have great interest in the project'.

Thomas Bouch then addressed the meeting and outlined the route of the railway. Bouch had been acclaimed in other quarters as a man who could plan and build good railways at comparatively low costs and in speaking he was at pains to point out how little the cost could be. 'The secret', he explained, 'is that railways with a large traffic, notwithstanding their great returns, had in the first instances incurred such heavy outlay and expenses that nearly the whole of what they realised was absorbed by their liabilities before any of it found its way into the pockets of shareholders but I have not the slightest doubt that this line can be made for less than £200,000'.

He went on to explain that his plan involved a single line and the cost of doubling it was estimated at about one-third more. Great applause followed when he finished with the words 'If the traffic were so great as to necessitate its being doubled, it would be one of the best paying lines in the Kingdom'. Bouch's scheme included a short tunnel to the east of Keswick which was perhaps not surprising given the terrain but another feature which was rather unusual was an aqueduct. This would carry Combs Beck over the line at Thornthwaite, just to the west of Keswick.

Other speakers made contributions, all speaking in favour of building the line. The view that coal, flour and meat might well be cheaper in Keswick if the line was built, seemed to carry a lot of weight. When the various contributors had had their say, the following resolution was passed. 'This meeting pledges itself to support the formation of a line between Cockermouth, Keswick and Penrith as being conducive to the landlords, tradesmen and inhabitants of the district and of the County generally'. Mr J. Fisher, of Crosthwaite, proposed R.D. Marshall, John Steel MP, Isaac Fletcher, John Harris, Isaac Gray Bass, William Fletcher, Arthur Dover, John Crozier, W.B.Gordon, Isaac Gate, J. Teather, Peter Crosthwaite, Joseph Todd, J.P. Crosthwaite, M. Cockbain, Jonathan Frank, S. Ladyman, I. Lowthian and E.Poole should be made provisional Directors. This was seconded by Edward Waugh and carried unanimously. This number was, however, later reduced to 15 and with other names appearing.

In drawing the meeting to a close, Henry Howard thanked the chairman and expressed the view that 'Mr Bouch's survey was more satisfactory that the one of 1846 because it was more economical and direct'. Howard then assured the scheme of his support stating that the line would be a great asset. As a landowner he was ready to buy shares.

Edward Waugh must have felt very pleased with what he had achieved. It seems rather strange that at this stage he was not made a provisional Director.

The 1846 and Earlier Schemes

The proposal of 1846 referred to by Henry Howard involved a plan to build a railway from Cockermouth to Keswick, linked to the Cockermouth and Workington Railway. The list of the first Directors included John Gandy, James Gandy and John Wilson Fletcher. The Bill for the line received the Royal Assent on 3rd August, 1846 [Act : 9th & 10th Vict., cap. cccxlii]. It is entitled 'An Act for making a Railway from the Borough of Cockermouth to the town of Keswick, all in the County of Cumberland, to be called "The Cockermouth and Workington Extension Railway"'. The route took it to the towns or through the parishes of Papcastle, Brigham, Bridekirk, Dovenby, Hames Hill, Setmurthly, Isell, Isell Old Park, Bassenthwaite, Underskiddaw, Crosthwaite and Keswick. The estimated cost was £195,000; the capital of the company to be £200,000. It was intended to issue 10,000 shares of £20 each. Completion time was put at five years. This scheme may well have been planned with a view to a through route but it was promoted on the strength of being 'of great public Advantage, by opening an additional, certain and expeditious Means of Communication between the said places . . .' The scheme was abandoned because there was insufficient support; a number of influential landowners taking exception to a route which went on the east side of Bassenthwaite Lake.

This scheme seems to be the culmination of others, each in its own way destined to become archive fodder. On 21st April, 1845 John Dixon, from Darlington, presented a report to John Steel of Cockermouth on the possibility of building a line commencing at Cockermouth and ending at Bowness to make a junction with what was hoped would be an extension of the Windermere branch. It was referred to as 'The Cockermouth and Keswick &c &c Railway'. The route took it to Keswick, approaching the town along the eastern side of Bassenthwaite and then after Keswick followed the Vale of Naddle by Thirlmere to Wythburn. It was from here that Dixon faced a dilemma. The terrain becomes extremely difficult. He pointed out that there was no locomotive powerful enough to tackle the sort of gradients which would be necessary. Some form of assistance might be possible with a cable on an incline but the obvious alternative was to make a tunnel. This would prove to be very costly, given the hard nature of the rock but was not out of the question. The total cost of construction was put at £548,000 with 29 miles costing £12,000 per mile, three miles of tunnel, £180,000 and engines, waggons, stations and other items, £20,000. No doubt John Steel was rather taken aback at the price. During 1845, also, applications were invited to buy shares in the East and West Cumberland Railway (E&WCR) and certainly by 4th November a number of

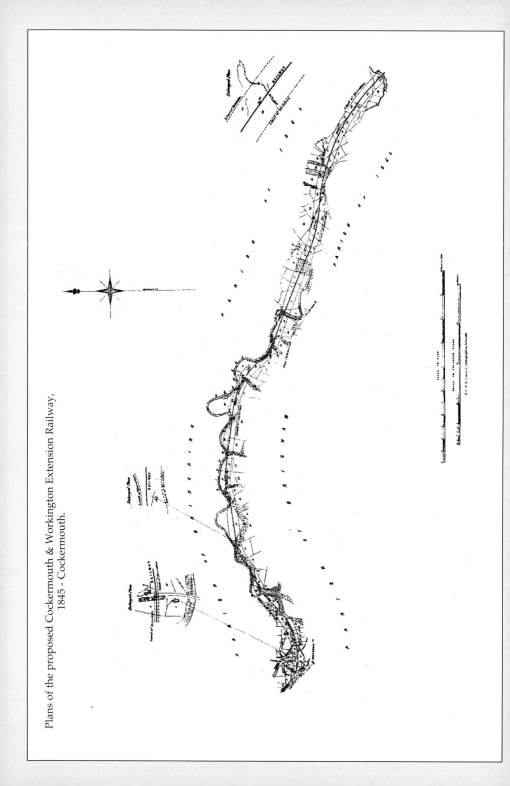

Plans of the proposed Cockermouth & Workington Extension Railway, 1845 - Cockermouth.

ANNO NONO & DECIMO

VICTORIÆ REGINÆ.

***,

Cap.cccxlii.

An Act for making a Railway from the Borough of *Cockermouth* to the Town of *Keswick*, all in the County of *Cumberland*, to be called "The *Cockermouth and Workington Extension* Railway."

[3d *August* 1846.]

WHEREAS the making of a Railway from the Borough of *Cockermouth* to the Town of *Keswick* in the County *Cumberland* would be of great public Advantage, by opening an additional, certain, and expeditious Means of Communication between the said Places, and also by facilitating Communication between more distant Towns and Places: And whereas the Persons hereafter named are willing, at their own Expence, to carry such Undertaking into execution, but the same cannot be effected without the Authority of Parliament: May it therefore please Your Majesty that it may be enacted; and be it enacted by the Queen's most Excellent Majesty, by and with the Advice and Consent of the Lords Spiritual and Temporal, and Commons, in this present Parliament assembled, and by the Authority of the same, That the several Acts of Parliament following, (that is to say,) the Companies Clauses Consolidation Act, 1845, the Lands Clauses Consolidation Act, 1845, and the

8 & 9 Vict. cc. 16. 18. and 20. incorporated with this Act.

[*Local.*]   68 *N*

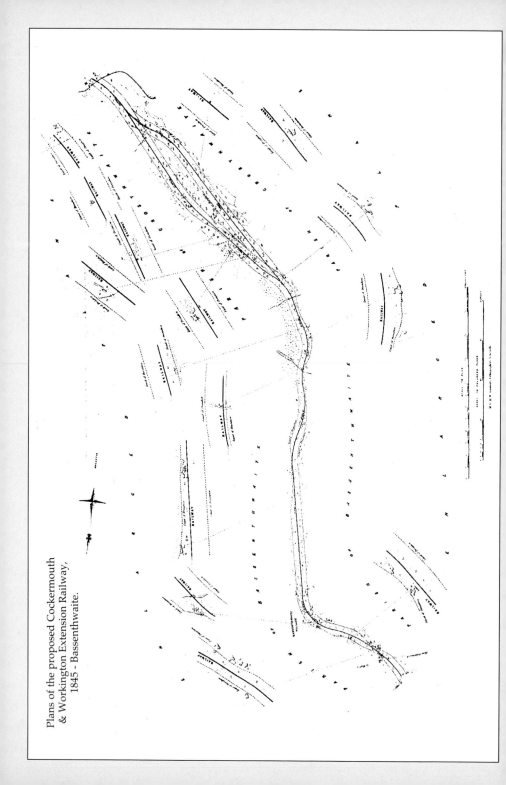

Plans of the proposed Cockermouth & Workington Extension Railway, 1845 - Bassenthwaite.

£20 shares had been sold. The E&WCR would go from Penrith to Keswick and progress seems to have been made in the planning stages. On 1st December, Lonsdale received a notice informing him that an application would be made for an Act of Parliament to build this railway and asking whether he would assent or dissent to the proposal. In the event, the line was not built. With all this in the past, it was up to Edward Waugh!

The Prospectus (1860)

It would seem that even by the time of the meeting held on 28th September a Prospectus was virtually ready and was issued shortly afterwards. It is in the form of a letter, approximating to folded A4 size. The typeface is Splendid in style and at times proves difficult to read. The text is as follows:

Cockermouth
September 1860

The formation of a Railway from Cockermouth to Keswick and Penrith has long been a desideratum and with a view to its accomplishment Mr Thomas Bouch the Engineer for the Eden Valley and other Lines has made a sectional survey which not only demonstrates the practicality of the scheme but his estimate of the cost of construction (under £200,000) offers a fair prospect to shareholders of a remunerative Dividend.

The Line will complete the communication between the Iron Ore Districts and Blast Furnaces of Cumberland and the Iron and Coke Districts of the Middlesboro' and South Durham, materially lessening the Railway transit to and from these places an advantage of the greatest importance in the carriage of heavy materials such as Coke and Iron Ore. Sixteen Iron Blast Furnaces constructed and constructing will consume 140,000 tons of South Durham Coke per annum and upon a low estimate it may be assumed that the proposed Line will secure one half of that traffic besides the return traffic of West Cumberland red ore to the Middlesboro' District where 80 furnaces are constructed. Direct communication will also be established with the centre of the Lake District from various points at both ends of the proposed Line which cannot fail to develop a profitable traffic.

The weekly average of railway receipts shows that £30 per Week per Mile is a moderate return but if the proposed Line yields only £15 per Week per Mile (an exceedingly low estimate) a dividend of 5 per cent per annum would be received on the estimated cost after allowing Fifty per cent of the gross revenue for working expenses. A gross return of £20 per Mile per Week would yield a Dividend of at least 7 per cent on the estimated capital and we are assured by the Engineer that such an Estimate has been most carefully ascertained, and though low, as compared with the cost of construction some years ago, it should be remembered that the principles of construction are now better understood, heavy cuttings and embankments are avoided, steeper gradients admitted and the cost of Rails which was formerly £12 to £14 per ton is now £6 per ton.

An income of one third of the present Receipts of the Maryport and Carlisle Railway or less than one half of the Mileage receipts of the Cockermouth and Workington Railway would, on the estimated cost, secure a Dividend of 5 per cent and with the Lancaster and Carlisle Railway Company divide [*sic*] 9 per cent, the Maryport and Carlisle 6½, the Whitehaven Junction 8, the Cleator and Egremont 10 and the Cockermouth and Workington 5 per cent upon an excessive mileage cost of

Plans of the proposed Cockermouth, Keswick & Penrith Railway, 1860 - Cockermouth.

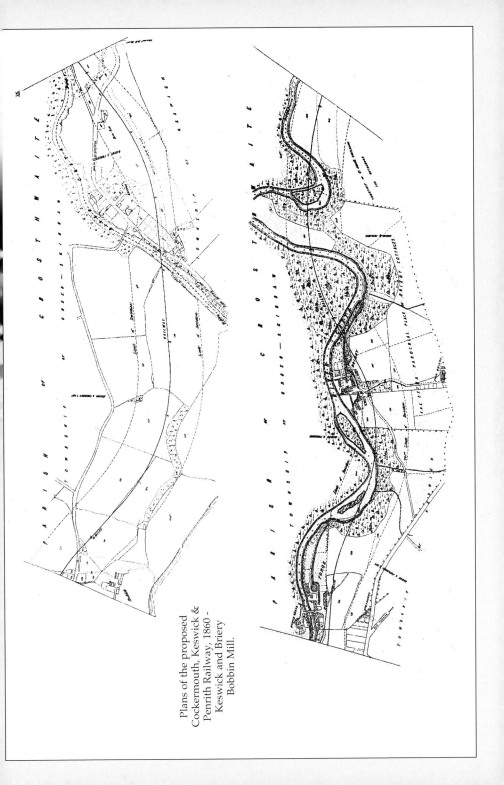

Plans of the proposed Cockermouth, Keswick & Penrith Railway, 1860 - Keswick and Briery Bobbin Mill.

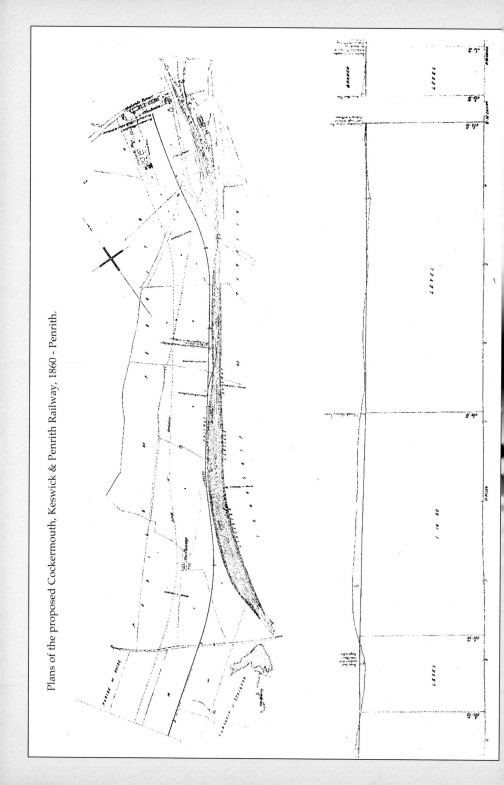

Plans of the proposed Cockermouth, Keswick & Penrith Railway, 1860 - Penrith.

construction, the Scheme, as an Investment deserves the attention of the Public independently of the benefits which will certainly result to the Landowners and Inhabitants of the District as well as the tradesmen of the Towns of Keswick, Cockermouth and Penrith.

It is proposed to raise the capital by 10,000 shares of £20 each.

We trust the Scheme will receive your support and beg to enclose a form of application for Shares which we shall be glad to receive after inserting the number of shares you propose to subscribe for.

No deposit for preliminary expenses is required but if subscriptions be received for a sufficient number of shares a deposit of £2 per share will be called for, previous to the application for an Act of Parliament.

    We are
      Your Obt Servants
        Steel, Waugh and Hartley

As plans moved ahead to present a Bill before Parliament, it is perhaps a little surprising that the scheme seemed to stir up virtually no local opposition or strong feelings. Although the route from Penrith to Keswick, in particular, passed through less striking terrain than other proposed schemes it would enter what many considered to be the heartland of the Lake District. As mentioned earlier, a previous scheme had met with some opposition and the initial proposal to build the branch line to Windermere and just beyond, in the previous decade, had been met with cries of alarm and horror from those who felt the tranquillity of the area would be lost as marauding bands of visitors whom, it was claimed, would not appreciate the amenities anyway, invaded the district. This time there seems to have been no poetic protestations; no metrical melancholy at the thought of what would happen if the proposal was realised. It has to be said, such feelings were far from dead, merely dormant, as the proposers of the Ambleside Railway and other schemes were to discover some 10 years later. Those who planned the CK&PR seemed to get off very lightly even though they openly advocated tourism (and therefore, presumably, 'marauding bands of visitors') in their plans from the out-set.

Yet why bring coal and coke over to West Cumberland at all, bearing in mind that by this time there were collieries in the area mining considerable quantities of it ? The need to import coal and particularly coke to this region arose from the type and quality of the West Cumberland coal. The Cumberland coal had a high phosphoric content and consequently much of it was unsuitable for producing the quality of coke required for use in the blast furnaces during the period when the Railway was planned. Later, in the early 20th century, when a coking process was found which did make such coal suitable, there was, inevitably, a detrimental affect on mineral traffic westwards. It has been suggested this factor was the prime reason why coke traffic westwards was virtually halved over a very short period of time.

For the moment, however, there was the prospect of trade and tourism. What better combination for ensuring a successful scheme?

PROSPECTUS OF THE

COCKERMOUTH, KESWICK, and PENRITH RAILWAY.

Capital £200,000, in 10,000 Shares of £20 each.

Length of Line, 31¼ Miles.

PROVISIONAL DIRECTORS.

Sir Henry Ralph Vane, Bart., of Hutton Hall, Penrith.
Reginald Dykes Marshall, Esq., of Leeds.
John Steel, Esq., M.P., of Derwent Bank, near Cockermouth.
Thomas Allison Hoskins, Esq., of Higham, near Cockermouth.
John Harris, Esq., of Greysouthen, Workington.
Isaac Fletcher, Esq., of Tarn Bank, Workington.
John Unsworth, Esq., of The Thorn, Penrith.
John Harris, Esq., of Woodside, Darlington, Civil Engineer.
Joseph Beaumont Pease, Esq., Ironmaster, of Middlesborough-on-Tees.
John Whitwell, Esq., of Kendal.
John Jameson, Esq., of Moorhouses, Penrith.
Edward Bowe Steel, Esq., of Cockermouth.
Arthur Dover, Esq., of Skiddaw Lodge, Keswick.
Isaac Gate, Esq., of Spring Bank, Thornthwaite, near Keswick.
William Bonnallie Gordon, Esq., Banker, of Workington.
John Simpson, Esq., Banker, Penrith.
John Crozier, Esq., of Riddings, Threlkeld, near Keswick.
Isaac Gray Bass, Esq., of The Craggs, Broughton, near Cockermouth.
Thomas Simpson, Esq., of Hazel Bank, Borrowdale.
William Cooke, Esq., of Camerton Hall, near Workington.
William Wilkinson, Esq., Banker, Penrith.
Henry Fletcher, Esq., of Workington.
N. Arnison, Esq., of Penrith.
John Musgrave, Esq., of Whitehaven.
William Bleasmyre, Esq., of Penrith.
William Fletcher, Esq., of Tarn Bank, Greysouthen.
Lawrence Harrison, Esq., of Penrith.
Christopher Fairer, Esq., of Penrith.
Joseph William Harris, Esq., Manufacturer, of Cockermouth.
William Thornburn, Esq., Jun., of Papcastle, near Cockermouth.
James Atkinson, Esq., of Winderwath, near Penrith.
Isaac Lowthian, Esq., Manufacturer, of Penrith.
Robert Scott, Esq., of Hayclose, Penrith.
John Robinson, Esq., of Whitbarrow, Penrith.
Robert Brostch, Esq., Solicitor, Keswick.
Dr. William Irving, of Penrith.
William Guy, Esq., of Keswick.
Mr. James Graham, Grocer, of Penrith.
Mr. Thomas M'Glasson, Brewer, of Penrith.
Mr. John Teather, of Keswick.
Mr. John Frank, of Keswick.
Mr. Peter Crosthwaite, of Keswick.
Mr. Samuel Ladyman, of Keswick.
Mr. Edwin Poole, of Keswick.
Mr. John Fisher Crosthwaite, of Keswick.
Mr. Joseph Todd, of Keswick.
Mr. Mark Cockbain, of Keswick.

BANKERS.

The Cumberland Union Bank, Workington, Cockermouth, Keswick, and Penrith.
Messrs. Barclay and Co., Lombard-street, London.
The Carlisle City and District Bank, Carlisle and Cockermouth.
Messrs. Glyn, Mills, and Co., Lombard-street, London.

ENGINEER.

Thomas Bouch, Esq., M.I.C.E., Edinburgh.

SOLICITORS.

Messrs. Steel, Waugh, and Hartley, Cockermouth.

The object of this undertaking is to extend railway communication with the Lake District, and to connect the railways of West Cumberland with those in the east of the county and the Eden Valley line, which communicates with the South Durham and Yorkshire systems, thus completing a direct chain of railways between the German Ocean and the Irish Sea, terminating with the harbours of Hartlepool and Stockton on the east, and the ports of Whitehaven, Workington, and Maryport on the west. Another object is to establish the shortest route between the valuable coke producing districts of Durham and the iron furnaces of West Cumberland, and between the hematite ores of Cumberland and the iron furnaces of Middlesborough and Durham.

The Line will commence by a junction with the Cockermouth and Workington Railway, at Cockermouth, and proceeding by way of Embleton, Wythop, Thornthwaite, and Braithwaite to Keswick, and thence by Threlkeld, Penruddock, Greystoke, and Stainton, will unite with the Lancaster and Carlisle Railway at Penrith, passing through the most attractive part of the Lake District along the margin of Bassenthwaite Lake on the west, at the foot of Derwentwater, and within 2½ miles of Ullswater. The passenger traffic from Scotland, the south and east of England, and from the west of Cumberland, will be considerable. There are built and building 16 blast furnaces at the western extremity of the line, principally at Workington. The coke for these works is obtained partly from the neighbourhood of Newcastle, and partly from the great coalfield of South Durham. The total consumption of coke, assuming no increase in the number of furnaces, will be 130,000 tons per annum, and as the proposed line shortens the distance to the South Durham coalfield 25 miles, the principal part of this traffic will come over this line at through rates.

The gross revenue, from 100,000 tons of coke per annum,

will be equal to 5 per cent. on the cost of the whole line and works.

There is now a large traffic in hematite iron ore from the mines near Whitehaven to the iron works in Durham and Cleveland, where upwards of seventy furnaces are in blast. The line will shorten the distance to nearly all these furnaces. Besides no material a saving in distance, the line offers peculiar advantages for the carriage of this traffic from the circumstance of having a large coke traffic in the opposite direction. The ore will be sent in return waggons. 50,000 tons of this ore per annum may be safely calculated upon.

The local traffic will be considerable, from coal, lime, and passengers, as well as from minerals. The mines of Newlands, Borrowdale, Skiddaw, and neighbourhood, have as yet been scantily and imperfectly explored, from the want of easy and cheap transit to the markets for lead ore and other products of these wealthy districts, and the country from Cockermouth to Penrith abounds with timber, some of which is valueless without a Railway.

The Line will effect a saving in distance:—

Between Cockermouth and Lancaster, Liverpool, and London	of 10 Miles.
Between Workington and Whitehaven, the Ports on the west coast, and Stockton and Middlesborough, the Ports of the east coast	of 30 „
Between the Blast Furnaces of Cleveland and the Whitehaven Hematite Iron Ore Mines	of 30 „
Between the Blast Furnaces at Norton, Stockton, and Darlington, and the Whitehaven Hematite Ore Mines	of 30 „
Between the Blast Furnaces at Witton Park Iron Works, and the Whitehaven Hematite Iron Ore Mines	of 24 „
Between the Blast Furnaces at Towlon and the Whitehaven Hematite Iron Ore Mines	of 20 „
Between the South Durham Coke and Coal field, and the Blast Furnaces at Workington and the West of Cumberland	of 25 „

No detailed estimate of the probable receipts of the Line has been made, but excluding the through mineral traffic, to which allusion has been made, the safest means of judging of the traffic is by a comparison with neighbouring railways. For example, the receipts of the Windermere Railway, which are chiefly derived from tourist traffic, were upwards of £20 per mile per week before it was merged in the Lancaster and Carlisle.

A similar traffic on this Line would yield a dividend of 8 per cent. on the whole capital, but a portion only of the mineral through traffic in addition would make it the best railway property in the kingdom. This is no exaggerated estimate if the actual receipts upon the following lines be compared with the expected receipts upon this, namely:—

Lancaster and Carlisle Railway	......	£70 per Mile per Week.
Whitehaven Junction	54	„ „
Whitehaven, Cleator, and Egremont	74	„ „
Cockermouth and Workington	31	„ „
Maryport and Carlisle	42	„ „
Stockton and Darlington	74	„ „
Kendal and Windermere	24	„ „
Furness Railway	54	„ „
Whitehaven and Furness Junction	18	„ „
Caledonian Railway	64	„ „

All the above receipts demonstrate the remunerative character of railway property if economy of construction receive proper attention. To this the efforts of the Provisional Directors will be studiously directed, and upon reference to the actual cost of construction of Lines recently made, the estimated cost of this Line may be confidently relied on as a close approximation to the actual cost.

The inhabitants of Cockermouth and Penrith, and of Keswick especially, are deeply interested in the formation of this Railway, and the landowners of the district will derive material advantages in the increased value of their land and its products. No opposition, but hearty co-operation is expected from them, and as this Line will complete the railway communication of Cumberland, thereby promoting increased commercial activity, it is expected that the project will receive a large amount of support from the capitalists of Cumberland.

Applications for Shares may be made in the form below to Mr. John Mayson, Secretary to the Cockermouth and Workington Railway, Cockermouth; or to Messrs. Robert and William Thompson, sharebrokers, Darlington; Messrs. Bragg and Stockdale, stockbrokers, Throgmorton-street, London; Mr. Jonathan Drewery, sharebroker, Newcastle-on-Tyne; Mr. John Laver, sharebroker, Carlisle; Mr. Nicholson, sharebroker, Whitehaven; Mr. William Welch, sharebroker, Lancaster; or Mr. William Wilkinson, bank agent, Penrith; Mr. John Fisher Crosthwaite, Keswick; Mr. Broatch, solicitor, Keswick; or Messrs. Steel, Waugh, and Hartley, solicitors, Cockermouth.

THE COCKERMOUTH, KESWICK, AND PENRITH RAILWAY.

To the Provisional Directors.

Gentlemen,—I request that you will allot me —— Shares of £20 each in the above undertaking, and I undertake to accept the same or any less number that may be alloted to me, and to pay the Deposit and Calls to be made thereon; and I hereby undertake to execute the Subscription Contract and other necessary legal instruments when required.

Name (in full) ....
Trade, Profession, &c. ....
Residence ....
Date ....

The Prospectus of the Cockermouth, Keswick & Penrith Railway as published in the *Railway Times*, 3rd November, 1860.

The Bill and Act of 1861

On 24th December, 1860, Edward Waugh presented, in a Parliamentary Declaration, a list of those who had subscribed for shares. They were mainly people local to the line but some came from further afield, for examples, from Norfolk and Dublin. The list included people belonging to many trades and professions; a jeweller, a vet, bank agents and bankers, those who described themselves simply as 'gentlemen' and those who used the description 'esquire', millers, builders and a pencil maker (from Keswick; no surprise!). The Bill to construct the line was deposited in the Private Bill Office and William Fletcher was named as the main promoter. It started its journey through the Houses of Commons and Lords on 8th February, 1861. On 1st May, William Fletcher, Hoskins and Waugh were joined up in London by Bouch to appear before a Select Committee. Bouch had probably travelled from Edinburgh whilst the others had made their way by carriage to Penrith and thence to the Capital by train. The first part of the journey had served to strengthen Waugh's resolve to gain rail facilities for Keswick and district! The Select Committee was chaired by Michael Dobbyn Hassard; Dyson and Company appeared as agents for the Bill. In the opening stages, petitions against the Bill by the London & North Western Railway (LNWR), the Earl of Lonsdale, William Thornborrow and Lancelot Dent were all read but in each case nobody was present to support them. However, a petition brought by Henry Howard did have an agent to support it, in the firm of Dorington and Company.

Mr Hall opened the case for the promoters and William Fletcher was first to take the oath. He affirmed he was from Workington and engaged in coal mining (also, later, saying he had an interest in iron making). The initial examination centred very much on the local situation. Fletcher pointed out that there was a real need for the effective distribution of coal between Cockermouth and Penrith because (at the time) this could only be done by cart. The price of coal along the proposed line was between 10 and 15 shillings a ton compared with eight shillings in Cockermouth. By railway, the reduction could probably be between three and five shillings. He went on to stress the benefit to the agricultural community of getting coal easily. In addition, cattle would be more effectively moved by rail. The committee seemed to have a keen interest in timber and referred to this several times during the sitting. As to passenger traffic, the members of the committee seemed to be unsure how densely populated the region was and Fletcher assured them it was a place visited by tourists and even went as far as suggesting 'more so than any other place in the Kingdom'. Questioned about his own interest in the scheme he asserted that it would be for the benefit of the public that the railway would be built. There were questions about the number of shares sold and whether anyone was actively opposing the plan. (He thought not.)

Discussion then moved to a wider consideration of benefits to the iron works of West Cumberland. Fletcher informed the committee that the line would reduce the distance which coal was presently being transported from the Durham Coalfield by some 35 miles and this would result in cheaper coke. The committee, understandably, then asked why it was necessary to take coal from

ANNO VICESIMO QUARTO & VICESIMO QUINTO

VICTORIÆ REGINÆ.

****

Cap. cciii.

An Act for making a Railway from *Cockermouth* to *Keswick* and *Penrith*, with a Branch thereout, all in the County of *Cumberland*; and for other Purposes. [1st *August* 1861.]

WHEREAS the making of a Railway commencing by a Junction with the *Cockermouth and Workington* Railway at or near *Cockermouth*, and terminating at or near *Penrith* in the County of *Cumberland*, and also a Branch Railway commencing by a Junction with the *Lancaster and Carlisle* Railway at or near the *Penrith* Station, and terminating by a Junction with the Main Line in a Field called *Mains*, at or near *Penrith* aforesaid, all in the County of *Cumberland*, would be of great public and local Advantage : And whereas a Plan and Section of the Railway and Branch showing the Lines and Levels thereof with a Book of Reference to the Plan, containing the Names of the Owners or reputed Owners, Lessee or reputed Lessees, and Occupiers of the Lands through which the Railway and Branch Railway are intended to pass, have been deposited at the Office of the Clerk of the Peace for the County of *Cumberland*: And whereas the Persons herein-after named, with others, are willing at their own Expense, to carry such Undertaking into execution ; but the same cannot be effected without the Authority of Parliament: May it therefore please Your

[*Local.*]   33 *R*   Majesty

The title page for the Act of Parliament for the Cockermouth, Keswick & Penrith Railway 1861.
Public Record Office

Durham when coal was mined in Cumberland and Fletcher told them the local coal 'is too full of sulphur for the making of iron'. In a final statement he told the committee that the 10 furnaces at Workington needed upwards of 100,000 tons of coke from Durham and the shorter route was considered vital. The next person to be interviewed was Bouch. In reply to a series of questions he told the committee that he had planned what he considered to be the best route and had had the advantage of starting in the Spring of the previous year, which had given him plenty of time to consider the route carefully. Further, he was sure it could be built for £200,000 and had built other lines which cost less per mile than this one, at £6,500 per mile. In his view 'it is a very ordinary line' with no heavy bridges or works and no tunnels and viaducts (a strange thing to say) and no need for stationary engines. One aspect with which issue had been taken was the number of level crossings. Originally six had been proposed and the committee asked for an assurance this number could be reduced to two. In the summing up of his evidence, when asked whether he saw the line as a great public utility, Bouch's reply was quite simply, 'I think it only requires to look at the map to see that; it speaks for itself'.

At this stage Mr Ellicombe, representing Henry Howard, questioned Bouch. The issues raised involved the amount of Howard's land needed and the proximity of the line to Greystoke Castle. There were then questions about the number of intermediate stations Bouch had planned on the EVR. Finally Bouch, in reply, stated that though pleasure traffic would be important, the exchange of ore and coke would be more so. Edward Waugh in his evidence made it clear that some of the inhabitants of Keswick, especially inn-keepers, had petitioned him to promote a railway and described how difficult is was in the summer to have the use of horses and carriages because they were so much in demand. Having asked about passenger traffic, the committee once again touched on the matter of timber and whether the railway would enable people to dispose of it. Waugh said that not only would this be so but the price of carriage would come down as well. He went on to say that he was of the opinion that all the landowners felt the line should be made in spite of the fact that against the 118 assenting, there had been 20 dissenting, with 33 'neuters'. There was, he felt, no active opposition and amongst the occupiers, 343 assented whilst only 13 dissented, with 37 'neuters'. After further questions of a fairly pedestrian nature, relating, for example, to the number of shares sold, Hall informed the committee that the case for the promoters was concluded. The chairman then declared that the preamble for the Bill was proved.

This, however, was not quite the end of the proceedings. When the clauses for the Bill were read, Mr Ellicombe proposed two clauses on behalf of Henry Howard. These required the company to construct and maintain four stations between Keswick and Penrith and 'to stop a train each way at each such station once a day and on Market Days, twice a day'. Waugh informed the committee that market days were Tuesdays (Penrith) and Saturdays (Keswick). Hall objected to the clauses, arguing that the Directors should be 'unfettered' in their action. He was sure that if the Directors saw such stations as beneficial, they would construct them. Bouch, when questioned about this matter, pointed out to the committee that it was not the practice to put stations on plans and although he felt four might be desirable, there were other factors to take into account such as gradients at proposed station sites. Bouch told the committee that there had been a proposal for a station on Howard's land 'for his own accommodation' and when asked whether his tenants might use it, all he would reply was 'It is upon his estate'. The committee decided not to grant either of the clauses.

Bouch was questioned further about the level crossings which were clearly a matter for concern. As mentioned previously, six had been proposed, this number had been reduced to two and the Board of Trade was still objecting to one of these, near Bassenthwaite Lake. There had been suggestions that the railway should be lowered or possibly diverted but Bouch was opposed to both ideas because the area was one liable to flood and diverting the line would 'twist it more' and although the curve could be worked he wanted to minimise such curves. He was also against raising the line because this would result in an embankment of 18 feet. He went on to say that 'whilst in such a line as the Great Northern it would be objectionable to have many crossings [because there were so many trains] there would be few trains on this line and they would not be travelling at high speeds'. Further questions were asked about the terrain and costs of alternatives and then Hoskins was called to give evidence. (He might well have been wondering by this stage whether his trip to London had been worthwhile!) After taking the oath, he was questioned about the significance of the road to be crossed, how busy it was and where it went. His answers satisfied the committee that the level crossing could be included in the scheme. After a few further questions, addressed to Bouch, Hassard was directed to report the Bill to the House. Its first reading was on 27th May and the second reading on 6th June. It was committed on 17th June and amendments were made on 21st June. The third reading with these amendments and some additional ones, was on 18th July. The Bill was then passed and returned to the Commons. Amendments were agreed on 25th July and the Bill returned to the Lords. It received the Royal Assent [Act : 24th & 25th Vict., cap cciii] on 1st August. The passage had been straightforward and without complications. The Act names as the first directors Isaac Gray Bass, John Crozier, Mark Cockbain, Arthur Dover, Isaac Fletcher, William Fletcher, Isaac Gate, Thomas Alison Hoskins, John Jameson, Isaac Lowthian, Thomas McGlasson, John Robinson, John Simpson, John James Spedding and John Steel.

Chapter Two

Construction and Other Developments: 1861-1865

With the Act to build the Railway on the Statute Book, steps were taken to move ahead as quickly as possible with building the line. By the 10th August, 1861, when the Board first met after this significant development, the Secretary had acquired an impressive minute book, from J.W.Lancaster, Mercantile and Law Stationers, of 9 New Bridge Street, York, and made his first entry which he did in a neat and legible hand. (Sadly, some of his successors were not quite so meticulous and legible.)

The meeting was held at the Royal Oak in Keswick and those present were Thomas Hoskins (Chairman) Isaac Bass, Arthur Dover, Isaac Gate, Isaac Fletcher, Isaac Lowthian, Thomas McGlasson, John Robinson and James Spedding. In accordance with the accepted procedure at this stage, the officers stood down and elections were held.

Isaac Fletcher proposed Thomas Hoskins for Chairman. This was seconded by Isaac Bass and the proposal was carried. Isaac Fletcher was then appointed Vice-Chairman. Henry Cattle, who for the next 10 years proved a most industrious contributor to the scheme, became Secretary and Manager.

The rest of the Board was eventually made up of those Directors on the original list. Thomas Bouch was formally appointed the Engineer and Edward Waugh found a role as the solicitor. The Cumberland Banking Company became the bankers. There were, in fact, no surprises!

The next action was the formation of two land committees. 'The Land Committee for the Cockermouth End' had as its members Messrs (William) Fletcher, McGlasson, Gate and Bass. 'The Land Committee for the Penrith End' consisted of Messrs Jameson, Simpson, Robinson, McGlasson and Crozier. During the next three years, these committees met frequently, the committee for the Cockermouth end meeting 64 times, the one for the Penrith end meeting 36 times. Each devoted a great deal of time to the acquisition of land. They had to tackle a number of problems and did not always have an easy passage.

The finance committee was made up of Messrs Jameson, Simpson and Lowthian. The common seal, a design for which had been submitted, was approved and it was resolved the seal should be procured immediately. The Secretary was instructed to acquire books and stationery and with that the stage seemed set.

The first ordinary meeting of the company was planned for 31st August, 1861 at 2 pm and was held at the Odd Fellows Hall in Keswick. Bass and Fletcher agreed to prepare a report. In accordance with the Act, the Directors' appointments were put forward for ratification and all were approved.

Another very important committee was also formed, namely the Stations Committee and this arranged to meet at Cockermouth station on 16th August and thereafter to view the proposed sites for the stations on the line. There are no CK&PR station sites marked on Bouch's plans (only the C&WR station and Penrith). On the set of plans deposited in Cumberland there are two proposed sites in Cockermouth for the joint station pencilled in, although it is not possible to say when these were added. One indicates a site in close proximity to the C&WR site, the other, just to the south of the workhouse and much further east. This was the general area of the site eventually used but before this decision was made, the Station Committee became involved in a very protracted debate about the joint station. The committee met the Directors of the C&WR for a preliminary discussion and already there had been a deputation from some of the inhabitants of Cockermouth who wanted a joint station to be built between the River Cocker and the workhouse (possibly prompting someone to make the note on the plan). If this could be agreed, the deputation also requested a new street from the main street to this station. At first sight this seemed reasonable (to the CK&PR group) and it was resolved 'if a sufficient number of responsible gentlemen will, before August 31, enter into such a legal obligation as shall be satisfactory to the solicitors of the Company, agreeing to construct a complete, a good and sufficient approach from the Main Street, at their own expense, the Railway Company will undertake to erect a station in the locality pointed out by the deputation'. The site at this stage included a cricket field and drops for minerals would be constructed near the Kirkgate Road. The matter proved to be rather more involved than had been foreseen and a saga would ensue which would sorely try the patience of the Directors of the CK&PR.

As far as the other stations were concerned, it was decided to site these as follows. Embleton at Lamb Foot (where a level crossing would be needed), Brathey Hill station at Brathey Hill corner, the Lake station, to be placed at the most convenient position where it passed Smithy Green, Braithwaite station, to be adjoining Occupation Road, Keswick station, to be placed at Shorley Croft, Threlkeld station, 'near the public road', Troutbeck station, on the east side of the road, Penruddock station in the Parish of Greystoke. Later, there would be changes in some of these names. The Land Committee at the Penrith end was asked to take immediate steps to purchase land near Penrith station belonging to a Mr Moorhouse, for use by the Railway.

The situation relating to an agreement over station accommodation at Cockermouth became a matter for continuing concern and consequently it was resolved that 'if the Directors of the C&WR cannot agree with the CK&PR then the Cockermouth members of the Station Committee [Hoskins, Bass and Fletcher] have full power to act with the Directors of the C&WR with the understanding that if they cannot agree a full meeting of the committee be called'.

The resolution of the problem, essentially what appeared to be intransigence by the C&WR, did not prove at all easy. At a number of Directors' meetings discussion of the problem was deferred in the hope that a solution might be found. In the meantime, a call of £2 per share was made and this was to be effected before 1st October (1861). Concerns were being expressed that the share list was falling short of the target and so yet another special committee was formed (William Fletcher, Bass, Simpson, Lowthian, Crozier and Spedding) to try and attract more shareholders. A contract was confirmed with the Aberdeen Iron Company for the provision of rails and later this company was asked to provide the fish plates as well.

The Directors of the CK&PR expressed pleasure with the progress that was being made but they were even more encouraged when they met at 'The Bush' in Carlisle, on 31st October to hear that the EVR had decided to apply for an extension into Penrith in the ensuing session of Parliament. This step was taken by the EVR when it realised, subsequent to commencing building its line, that in the developing circumstances, the south-facing junction with the L&CR, near Clifton, was already, even before completion, virtually redundant in terms of through traffic. The earlier misgivings of some of the EVR Directors that the SD&LUR junction at Tebay would detract from the EVR as a through route had been raised again with the prospect of a line from Penrith to Cockermouth and a connection with this line was seen to make vital economic sense. There was, of course, the objection of the L&CR to contend with and to get round this the EVR initially planned to have its own line into Penrith, running in effect parallel to the L&CR. In the event, the EVR gained running powers over the L&CR into Penrith and so this duplication proved unnecessary. There would still be some inconvenience in entering and leaving Penrith, from the EVR to the CK&PR and vice-versa, but this, too, was to be easily resolved in the fullness of time.

The Cockermouth station project was still in some difficulty. Another proposal had been put forward that the new station should be built at the Cockerside site and the proposal to site it on the cricket field (no doubt much to the relief of the local eleven) was bowled out. Things now seemed to be moving in the right direction and on 30th November, the CK&KR Directors confirmed the proposal to build on the Cockerside site on land belonging to a Major Thompson and agreed the formation of a New Street Company to build New Street. It was at this meeting that the Board announced Keswick would be the place for the Head Office.

1862

Whilst all these many and varied deliberations had been taking place, Thomas Bouch had been pressing ahead with the arrangements for constructing the line, John Wood having been appointed the Resident Engineer. The latter was to have a long and distinguished career with the company.

Provision was made for the spiritual welfare of the navvies and a number of local clergymen became involved. Worship took place and instruction was given in several places, including the Forge [described as a suburb of Keswick, near the station] and in the huts at the side of Bassenthwaite Lake. It is reported that in general the behaviour of the navvies was 'good', in spite of the fact that many, perhaps not surprisingly, consumed considerable amounts of alcohol. They were particularly praised at one stage for 'the kindness which they manifested for any of their suffering fellow-labourers; especially as shown in their providing decent interment for such as had been victims of accidents on the line' [The Reverend Battersby]. Christmas parties were given for them by local people who tried to provide a little respite and these gatherings were attended not only by the navvies but also by their wives and children as well.

Bouch reported to the shareholders at their meeting on 28th February, 1862. He was a Cumberland man born and bred and so he must surely have been aware of the vagaries of the weather in that part of England. Perhaps he longed for more opportunities to build railways in better climes because he had continually to excuse lack of progress on the poor weather conditions. This was the case for the SD&LUR and also the EVR. It became the case for the CK&PR as well. Perhaps he was an optimist; he had plenty of experience to suggest he should be more generous with the time he allocated for completing construction. Even the staking out was delayed; an ominous sign, perhaps! Add to this the fact that in some sections this was a difficult route and problems seemed inevitable. It has already been mentioned that the first preference some years before had been for a line to pass along the east side of Bassenthwaite. The new route resulted in the village of Bassenthwaite being three miles from the nearest station. East of Keswick there were difficulties adapting to the course of the River Greta which had to be crossed nine times. Screw pile bridges were used on some sections to ensure that flood water would flow easily and not cause damage. These were to give problems later. There was a heavy gradient between Troutbeck and Threlkeld and this would give rise to operating difficulties. The summit level in this section is 889 feet. At the meeting of 28th February, Bouch could announce that they were ready to invite tenders for contracts for construction. There had been some modifications to the original route, especially in the Vale of Greta, near Keswick, but whatever the weather might do in delaying the staking out, at least it had not hindered the completion of the paper work. Bouch was able to inform the shareholders that 1,933¼ tons of rail had been delivered, some to Cockermouth and some to Penrith.

The Board awarded the contract to Boulton & Son. It was for £166,775 although this did not include the stations at Cockermouth, Keswick and Troutbeck.

Cutting the first Sod

'No undertaking was ever commenced under more favourable auspices than the line of railway the proceedings at the cutting of the first sod of which we record today . . .' So began one writer, setting down an account of the cutting of the first sod of the CK&PR. Even after taking into account the tendency for writers of the period to be florid and euphoric in their writings about such events, it does appear that it was certainly a memorable occasion and one which was long remembered by all those present. Wednesday, 21st May, the day chosen, was fine and sunny and the weather did much to help raise the spirits of those involved. The programme began at 11.30 am. The bands of the Cockermouth Engineers, the Cockermouth Rifles and the Skiddaw Greys played for a time in front of the town hall at Keswick and a large crowd gathered to listen. A stage coach arrived carrying on top the wheelbarrow and spade to be used in the ceremony. The mahogany barrow had been made in Keswick by Joseph Crosthwaite, a cabinet maker. The spade was supplied by Mr Altham, Penrith, and it carried a silver shield with the inscription 'Presented to T.A.Hoskins Esq., of Higham, J.P., on the occasion of his cutting the first sod of the Cockermouth, Keswick and Penrith Railway, May 21, 1862'.

At 12.30 pm, a procession formed up in the market place. This procession consisted of the Directors, clergymen, tradesmen, the riflemen, 800 Sunday school scholars, Oddfellows, Foresters and members of the temperance society. Heading the procession was a group of men described as 'genuine navvies'. These men, who appeared just before the procession started, to the delight and amusement of the crowd, wore 'new white slops and white poke caps with a red tassel hanging from the end'. One man carried the barrow on his shoulders whilst another carried the spade. With band playing and banners flying, the party moved to Great Crosthwaite. Here the main ceremony took place, with the children being placed at the front to enable them to have a good view of the proceedings. First the whole assembly sang Psalm 117 and then The Reverend T. Battersby said a prayer. It went on at some length asking God to bless the endeavours about to be undertaken and [presumably in case He had not realised] how important they were to all in the district and beyond.

Battersby then called upon Thomas Hoskins 'in the name of the committee who have been appointed to conduct the proceedings of this day and in the name of the shareholders of the projected line of railway' to cut the first sod. Before doing so, Hoskins spoke at some length. There are on record a number of orations he gave and he was an eloquent and convincing speaker. He had, what today would be referred to as 'a sense of theatre' carrying his listeners along with him and prompting reaction from them. In the speech he cleverly wove together religious and commercial themes and was not ill at ease in doing so, living as he did in an era which believed in a God who would view favourably robust enterprise which would improve people's lives. He started 'Ladies and gentlemen, my friends, my good friends and neighbours, without prayer no human effort, no human wisdom, I believe is of any avail. As with prayer we have begun so in the spirit of prayer may the work before us be carried on . . .' He went on to point out that it had been universally recognised that the first and indispensable requirement of any civilised community to further the advancement of its social condition is a railway and that Keswick will benefit with better contact with 'the stirring world around'. There were frequent shouts of 'Hear, hear', loud applause, ''vociferous cheers' with loud cheers at one point from the navvies. At the end he announced 'And now my friends, to work' whereupon he 'threw off his coat and sent the spade into the ground and cut the first sod in a most professional manner'. It was at this point that his remarkable sense of theatre emerged again because he then held the sod high on the spade, like some trophy, and shouted to he crowd 'Here it is!' The crowd went wild, there were three cheers, the Skiddaw Greys fired three volleys and the band played 'Rule Britannia' and 'God Save the Queen'. [It must have resembled, somewhat, the now familiar scenes at the last night of the proms!]

Hoskins placed a few sods in the barrow and wheeled them a short distance away and brought the barrow back, once more to loud applause. Isaac Fletcher then spoke, describing Hoskins as 'the very A1 of navvies'. He expressed his gratitude to the many present who had brought the scheme thus far and those whose enterprise in other parts of Cumberland would have a beneficial effect on the railway. He expressed the view that those who had recently been critical of the whole scheme (and he was sure were not present) would be proved wrong and he finished (again amidst cheers) by saying 'I sincerely hope that at no distant period we may all meet again . . . to celebrate the completion of our enterprise'. There was another rendering of the National Anthem, a further volley and, to cheering, the Misses Hoskins cut more sods and wheeled them away. The children were given cakes and people then dispersed to join in the dancing and 'other amusements'. The Directors went off to a dinner. This was provided at the Derwentwater Hotel, Portinscale, at 5 pm and in the interval between this and the sod cutting, the guests either walked in the grounds or spent time on the lake. During the meal, which Mr and Mrs Bell, the proprietors organised, the band of the Cockermouth Rifle Corps played suitable music in the garden. There were 80 people present and once again a clergyman, The Reverend A.R. Webster, took the chair. After dinner there were a number of toasts proposed by a variety of people. Battersby in replying to a toast to the Bishop and Clergy of the Diocese took the opportunity to praise the Bishop and Lieutenant Teather, proposing the health of the Earl of Lonsdale, pointed out that whilst the honourable gentleman had not bought shares in the line he had given a good reason for not doing so! Once again, much was said about the benefits the new line would bring to the district. Mr Boulton, senior, was not able to be present, having been called away to business in London. He was represented by his son who remarked that he came as a stranger among them but he hoped soon to be better acquainted. What a grand irony that was to become! Mr T.F. MacNay, Resident Engineer of the EVR, was also present. The whole day had been highly successful and a great boost to morale. In spite of the fact that some of the Directors had chosen to visit the Great Exhibition and could not be present, the future looked good. Hoskins concluded the festivities with the words 'To our next merry meeting' and with that everyone went home.

Bouch was back again on 30th August and was able to tell the shareholders that the heaviest class of work, the earthworks, had involved the removal of 80,000 cubic yards, this being about one-tenth of the total. He was anxious to point out this was not really a true measure of the real progress because a lot of time was usually involved in opening cuttings. The piers and west abutments of the viaduct over the River Cocker had been built to springing level and the east abutment and one of the piers of the viaduct at Penruddock were also up to springing level. A start had been made on four of the remaining piers, four small bridges had been built and others were in progress. Unfortunately, the Summer had been a wet one and so progress had been slower than he had hoped.

The Directors and shareholders seemed to be satisfied and, in fact, throughout most of the construction period Bouch came in for little criticism from the shareholders in spite of the work falling behind schedule. He must have found this a pleasant change after dealing with some of the shareholders of the EVR who, in similar circumstances, had been angry to the point of accusing him of rigging the reports and not presenting a true picture of what was going on in an attempt to cover up lack of progress. During this meeting it is notable that Hoskins waxed eloquent about Henry Howard's support for the scheme and this may well have been to reassure those who had wondered where Howard stood, following the events at the meeting of the Select Committee.

Cockermouth Joint Station

In June, there was a special meeting to discuss the arrangements for the joint station at Cockermouth. It was resolved . . .

that the original piece of land occupied by the present Cockermouth Railway and Station (which for this purpose shall commence at the point of junction of The Keswick Railway to be agreed upon and shall terminate at the Easternmost limits of the said Station) of all buildings and works . . . shall be bought by the first mentioned Company into a common fund. The price of Major Thompson's land, now offered to the CK&PR and such other land on the East side of the Cocker and the Lorton Road as the two companys [sic] may hereafter mutually agree to purchase for enlarging the Joint Station . . . shall be paid for and bought by the Keswick Company and added to the same fund. Each company shall receive interest of 5 per cent.

The C&WR Board were able, in principle, to agree to this.

[In 1863, Wood's plans for the proposed new station at Cockermouth, with some modifications by Mr Drane, were put forward for approval. The matter of a house for the station master was raised and it was agreed to leave it to Wood to decide whether this should be part of the station or a separate building. A beautifully executed drawing of this new station, signed by Jonathan Cape, still exists.]

An Important Decision

On 12th December , an EGM of the shareholders of the CK&PR was called, the venue being the Odd Fellows Hall. The purpose of the meeting was for the Directors to discuss with them and submit for their approval a significant proposal involving the LNWR and the S&DR along with the CK&PR. Memoranda of agreement were put before the meeting.

The LNWR would provide £25,000 in share capital in return for various conditions. The LNWR would work all passenger and some goods traffic and provide engines and rolling stock for this purpose. It would also provide the coal and coke for its engines, together with the necessary man-power and the required stores to work and keep the stock in good repair. It would, in addition, provide guards for its trains. The CK&PR would, for its part, provide the staff for working the line and manning the stations as well as the appliances to supply water for the engines and steam sheds with any equipment needed.

The LNWR would fix rates and fares on through traffic (except minerals) carried to and from its system and to and from the CK&PR; also through mineral traffic from its own system over the Keswick line to and from Cockermouth and beyond. The exception to this would be traffic carried over the S&DR (the EVR). The minimum of these through rates allowed to the CK&PR being not less than ⅝d. per ton per mile.

The shareholders were also asked to agree to granting the LNWR full running powers in perpetuity.

The CK&PR would retain two-thirds for the use of its railway, the LNWR one-third for engines, rolling stock and other expenses, this of the gross mileage receipts arising from all fares, rates and charges for passenger and goods traffic over the CK&PR. The LNWR would be able to nominate two Directors to the Board of the CK&PR and the Board would be reduced to 12 in all.

This Board would also include two members nominated by the S&DR with whom a similar agreement was also pending. This would mean that the Board would consist of eight members of the CK&PR, two from the LNWR and two from the S&DR. This Board would run the Railway and would fix the amount of services and the number of trains, although the LNWR stated that it did not propose to run more than three passenger trains each way in the Winter and four in the Summer with one goods train each way, each day. The memoranda had been signed by William Cawkwell for Euston and Henry Cattle for Keswick. The shareholders agreed unanimously to approve them.

The Directors then put before the shareholders similar memoranda of agreement with the S&DR.

It, too, would contribute £25,000 of share capital. In exchange it would operate the mineral traffic and provide the engines and the men. As with the LNWR, it would provide coal, coke and stores and would fix the rates of all through mineral traffic. The S&DR also looked for full running powers in perpetuity. The shareholders approved, again unanimously. The Directors of the S&DR, in particular, must have felt very pleased. It was reckoned that the mineral traffic was going to be the most lucrative element of the line.

The acceptance of these memoranda marked a key stage in the development of the CK&PR. It meant, quite simply, that the responsibility of running and maintaining engines and rolling stock was someone else's worry. The situation might well be compared to that of Railtrack, following the privatisation of the railways at the end of the 20th century. It was agreed that the Bill for these decisions to be made legal would be put before Parliament at the earliest opportunity.

During 1862 there were a number of other significant developments though none as significant as the one described previously. In February it seems another group had been set up to discuss further and settle the matter of the joint station at Cockermouth with the C&WR. This met again on 31st May but no agreement could be reached. The representatives for the CK&PR in desperation decided to abandon the negotiations. In the circumstances a decision was made to look at land acquisition elsewhere to enable the CK&PR to proceed immediately in making the line to the Parliamentary point of junction on the C&WR. This action jolted the C&WR and it came back with a request for further talks. At a further meeting held on 16th June at Cockermouth, the resolution of the CK&PR to discontinue negotiations was withdrawn and new proposals considered. The plans for Cockermouth joint station would be submitted to the C&WR Directors for approval but if there continued to be differences, it was suggested an 'umpire' should be found for further consultation with the C&WR Engineer.

On a more positive note, the Directors of the C&WR informed the Directors of the CK&PR (on the 10th June, in readiness for a meeting on 16th June) that they had agreed unanimously to grant facilities for through traffic from Cockermouth to Workington for the CK&PR, the S&DR and the LNWR.

Mineral traffic through to Workington would be at the rate of 3*d*. per ton plus a mileage rate. Details were being finalised in other areas by the Works Committee which met regularly. It was agreed Bassenthwaite station and the mineral depot would be on the north of the line (meeting, 10th November, 1862) and a siding for timbers on the south side. A level crossing would be substituted for a bridge over the line, assuming the trustees of the turnpike road would agree. It was decided Keswick station would have accommodation for company headquarters. In early 1863 a decision was made to accept Bouch's plan for the station with two exceptions, namely a kitchen must be provided for the refreshment room and the refreshment room and porters' room should be made into one big room. For the eastern end of the line, three plans were submitted for Penrith station, two by Bouch and one by Worthington. One of Bouch's plans was accepted. In connection with the CK&PR plans at Penrith, the setting up of a committee was proposed to discuss with the LNWR the whole of the station arrangements at Penrith. Leases for accommodation by station masters were considered in June, with a decision to actually purchase at Penruddock, Threlkeld and Troutbeck.

When it met on 25th June, the Board agreed that the company should seriously consider building a hotel at Keswick and Bass, Hoskins and Isaac Fletcher became the members of a newly formed hotel committee. They began their work by inspecting hotels at Windermere, Grasmere and Ullswater.

1863

Bouch, meanwhile, was having better luck with the weather. In February he was able to report there had been good progress made during the Winter months. As a result, half the earthworks had been completed, as had 40 bridges (or some nearly so). The viaduct over the River Cocker was virtually finished and the arches of Penruddock viaduct had been closed. Preparations had been made for starting the viaducts over Mosedale Gill and Trout Beck and the iron work of the several bridges crossing the River Greta was being progressed. The 114 ft-span viaduct at Brigham was complete except for the parapets and planking and of the screw piling 50 piles had been screwed to the requisite depth and about 140 feet of superstructures had been completed. Bouch was optimistic. If there was a fine Summer, he would be able to report favourably next time as well!

In early 1863, Mr Boulton senior died. The Directors were generous in their praise. They referred to him as a man 'of great business, tact and energy, particularly highly esteemed for his punctuality'. They were careful to add that his death should not delay the work and opening of the line. As things turned out, his son did not come up to their expectations and relationships between the company and the contractor deteriorated considerably.

The Bill relating to the joint working by the S&DR and LNWR went through Parliament unopposed and received the Royal Assent on 29th June.

In August, Bouch was still pleased with the progress. He was able to report that the earth-works should be finished before the onset of Winter as only about

Penruddock Viaduct - Cockermouth, Keswick & Penrith Railway

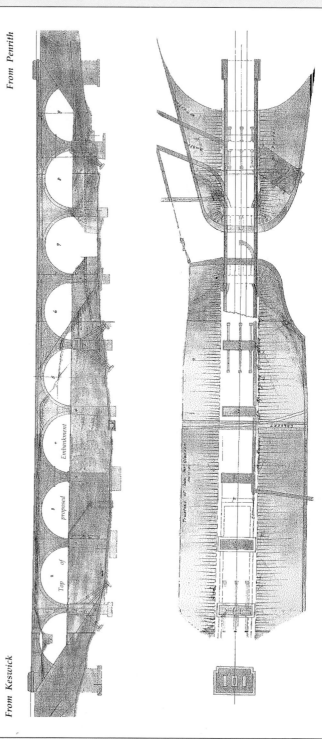

From Penrith

From Keswick

Penruddock viaduct. This plan is dated 1917 and shows proposed modifications.

Cockermouth viaduct taken in 1966. The building on the left of the picture was formerly the goods shed, but before this it had been an engine shed for the Cockermouth & Workington Railway. *Ian S. Carr*

one-fifth remained to be done. Viaducts at Penruddock and Cockermouth were now complete and already, since the last report in February, the ones at Mosedale Gill and Trout Beck had piers and abutments up to springing level. Eight of the nine bridges over the River Greta were almost complete. Seventy-five other river and road bridges were complete but 28 had yet to be started. Twenty miles of track had been laid, the station house at Newbiggin had been roofed and although the other stations had not been started, this situation would be rectified immediately. Bouch felt, nevertheless, the need for caution. 'With the uncertainty of Winter before us, it is impossible to speak with confidence as to the time of completion but the progress made is so satisfactory that there is a reasonable prospect of the works being completed in the stipulated time'. That statement may well have made a significant contribution to what later became a very embarrassing mistake.

Penruddock viaduct. There were problems with this structure which are referred to on Page 125. *Cumbrian Railways Association*

Although the Directors expressed satisfaction with the general situation, there was some uneasiness. The Works Committee inspected the state of the works between Threlkeld bridge and Penrith on 8th July and found cause for concern with the lack of satisfactory progress. It recommended that more workmen should be employed. This was just the thin end of the wedge.

The Penrith Station Committee met later in the month (on 24th July) with the group consisting of four representatives from the CK&PR, two from the S&DR and five from the LNWR. Plans were approved for a platform 12 ft wide, with a siding for spare carriages at the south end. There would be a booking office, a large general waiting room, a ladies' waiting room and a waiting room for gentlemen travelling first class. It was agreed that the cost of altering the existing accommodation should be valued 'as between friendly companies' 5 per cent per annum of the value or cost, being paid in equal proportions, that is one-third each. The cost of enlargements would be defrayed by the LNWR and the interest paid in equal parts by the three companies.

On 25th September, the Works Committee was out and about again, this time looking, in particular, at the section from Monks Hall to Thornthwaite. The members were not impressed. In their view, the work was so far behind that it was hinted there had been an element of neglect by the contractor. They were especially critical of the state of the station bridge over the River Greta which seemed to be no further advanced than it had been three months previously. Growing lack of satisfaction with the work of Boulton junior would eventually lead to something of a showdown.

It has to be said, in defence of the Boultons, that in some aspects they had shown considerable initiative. During the Autumn of the previous year (1862) there had been considerable discussion about the installation of the telegraph. The Boultons wanted to install this as soon as possible and had corresponded with The Electric and International Telegraph Company. The Boultons were of the opinion that being able to communicate along the line of the works during the period of construction would enhance the efficiency of the operation. The Works Committee had, understandably, agreed and sanctioned £418 for the purpose.

Another aspect raised by the Directors at this stage was the lack of provision of engine sheds and on 31st October, Wood was instructed to investigate the matter.

In November, the Works Committee opened the tenders which had been invited for the building of the houses for the station masters at Lambfoot, Piel Wyke, Braithwaite and Threlkeld. They were all considered to be too high and none was accepted. They did approve the building of an engine shed, a shed for six carriages and a turntable at Keswick. A tender by Grave and Cape for the building of station buildings and a station master's house at Cockermouth for £1885 was also accepted. There was still, however, no real solution to the problem of Cockermouth joint station. The Directors, meeting on the 3rd December, discussed the problem and another group for joint talks was mooted. During 1863 the four Directors assigned to assess the provision of hotel accommodation in Keswick did so and found it wanting. As a result, on 27th August, the Directors put before the shareholders, for approval, a project for the building of 'a first class hotel' in connection with the station. This was agreed. An architect, Mr Ross, had already been consulted and he had drawn up a plan. Once this was approved, Cattle was authorised to invite tenders. Meantime, Boulton's tender of £3,500 for the station at Keswick was accepted with the provisos that the booking office and other offices be ready by 31st March, 1864 and the rest completed by 1st June. When the tenders for the hotel were opened on 25th September all were much higher than anticipated and so Wood was instructed to modify the specifications. The completion time was set at 1st January, 1865. In fact Wood was given authority to make any changes he felt necessary provided the essential design was not affected. In November, fresh tenders were opened and David Hall of Carlisle was successful with a figure of £8,800. James Gouge was appointed clerk of works at 50 shillings a week. On 2nd December Bolton and Graham were given the contract to build the station masters' houses at Lambfoot and Piel Wyke for £333 each although Braithwaite and Threlkeld still had to be settled.

As 1863 drew to a close there were growing concerns about the lack of substantial progress. The Directors were very keen to have the line open before the summer season of the following year. With this in view, the Works Committee, meeting in December, proposed that the contractor be given incentives to achieve this. There would be £750 if the Directors could give notice to the Government Inspector that the works would be ready for inspection on 1st May. However, if the date was 23rd April there would be a payment of £1,150 and for 16th April, £1,750.

1864

The dawning of 1864 did bring some encouragement for the Directors of the CK&PR. The North Eastern Railway (NER) decided to promote a Bill to provide a link from Eamont Bridge to Redhills (Act Vict. 27 & 28 cap. cxviii; June) thus promising a connection from the EVR onto the CK&PR without the need to pass through Penrith. On 7th January the 'Parliamentary Committee', which consisted of the Chairman, Vice-Chairman, Bass and Lowthian was reconvened with full powers to instruct the company's solicitor to provide whatever assistance was deemed necessary.

The relationship between the contractor and the company deteriorated further in the early part of the year. On 4th and 5th February, the Works Committee inspected the whole of the line. They expressed a measure of satisfaction but urged the contractor to push hard the works in the Greta, the pitching of the embankment on the lake and the general ballasting. When they returned on 24th February there seemed no sign that any of the recommendations had been carried out. They suggested that a double shift be used, night and day.

On 25th February the matter of whether or not to double the line was raised again. It seems there were those who had been pressing for this step to be taken and the time for the purchase of land in the terms of the Act was running out. A figure of £8,000 had been quoted but as no capital had been provided or was available and as it was considered many years would probably elapse before doubling was needed and, further, because there was an assurance that doubling could be carried out at a later date without disrupting traffic, it was agreed not to purchase the land.

When the Engineer reported to the shareholders at their meeting on 25th February the content was disappointing. Bouch did not, in fact, attend but sent his report from Edinburgh. Once again there had been delays caused by very unfavourable weather. The progress had been slower than anticipated. 'Still, if the weather is moderate from now', he wrote, 'the line could be completed by June'. So much for the incentives! The report pointed out that several embankments remained unclosed. Troutbeck viaduct, with its four spans, was still unfinished but would only take about one month. The masonry over all the bridges over the Greta was almost finished. All the screw piles had been sunk. Only a small fraction of the superstructure had to be completed. There were several bridges to be started but these were only small ones. All the stations except Braithwaite were under construction, with Newbiggin, Troutbeck and Penruddock almost complete. The late frosts had hindered the completion of loading banks and platform walls. Twenty seven and a half miles of track had been laid and 18 of these had been ballasted. It hardly seemed like a railway that was 'near to completion'! The Directors were obviously disappointed and made it clear they had been urging the contractors to make a vigorous effort to complete for some time. They repeated their aspiration to secure the tourist traffic for the forthcoming season. To any discerning person, the prospect of that now seemed remote. On a more positive note, it was possible to report the progress made in providing a hotel at Keswick. The only consolation the Directors could offer, at the end of the meeting, was that the line would be ready to meet the demands of the tourist traffic in the Summer of 1865.

At this stage the Works Committee felt the need to provide even greater incentives. Boulton was interviewed personally by the members and told that if the line actually opened for passenger traffic by 1st July the company would pay him a premium of £2,000. There was, however, a downside. If the line did not open by then, the company would insist on all the penalties for non-completion being rigidly enforced.

At the beginning of May, the Works Committee inspected again. Bouch was informed that the pitching of the line along Bassenthwaite was so inferior that the contractor must renew it. In other respects there was guarded optimism that the deadline for 1st July might be met. There was much ballasting to be done and the committee proposed that the contractor be given a powerful locomotive and 30 waggons to effect this. The Board readily agreed. At a meeting on 4th May, there was a proposal that the stations should be formally named Embleton, Bassenthwaite Lake, Thornthwaite, Keswick, Threlkeld, Troutbeck, Penruddock and Greystoke or Dacre. The following day, the Board accepted these recommendations and, in addition, agreed the NER could form a junction at Redhills with a bridge over their line.

On 24th July it was agreed by the Works Committee that the company would purchase Boulton's plant for £14,000 and this was to be paid into the bank to be credited to Boulton. When the plant was sold on, Boulton would be credited with any shortfall. In the meantime arrangements for the joint use of the station at Penrith were approved on 2nd April with the additional requirements that the connection between the down main LNWR and EVR line should be near the turntable, there should be three connections between the EVR and CK&PR to enable passenger and mineral traffic for Keswick to occupy the sidings (this until the new junction at Stainton and Yanwath (Eamont and Redhills) had been completed), a water column be provided between the turntable and the Keswick line, an engine pit in the turntable siding, an extra foot be added to the width of the Keswick platform and there be an extra room for ladies.

By this time it had been resolved that at Cockermouth the C&WR station would become a goods depot and the joint station would occupy a site almost the same as that originally proposed. About this time, the Keswick Gas Company was asked to supply gas to the station and hotel at Keswick. On 1st June the Works Committee was at last able to inspect the line from Penrith to Keswick by engine. The members, however, were not impressed by every aspect of the works and later described the quality of the work along Bassenthwaite Lake as 'objectionable'. As far as Keswick station was concerned it was decided that the ticket office should be placed in the general room and that the kitchen should be converted into a gentlemen's waiting room.

In spite of the perceived short-comings, the members of the Works Committee remained very optimistic and recommended to the Board that, subject to the Engineer's approval, the Board of Trade should be given notice that the line was ready for inspection. At this point it seems there was some sort of breakdown in communication! The Board of Trade was indeed contacted but without reference to Bouch. The Board minutes of 31st August report that 'the Government Inspector has been over the line within the last few days. No definite report has been received from him but it is understood he will recommend certain alterations . . .' In fact this whole matter caused Bouch considerable embarrassment. The inspector had, as far as he was concerned, arrived unannounced. In his report for the following shareholders' meeting, he wrote 'From a misunderstanding of the instruction of the Board of Trade, too early notice has been given to our readiness to open the line and as a consequence of which, the Board of Trade Inspector has arrived before he was expected and before we were ready to receive him. He has, however thoroughly inspected the line and subjected the bridges to a severe test the result of which was quite satisfactory and only suggested some slight alterations in minor details . . .' He then goes on in an attempt to be more positive 'I think I may congratulate you that when the line is finally completed you will have a railway more substantial than ordinary and the more so that the Government Inspector stated he had never inspected a line of the same length on which the works were so numerous'. Bouch had explained to Captain Rich, the Board of Trade Inspector, before the inspection, that the line was incomplete and it was hoped all would be ready by the second week in September. The Directors excused the lack of completion on the shortage of manpower.

One modification the Board of Trade had insisted on was the replacement of all the chairs by a heavier version. The £200 allocated for the opening ceremony would not be needed for a while and the plans to send out invitations for a 'cold collage' (collation plus wine, no more than 5 shillings per head) at Keswick with the opening train to start at Cockermouth, with Penrith guests and those on the route being conveyed to Cockermouth first by a special train, had to be put 'on hold'! So did the free train travel (for those who applied for tickets from the Secretary) on the following day.

Whilst all this was taking place, other essential business was being progressed. On 2nd June the station masters were appointed. John Latimer at Keswick, on 30s. per week with an allowance of 3s. per week for house rent until a dwelling could be erected for him, he would also be provided with uniform; Henry Sutcliffe for Newbiggin, on 19s. plus a house and uniform; for Penruddock, William Reay on 21s. with a house and uniform; William Richardson for Troutbeck, on 19s. with house and uniform; Richard Hopes for Braithwaite, also on 19s., house and uniform. Bassenthwaite Lake was put in charge of Samuel McKenzie, 21s., house and uniform and Embleton went to John Scott on the same terms as Newbiggin. It will be seen that by this time, the proposal (on 4th May) to use the name 'Thornthwaite' had been dropped in favour of 'Braithwaite' (as originally suggested by the Station Committee) and a similar one to use either 'Greystoke' or 'Dacre' dropped in favour of 'Newbiggin'. In the end, the name 'Blencow' was favoured and so, in turn, 'Newbiggin' was abandoned as well.

At the same time the Directors instructed the Engineer to survey a line from some point on the CK&PR at or nearby Cockermouth and Embleton to a point on the projected extension of the Cleator Railway near Ullock. This was one of a number of schemes over the years which came to nothing. By the 30th June, a scale of local fares and a scale of rates had been agreed, as had a timetable for passenger trains. The latter were agreed at a meeting at Euston on 9th June and were as follows:

	am	am	pm	pm
Depart Penrith	6.45	9.37	1.40	6.00
Reach Cockermouth	8.05	10.57	3.00	7.20
Leave Cockermouth	7.00	9.00	11.45	6.10
Reach Penrith	8.20	10.20	1.05	7.30

Fares were based on 2½d. per mile for first class, 1¾d. for second class and 1d. for third class. Return tickets would be 'a fare and a half'.

As far as the actual working procedures on the line were concerned, the LNWR system would be used and G.P. Neele of the LNWR agreed to send Henry Cattle a copy of the regulations. Another decision made was that Government classes would only be available on the first and last trains each way each day. On the other trains only first and second would be available. Through bookings would be possible for Carlisle, Lancaster, Preston, Liverpool, Birmingham, Manchester and London with Keswick, Cockermouth, Penruddock and Bassenthwaite Lake. Consideration would be given to including the other 'minor' stations in the future. Tourist fares to Keswick from stations south of Preston would be the same as those to Penrith and passengers would be able to return by Windermere without extra payment. Tourists would also be able to break their journeys between Keswick and Penrith. A rather nice turn of phrase came at the end of the deliberations when it was stated 'Rolling Stock of the LNWR to be considered at home on the CK&PR'.

At a meeting in Penrith on 20th July it was agreed that through bookings would be made from the CK&PR to Appleby, Kirkby Stephen, Barnard Castle, Darlington and places beyond. The issuing of tourist tickets was discussed and it was agreed these should be valid for one month and cost the equivalent of two returns plus 25 per cent.

Further discussions had also been taking place during this period involving the stations at either end of the line. On 25th July it was decided a station master should be appointed for Cockermouth. The person appointed would answer to the joint station committee 'with occasional Lawful requests from each of the companies' and receive a salary of £100 per annum. The CK&PR Board were told on 31st August that the Penrith joint station committee felt it would be impossible to work the traffic of the EVR and CK&PR on the LNWR main line and had urged the LNWR immediately to continue the CK&PR line down to the station and make a temporary platform until the permanent work had been completed.

There had also been problems relating to the engine shed at Penrith. On 11th August, Hoskins reported on a visit he had made to Euston on 14th July to try and settle the matter. He met Richard Moon and William Cawkwell and found them difficult. They were reluctant for the CK&PR to build a shed on their land, the suggestion being that if they did, it would belong to the LNWR. However, building a shed on CK&PR land would result in it being too far from the station. There was also the matter of who should actually be responsible for building it. After some considerable wrangling it was eventually agreed that the shed should be built on LNWR property with undertakings about rent (for other companies' use) and removal, if ever necessary. In fact, the deliberations before this meeting had become so difficult at one stage that Christopher Johnstone, of the Caledonian Railway, was asked to arbitrate and he had come to the view, before the meeting on 14th July, that the onus to build was on the CK&PR. It had been argued that if the LNWR was working the CK&PR it should provide the shed at Penrith, particularly as it ought to be on LNWR property. It was agreed that the LNWR would build the shed and charge 5 per cent upon the outlay for rent as long as the shed was used exclusively for the CK&PR. This later presented problems for the NER when they wanted use of the shed and another long wrangle ensued.

A decision was made at a meeting on 23rd September which was to give rise to a number of issues a few years later. The meeting involved representatives from the Furness Railway, LNWR, C&WR, CK&PR, the Whitehaven Junction and the Whitehaven and Furness Junction railways. It was noted that from Whitehaven to Carnforth was 74 miles whereas via Keswick the journey was 85 miles making the Whitehaven route the more favourable. Fitzsimmons for the LNWR proposed that all traffic to and from Workington should be conveyed by the shortest route and that all existing rates by the longer routes be cancelled after the opening of the CK&PR and this was agreed.

In October, Captain Rich returned to carry out a further inspection of the line . . . but the work was still unfinished. There had been a number of steps taken to speed up the process. Between £300 and £400 was made available to pay additional wages and the Works Committee had instructed the contractor to get in platelayers from other railways to facilitate completion. All to no avail. After his visit on 23rd and 24th October, Captain Rich, on this occasion, did produce a report. This is dated 25th October so he certainly wasted no time! His first observation, not surprisingly, was that the line was incomplete. He went on to indicate where there were areas of weakness which would need to be rectified. There was concern about the signalling and he warned of possible collisions with trains on the CK&PR and the L&CR. In addition there were 10 main areas for attention. He noted that there was at least one viaduct where an abutment wall had collapsed. Retaining walls had also collapsed in some places and parapet walls were incomplete in others. The pitching of the bank at Bassenthwaite was unsatisfactory (the Works Committee must have felt vindicated) and the west distant signal at Blencow would have to be raised and moved to a greater distance. His conclusion that 'the railway would be a danger to the Public and therefore cannot be opened to passengers' was, in effect, a foregone conclusion. Shortly after Rich's visit, the retaining wall at Cockermouth viaduct collapsed.

The Works Committee met on 29th October to consider the report. As far as Bassenthwaite was concerned, enough was enough. They recommended that the contractor be relieved of the work and help should be sought elsewhere. Wood was authorised to act. It is perhaps surprising that in spite of all these problems, their advice was that goods trains should commence running, which they did the following month. When the Board met on 3rd November, disappointment in the contractor was expressed strongly and there was a resolution to take drastic action. It was decided that Boulton should henceforth be paid only on a week by week basis. No plant was to be recovered by him from the works without written authority and no sale was to be made without confirmation. All monies due for the plant were to be paid to the Secretary direct by the purchasers. This action sowed the seeds for what was to become a lengthy and acrimonious legal battle between the company and the contractor and this continued long after the railway opened.

On another front, on 1st December, Cattle had occasion to report to the Board the behaviour of John Latimer, the man appointed to be station master at Keswick. Cattle had taken the step of dismissing him for being on the station platform 'in a state of intoxication' (in violation of Rule 4). Latimer had appealed to the Board against this decision (Rule 10) and asked to be reinstated. The Board, perhaps with more pressing issues to consider, decided to defer a decision.

Back at the works, Bouch carried out a careful inspection on 15th December in the company of the Works Committee, declared the line was ready for inspection and that the Board of Trade should be informed. Captain Rich returned for a third visit on 22nd December and wrote a report on the 23rd December. In it he informed the company that the line was ready for opening to passenger traffic and the Works Committee decided 2nd January, 1865 should be the day. There is no evidence but it is not unreasonable to assume that the Directors, and no doubt others involved in the project, had a happier Christmas than usual and may well have stood by their Christmas trees, in accordance with the custom recently introduced by Prince Albert, but with the traditional toasts of the season being augmented by one to 'The Railway'.

Chapter Three

The Railway Opens - Rise and (some) Fall
1865-1880

1865

There was no time to organise cold collations. Passenger trains started running, as planned, on 2nd January, 1865, 10 days after the inspector's report had been received. It is fortunate there is still extant an eloquent account of the first journey which gives detail not only of the event but of the line itself. The language is sometimes rather florid and there are some rather amusing, if unusual, turns of phrase but the account catches the mood of the event.

The regular passenger trains commenced running on the line yesterday [Monday] and there will be three trains from Penrith to Cockermouth and back daily, which have been arranged so as to meet the more important trains from north, south and east. At ten o'clock yesterday [Monday] morning the first regular train, consisting of eight carriages started from Penrith station and though the weather was the reverse of favourable for those who were inclined to travel for pleasure only, the carriages were well filled, chiefly by those who had an interest in the line and were determined to know somewhat of its capabilities. Waiting the arrival of the 'Eden Valley' the train started precisely at ten o'clock and a lusty cheer from the friends on the platform and in the carriages was the only token that anything unusual was taking place. Up the incline from Penrith to Troutbeck there is nothing particularly striking or in any way different from many other lines, but as soon as the summit is attained and the train approaches Threlkeld, the scene changes and even as viewed in its present aspect the great diversity of the scenery cannot fail to be appreciated by those for whose convenience and profit the line has been originated and so successfully carried out. Leaving Threlkeld, the line at a gradual decline approaches Keswick skirting for some distance and frequently crossing the River Greta whose banks are well wooded and the scenery picturesque. Again crossing the Greta, close to the town, we draw up at Keswick. There we find a large and convenient station with Mr Latimer as master. Closely adjacent is the hotel capable of accommodating hundreds of visitors and which, from its many conveniences cannot fail, under judicious and liberal management, to attract to it a large portion of the tourists who annually frequent the delightful summer resort. Its erection, now that the line has been established, was a necessity, for even previously complaints had been made of the want of sufficient hotel accommodation at Keswick. Here the event seems to be regarded as most auspicious, the station is garlanded with evergreens, the large platform which is almost entirely protected from the elements is densely crowded. Loud cheers rent the air and the melodious strains from the instruments of the Rifle Corps Band, proclaim that a new era has dawned for Keswick. The scene contrasts favourably with the cheerless prospect outside, for the snow is still falling heavily covering with its white mantle hill and valley and even in some instances presenting itself unsolicited in the carriages as they dash along the line and making the window seats anything but pleasant and yet, what a change for the better ! How much more comfortable to journey from Penrith to Keswick under the hour in spite of wind and weather than to be outside passenger on a coach trying in vain to protect oneself from the wind and snow for three weary hours. In this respect at least we may well ask that old times may come again no more. Leaving Keswick we pass along one of the most delightful portions of railway in the world; on one side a majestic range of mountains, their summits, clad with snow,

Cockermouth, Keswick and Penrith Railway.

TIME-TABLE for JANUARY, 1865.

UP.	1	2	3		DOWN.	1	2	3	
Classes refer to the Cockermouth, Keswick & Penrith Railway only.	1&2 Cl. & Gov.	1&2 Cl.	1&2 Cl.		Classes refer to the Cockermouth, Keswick & Penrith Railway only.	1&2 Cl. & Gov.	1&2 Cl.	1&2 Cl.	
	a.m.	a.m.	p.m.			p.m.	a.m.	a.m.	
Maryport..........leave	...	...	4 28	...	London, (Euston) l've	9 0	...	9 0	...
Whitehaven..............	...	10 40	4 20	...	Birmingham.............	10 30	6 0	11 15	...
Workington..............	...	11 2	4 45	...		a.m.			...
Cockermouth arrive	...	11 30	5 15	...	Manchester..............	2 0	9 30	1 40	...
					Liverpool, (Lime St.)	1 15	9 10	1 0	...
Cockermouth l've	7 0	11 40	6 40	...	Wigan.....................	2 47	10 12	2 6	...
Embleton,......... „	7 8	11 48	6 48	...	Preston....................	3 25	10 50	2 45	...
Bassenthwaite Lake	7 15	11 55	6 55	...	Lancaster................	4 0	11 32	3 18	...
Braithwaite...... „	7 30	12 10	7 10	...	York, v. L'ds & Inglt'n	...	...	11 45	...
Keswick........ „	7 42	12 22	7 22	...	Newcastle, v. Carlisle	...	10 15	1 45	...
Threlkeld......... „	7 53	12 33	7 33	...	Do. v. Bp. Auckland	5 15	...	...	...
Troutbeck ...... „	8 7	12 47	7 47	...	Edinburgh	...	10 0	1 0	...
Penruddock..... „	8 13	12 53	7 53	...	Glasgow, v. Caledon.	...	9 45	12 15	...
Blencow .... „	8 22	1 4	8 4	...	Do., v. G. & S.-W.	...	8 0	10 30	...
Penrith ...arrive at	8 35	1 15	8 15	...	Leeds, v. Ingleton....	...	5 35	2 5	...
					Darlington	7 25	...	1 0	...
Penrith, dep., North,	8 47	1 23	8 37	...	Barnard Castle	8 1	...	1 35	...
Do., do., South,	8 43	1 37	8 20	...	Kirkby Stephen	8 45	...	2 22	...
	8 50				Carlisle....................	8 10	1 5	5 0	...
Do., do., E. Valley	10 0	3 30	...	...	Penrith, arr. E. Valley	9 35	...	3 20	...
Carlisle......arrive at	9 35	1 55	9 10	...	Do., do., South, {	5 45	1 23	5 12	...
Edinburgh	...	5 45	12 25	...		8 47			
Glasgow, v. Caledon.	...	6 15	12 35	...	Do., do., North, {	8 43	1 37	5 33	...
Do. v. G. & S.-W.	3 55	8 50	...	...		8 50			
Lancaster	10 26	3 9	10 5	...					
Preston...................	11 10	3 44	10 45	...		a.m.	p.m.	p.m.	
Wigan....................	11 47	4 15	11 18	...	**Penrith**........leave	9 40	1 45	5 40	...
Liverpool, (Lime St.)	12 40	5 10	12 15	...	Blencow .... „	9 51	1 56	5 51	...
Manchester	12 45	5 0	12 10	...	Penruddock..... „	10 3	2 8	6 3	...
Birmingham............	3 15	7 20	2 31	...	Troutbeck........ „	10 10	2 15	6 10	...
London, (Euston).....	5 50	9 50	5 50	...	Threlkeld........ „	10 23	2 28	6 23	...
Kirkby Stephen.......	10 55	4 21	...	...	**Keswick**........ „	10 32	2 37	6 32	...
Barnard Castle........	12 7	5 35	...	...	Braithwaite..... „	10 40	2 45	6 40	...
Darlington..............	12 45	6 15	...	...	Bassenthwaite Lake..	10 55	2 59	6 55	...
Redcar....................	2 55	7 52	...	...	Embleton........ „	11 3	3 8	7 3	...
Saltburn.................	3 10	8 5	...	...	**Cockermouth**..arr.	11 15	3 20	7 15	...
York, v. Darlington..	3 5	8 55	...	...					
Do., v. Inglt'n & Leeds	4 15	6 35	...	...	Cockermouth ... leave	11 40	6 10	...	...
Newcastle, v. Carlisle	1 10	5 35	...	...	Workington arrive at	12 5	6 40	...	...
Do., v. Bp. Auckland	4 0	7 55	...	...	Whitehaven.............	12 30	7 10	...	...
Leeds, v. Ingleton ...	3 0	4 30	12 5	...					
Do. v. Lancaster...	3 0	...	...	...					**OVER**

Cockermouth, Keswick & Penrith Railway Timetable, January 1865. Note these times do not agree with the ones decided at Euston, the previous June.

frown upon us whilst on the right is the beautiful Bassenthwaite Lake, its surface now ruffled by the wintry wind and covered with innumerable flocks of wildfowl. Here, for several miles, the line is almost level and we glide swiftly over its surface with almost imperceptible motion. The opposite shore of the lake (which we never lose sight of till we arrive at Bassenthwaite Station) is thickly dotted with gentlemen's seats which rear their heads above, or peep inquisitively from the woods by which they are surrounded. Shortly Embleton is passed, at this season of the year, a wild infrequented country, rarely visited by strangers. A few miles more and we reach Cockermouth, when the whole of the passengers disembark and the neat and pleasantly little station is at once crowded. Further additions to the group are made by the arrival of a train from Workington which deposits its living freight, gathers up the new arrivals and at once returns, whence it came. The Cockermouth Station stands on an eminence nearly opposite the old castle and is within five minutes walk of the town and closely adjoins the recently erected church which has been such a cause of dissension between the inhabitants of Cockermouth, more particularly those who belong to the masonic order, and their diocesan. After a stay of fifteen minutes, the weather prevented any attempt at conviviality, for refreshments which would have been eagerly welcomed, were unfortunately not within our grasp, we take our seats for the return journey. The route is the same, the weather has not improved, half an hour brings us to Keswick when a scene similar to the former is enacted , the cry 'take your seats' is heard, from voices not as yet accustomed to its utterance, the whistle screeches horribly, as our Dean would say, and we are once more en route for Penrith. As we approach Newbiggin the breaks [*sic*] are applied, immediately there is a diminution of speed, the train runs into Penrith exactly at the time specified 1.15 pm and the journey to Cockermouth has been accomplished in time to prevent any delay in the serving up of our New Year's dinner. The line throughout, incline and decline, is perfectly steady; there is none of that unpleasant jolting that railway passengers have frequently to endure. The first and second class carriages have been fitted up with more that the ordinary attention paid to the comfort and convenience of the public; in fact the directors seem to have taken every pains, foreseen every requirement and endeavoured to make the line one of the most attractive and enjoyable in the whole Kingdom. Great credit is given by The Government Inspector to the contractors and engineer for the manner in which they have completed their respective undertakings.

Sadly the writer's identity is unknown. The coach referred to in the account was scheduled to leave Penrith at 8.53 am and arrive in Keswick at 11.50 am. It returned from Keswick at 3.00 pm and arrived back at 6.00 pm. As implied in the account, it would be no match for the railway.

Although still in office, it would seem, on the opening day, poor John Latimer was not destined to share in the new euphoria. On 5th January the Board upheld Cattle's action and his dismissal was confirmed. Bouch, it was agreed, would stand down with the full opening of the Railway and Wood was appointed Resident Engineer on a salary of £250 per annum. Boulton, it was decided, would have to relinquish his agreement to maintain the line. This did not mean they had heard the last of him! The main business, now, was getting the railway fully operational. Even though railways were no longer in their infancy, those who were employed to work on them in this period usually had no previous knowledge of procedures and so it was imperative that careful and clear instructions were given at all levels, especially to the more senior employees such as the enginemen and station staffs. The man entrusted with much of this work was Henry Cattle, the first Secretary and Manager.

The First Rule Book (1864) and Mr Cattle's Circulars (1865-1870)

The contents of the first Rule Book were approved by the Directors at a meeting on 2nd June, 1864 and the authorisation for it was signed by Henry Cattle. It is very user-friendly. There are 101 pages written in simple language which even those with only rudimentary reading skills, given the state of literacy of the period, probably found reasonably easy to follow. The print is clear and quite large and key words and sections are printed in heavy type. The book is divided into sections, each clearly marked. Rules 1-10 are about general matters and relate to issues such as duty and behaviour. For example Rule 4 states 'No instance of intoxication on duty will ever be overlooked - such an offence will render the party committing it liable to instant dismissal and to punishment by a magistrate'. Rule 5 cautions against the use of improper language, cursing and swearing, rudeness or incivility to passengers and receiving gratuities. Any may result in dismissal. There is opportunity for redress. Rule 10 points out that 'should any servant think himself aggrieved at any time, he may memorial the Board; but in such case the memorial must be sent through the head of the department'. Rules 11-39 deal with signals, with a section at the end on special signals for the junction at Cockermouth. Rules 40-46 deal with points, 47-65 station masters and clerks. Rule 57 is printed in very heavy type and states 'Every exertion must be made for the expeditious dispatch of the Station duties and for ensuring punctuality in the Trains'. 59 'As a general rule Passenger Trains are to take precedence of Luggage, Cattle and Coal Trains and such Trains must not be started from any Station when Passenger Trains are due'. This rule is then qualified with certain exceptions but the Directors of the CK&PR make it clear where priority lies. Rules 66-77 relate to policemen, signalmen and pointsmen; 78-83 to gatemen and level crossings and 84-119 to enginemen. In this last group, Rule 84 states 'All Engines or Trains following each other shall keep at least 1,000 yards apart'. Rule 86 makes it clear that a driver must be with the engine 30 minutes before the journey is due to start; the fireman 45 minutes. Both must be 'as clean as circumstances will allow'. Rules 120-150 are for guards and breaksman; 151-187, platelayers and others. There follows a section on train staff regulations: 'The Directors having ordered that a signal staff or Train Staff Ticket is to be carried with each train or Engine, to and from, without this Staff or Ticket no Engine or train is to be allowed to proceed'. Twelve rules are contained in this section. There follows a section listing certain bye laws; there are eight of these. Rule 4 is interesting in that it forbids passengers to smoke both in carriages and in the company's stations. Again there are those forbidding intoxication and causing damage to items such as linings and cushions. Finally there are relevant extracts from Acts of Parliament on railway matters.

Evidence suggests that Henry Cattle carried out his duties in a most diligent and fastidious way. Fortunately, Mr Fawcett, the first station master at Penrith, was equally meticulous. When it appeared that in some ways the Rule Book might be too simple and addenda were necessary, or if there was a suggestion that the rules were not being applied properly (not suggested but perhaps because some had problems resulting from a lack of literacy) Henry Cattle issued circulars. These appeared on a regular basis and on a variety of topics. On receiving his copies, Fawcett carefully stuck them into a well bound book for reference. The book, albeit now in a rather dilapidated form, exists today and the circulars give us an insight into operational practice, the short-comings and Henry Cattle himself, as he endeavoured to ensure the Railway ran smoothly, efficiently and safely.

Most of the circulars are printed on blue paper in what approximates to A5 size, although some are written by hand. As far as the latter group is concerned, it would seem they are not in Cattle's hand; only signed by him. Some of the early ones deal with very routine matters but, again, it should be borne in mind they were, in effect, training documents for employees almost completely unfamiliar with procedures on a railway.

Circular 13, issued on 30th December, 1864, just before the railway opened to passengers, deals with the collection of tickets. 'These must be collected before the holders leave the station'. 'Day and Market tickets are double . . . make sure the passenger gets the return half . . .' 'Passengers who travel in a more superior class (than the ticket purchased) must be charged the difference'. 'A passenger with no ticket must be charged from the starting point of the train, unless the starting point is known and there is no intention to defraud the Company'.

The Volunteer Rifle Corps formed the subject of No. 16 issued on 23rd March, 1865. When these men were in uniform they were able to take a double journey for the price of a single ticket from where they reside to 'the place which the Station Clerk knows is appointed for the Corps to assemble'. 'As all trains have 1st and 2nd Class carriages attached, Tickets of these classes may be issued by any Train, 3rd Class tickets may also be issued by such Trains as will admit of the volunteers travelling *in each direction* by that class carriage. Volunteer tickets will be supplied to the stations'.

The following circular, No. 17, applies to military, marine and police forces and states that each commissioned officer is able to travel '2*d*. per mile, 1st Class and each soldier, marine or private of militia or police force and each wife widow or child (above 12) is authorised to travel 1*d*. per mile 2nd or 3rd Class. Children under 3 travel free'.

Circular No. 18 deals with excess luggage rates whilst No. 19 deals with the sombre business of transporting corpses. The rate for the latter is 1*s*. per mile; 10*s*. minimum. A circular issued in May looks very jolly. It is printed on pink paper and the print face is decorative. It is headed Pic-Nic or Pleasure Parties. 'During the Summer Months, starting on 1st June, parties of not less than six who intend to return the same day will be able to purchase 1st and 2nd Class Return Tickets at a single fare for the double journey'. These tickets, which had to be bought two days in advance, were issued at all stations to Keswick and Bassenthwaite Lake and also to Ullswater and Brownriggs Hotel, the coach fare being included.

Other circulars deal with routine operational matters. Number 22, issued on 27th September, 1865 refers to waggons set aside for the use of coal and lime traffic between coal pits and lime quarries on the C&WR and the CK&PR and instructs that all waggons have to be unloaded on the day of arrival and sent back the following day.

In a different vein, Circular 25, issued on 5th October, 1865, may strike a chord with anyone who has been on the receiving end of memoranda dealing with difficult, urgent matters. He writes, 'Having received some terrible frights lately from the way in which letters have been addressed to me, the words 'IMPORTANT' and 'VERY IMPORTANT' written in red ink outside the cover, when the matter was of the most trifling importance, I beg to request that you will not address your letters in this way unless the subject *is* very important'.

Circular 26 is somewhat seasonal, being issued, as it was, on 10th October (1865). 'As the season of the year is now approaching when foggy weather may be expected . . . keep up the supply of detonators for those who need them'. He goes on to remind the recipients that Rules 156 and 157 forbid ballasting or the removal of rails in such conditions unless there are exceptional circumstances. Facilities must be provided for the sanding of the rails and waggons in sidings must be secured with scotches during high winds to prevent them being blown onto the main line.

On the same day, he issued Circular No. 28: 'I find many of the Company's servants travelling without tickets or passes. No-one will be allowed to travel without the same - if they do so they may be fined'. At one point Cattle is clearly displeased by what he considers sloppy behaviour by the company's employees, especially those who act in any way in an administrative capacity but also by those who operate the Railway as well. In Circular 31 he addresses such issues 'I find that a very unbusinesslike way in replying to letters particularly in the Passenger Department prevails at our stations. What I mean is the replies being written across inward letters and the letters being returned to the sending stations. This must at once be discontinued and all replies written on the proper memorandum forms. All inward letters to be carefully preserved for in some cases letters have been sent back and we are thus left without any reference whatsoever'. He also insists that copies of outward letters are kept as well. It is perhaps significant that it is at about this time that Mr Fawcett starts to stick the circulars into a book and may explain why most of the circulars before this point do not appear to have been retained. On matters of what he perceives is poor practice and slackness he has occasion in Circular 46 to point out 'I have observed trains arriving at Keswick and other stations following a preceding train within the time named in Rule 23. Drivers ignoring signals are to be reported'. Then again, 'I find the practice prevails of parties holding Facing Points when trains are passing over them by simply placing the knee against the handle instead of firmly holding it in the right hand'.

To engine drivers he has the following to say in Circular 47: 'I find a practice prevails with Drivers of Assistant Engines of uncoupling their engines from the train on reaching the top of an incline and allowing the leading engine with the train to proceed, their engine following a short distance behind. This is highly dangerous to Platelayers and at Level Crossings (because a following engine may not be expected)'. Station masters are chided in Circular 49 for interrupting clerks who are attempting to send messages on the telegraph.

Circular 33, issued on 26th February, 1867 deals with telegraphing trains. 'All trains, goods and mineral, as well as passenger and regular, as well as specials, must immediately, on passing any station, be telegraphed to the next station.

Penrith and Cockermouth must announce to Keswick the departure of all trains' [which was the existing practice]. A 10 minute rule was introduced. 'Those attending the Telegraph must check it at no more than ten minute intervals'.

In an attempt to iron out a number of problems relating to operating procedures, a lengthy Circular, 34, was issued on 19th February, 1867. It stated that amended regulations would come into effect on 1st March. The engineman would be the person on whom responsibility must rest on the train. A train must not leave a station without the train staff (that is, baton) for the appropriate section. The station master would be the sole person in charge and authorised to deal with this. The engineman was to receive the staff and place it in the special socket on the engine. If other trains travelled in succession before the staff could be returned, a train ticket was to be issued to the leading train (or engine) indicating 'Staff Following'. 'The staff *must* be shown to the engineman to whom the ticket was issued and the staff must be given to the last train' (in the group). Once the staff had been issued, no other engine or train must leave the station until the staff was back. Provision would be made so that tickets could not be acquired without the staff, which would also act as a key. Colour codes would be adopted, each section having its own colour. A red staff, for example, would only open a red box. In addition, colours would be alternated so that the same colour would not be used for two sections at one station. The ticket boxes would be fixed in the office. As far as ballast trains were concerned, these must proceed to the next station after depositing their loads and the staff must be handed over there. Cattle was adamant these regulations should be obeyed to the letter and his desire to see a properly run railway becomes clear again when he states 'Dismissal will follow for any engineman who disobeys regulations even though no accident occurs'. He then points out that 'taking a Staff beyond a station at which it should be left is also a grave offence'. Further, such action 'will be severely dealt with' although the inference seems to be that there will not be automatic dismissal in this case. As far as guards are concerned, they are instructed they must not give the signal to depart until they have been shown the staff or ticket by the engineman. Again, any disregard of this would result in either a fine or dismissal. As far as the telegraph was concerned, this must still be used to announce the departure of every train. When a train had a pilot engine, the front engine must carry the staff or ticket. If an engine failed, the fireman must take the staff to the station 'whence assistance is expected that the Staff may be at the station on arrival of the engine'. If the engine is in possession of a ticket, 'assistance CAN ONLY COME FROM THE STATION AT WHICH THE STAFF HAS BEEN LEFT'. The fireman was to accompany the assistant engine to his own. On 17th July, 1870 a further instruction was issued in addition to Number 34 (although not numbered) regarding pilot engines. 'When a Pilot Engine is assisting a train and is attached to the front of the regular engine, the Pilot or front engine will carry the Staff or Ticket but in the event of the assistant engine being behind the train, he must carry the Staff or Ticket and a Ticket must also be given to the engine on the front of the train'.

Cattle seems to have afforded what might be termed privileges to certain individuals. Two of these are indicated in hand-written (and so unnumbered) circulars. The first, dated 6th September, 1866 states: 'You may allow Mr Joseph Cochain, Wine and Spirit Merchant, to travel by goods train at any time on his taking a Ticket'. The second 'I have agreed with Mr Mark Cockbain of Souterfell to convey a newspaper for him from Penrith to Troutbeck once a week for a year commencing February 1st 1868 and ending January 31st 1869. Our Stationmaster at Troutbeck will collect the amount, 2s. 6d. and debit himself through parcels. Always enter the newspaper free of charge'. Problems arose over the transport of luggage in private carriages on carriage trucks which prompted a hand-written missive (not actually written by Cattle, but signed by him). 'In no case must you allow the party or parties owning the carriage to have more luggage than is allowed according to the class they travel. All above must be charged as Ordinary Passengers Excess Luggage. The carriages must be looked into'. In 1868 it was agreed workmen's tickets would be introduced and Cattle outlined the conditions for these in Circular 36 of 20th May. They would be available from Saturday night until Monday morning to workmen employed in the neighbourhood 'of our Country Stations but whose families reside elsewhere' (Cockermouth, Keswick or Penrith). The fares were the same as Third Class market tickets. They would be available on the last train on Saturday evening and for return by the first train on Monday. The issue of these tickets was tightly regulated and required a special application being made. Each application had to be personally approved by Cattle before a ticket could be issued and the period of validity clearly indicated. Once a ticket had expired, a fresh application had to be made. In fact this circular was followed, a week later, by one from the accountant, Peter Thompson, pointing out that it would be Third Class Sunday tickets which would be issued to workmen. This concession was followed by another similar one in December of the same year. Station masters' and platelayers' wives attending market at Keswick or Cockermouth could purchase Government tickets at a single rate for a double journey. These tickets were required to have 'Return' and 'Station masters Wife' or 'Platelayers Wife' written on the back.

Cattle continued to issue a steady stream of circulars, some 53 in all, until he left the CK&PR in 1870. He was succeeded as manager by the man who during this time had been the accountant, Peter Thompson.

As the line settled down to the new found routines, there were other matters to be addressed. There were decisions to be made about the hotel. Major Spedding, together with the Resident Engineer and the Manager, were authorised to take immediate steps to furnish it and arrange for the laying out of the grounds. Mr Bap was set on to help with the former and Mr Kemp, of Birkenhead, was asked to lay out the grounds.

On 15th February (1865) Mr Jenkinson was appointed to fill the vacancy of station master at Keswick. Meanwhile other misdemeanours had been uncovered at the same station. John Atkinson, the booking clerk, and Joseph Thwaites, a porter, were accused of overcharging for the carriage of parcels and pocketing the excess. Thwaites was dismissed; Atkinson was demoted.

Station masters' houses were still needed at Keswick, Blencow and Threlkeld and on 29th March tenders were opened and Mr Harrison was awarded the contract for £1,037.

At the shareholders' meeting on 22nd February, the Directors excused the late opening of the line by pointing out that the Board of Trade Inspector had imposed stringent requirements on the company but, on the positive side, they were able to say the heavy mineral trains, which had been running for some weeks, had tried and proved the line. The projected cost was £297,420 8s. 10d. and this included the cost of the hotel which was almost finished.

In fact, at this point, there was a significant development involving the hotel. The Cumberland Lake District Hotel Company in Penrith put in a bid to purchase it. They gave an undertaking (rather rashly, as it turned out) to build a first class hotel at Bassenthwaite as part of the deal. The hotel company was prepared to take the hotel as it stood for cost price and to pay within two years with interest at 5 per cent. The Directors were agreeable to this, subject to the shareholders' approval. It was at this time the Directors decided to build a covered way between the hotel and the station, a shrewd move as the cost would be deemed part of the hotel outlay and therefore be charged to the hotel company!

On 23rd May, Cattle wrote to Fawcett at Penrith. 'You will have received my letter of last evening about The Eden Valley Train. Of course you will not accept orders from Mr Stephenson about our trains. Don't leave the train when you can possibly avoid it but don't stay after 10 o'clock unless you hear that there are passengers on the train'. The matter of not holding trains to allow the making of connections became quite a contentious one at times. Both companies were responsible for the practice, occasionally, and in 1894, the Chairman of the CK&PR, then H.C. Howard, speaking at a staff dinner where employees from all the companies (CK&PR, NER and LNWR) were present, caused laughter and cheering when he said 'The North Eastern is also a very important connection which only has one fault which, I hope, when I have mentioned it, will no longer continue. The North Eastern will never wait for the trains on the CK&PR although they always make the trains of that Company wait for theirs!'

During the first half of the year, Boulton's equipment was put up for sale (Wood was instructed to purchase any useful items) Cattle arranged for a bookstall to be put on Keswick station and it was agreed to put in a blind siding at Keswick. The Board, at a meeting on 11th May, expressed concern that the NER had not let them have a sight of the plans to form the junction at Redhills and urgent request was made for this. It was agreed a tank engine should be purchased, although there was some uncertainty about whether or not it could occasionally be used in service and it was resolved to approach the LNWR to clarify this. Staffing was reckoned to be too high although the Board had to concede it was difficult to see where reductions could be made. Period ticket prices were set as follows:

1st Class	12 months	£1 per mile
2nd Class	12 months	15 shillings per mile
For 6 months	Half the cost of 12 months plus 20 per cent	
For 3 months	Half the cost of 6 months plus 20 per cent	

The Cumberland Lake District Hotel Company ran into problems with the scheme to build a hotel at Bassenthwaite. Lord Leconfield objected to the proposal to put boats on the lake and this was deemed an integral part of the scheme! (This was not the first time Lord Leconfield had raised an objection relating to some aspect of the Railway.) More to the point, perhaps, only £9,000 had been subscribed for the project and so the hotel company asked not to be bound by that part of the proposals. At a special meeting of the shareholders on 17th June, the sale of the hotel at Keswick to The Cumberland Lake District Hotels Limited, was agreed in principle, the condition for the building of a hotel at Bassenthwaite having been waived. It was not, in fact, carried through.

On 16th September, Edmund Grayson was given permission to erect a drinking fountain on the road to Keswick station and a Mr Gibson of Dartford, Kent, made a claim against the Railway relating to the late arrival (on 11th August) at Keswick of the train due to leave Penrith at 5.40 pm. The solicitor was instructed to resist this.

On 26th August, at the shareholders' meeting, the financial aspects of building the line were outlined. There had been no final settlement with Boulton but it was reckoned the cost would be about £10,000 per mile. From the opening date until 31st July there had been receipts totalling £11,168 4s. 4d., expenses had been £7,086 10s. 1d. which left a balance of £4,081 14s. 3d. After interest on debentures £2,360 9s. 3d. remained for dividends. A dividend of 2 per cent was declared which left a little in balance. This was accepted as a satisfactory start.

All seemed set for a bright future. The railway was serving not only the local rural lakeland community but the mines and furnaces of two of England's most important industrial communities as well. Good returns in future seemed assured.

1866

Even so there were events to send ripples across the pond! The Cockermouth Joint Station Committee was still having problems and when it was discovered that Richard Moon, the Chairman of the LNWR would be visiting Whitehaven on 1st August, 1866, it was agreed a deputation of two CK&PR Directors, the Chairman and Thompson, should arrange to meet him and petition him to appoint some LNWR Directors to represent his company on the joint committee. Moon was never the easiest of men to deal with, especially when he was out of sorts. In some of his photographs, he actually has a rather mean appearance; looking for all the world like an archetypal Dickensian figure and the sort of person who might well have inspired the main character in 'A Christmas Carol'. On 1st August, Moon was not in a good mood. Perhaps he considered the deputation to be an intrusion. The Directors received short shrift. Richard Moon told them that in his view the joint committee was unnecessary and that the station could be adequately managed by the two managers, Cattle and Myson. Hoskins had certainly met Moon before and no doubt realised he was not a man with whom to trifle! A recommendation taking into account Moon's observations was placed before a meeting of the CK&PR Board on 18th August and carried. From there on Cattle and Myson would be responsible for running the joint station. However other joint committees would be set up later to deal with other matters.

At the same meeting the Directors felt they had to take the LNWR to task on another matter. This involved the movement of pig iron to Sheffield. It had been reported that pig iron was being taken along the Furness line instead of the CK&PR and this, in the Directors' view, was a contravention of the agreement the company had with the LNWR. A letter was promptly dispatched to the LNWR and an outcome awaited. Cattle meanwhile made attempts to secure a portion of the Consett ore traffic but in spite of his efforts, failed to do so. John Smith, the station master at Threlkeld, resigned and William Wolton was appointed to succeed him. The porters at Keswick station requested overcoats and the Secretary was authorised to provide these at 25 shillings each, on the understanding that the porters paid half the cost! A siding was authorised for the tile works adjoining Troutbeck station and the Secretary was instructed to purchase a horse and waggon for cartage at Keswick.

The LNWR appeared rather reticent in replying to the letter about the pig iron going to Sheffield via the Furness and so another letter was sent on the 20th October. The point was made that receipts were being affected by the practice being adopted. Still there was silence.

The proposal by the Midland Railway Company to construct a line from Settle to Carlisle led the Directors to consider constructing a connecting line to this. The matter was raised again in February (1867) when Wood was instructed to survey a line from Penrith to Langwathby or some other point on the Midland line as he saw appropriate. A petition from a group of residents in Penrith supporting this move, spurred them on. Confident in the support Richard Moon had given them, Messrs Cattle and Myson settled the rules for the operation of Cockermouth station.

Whilst Cattle made every effort to ensure the safe operation of the railway, nevertheless there were accidents. The first fatal accident to be reported occurred in December 1864 when James Thompson, a platelayer, was killed. His widow was awarded £5 compensation and 'all other expenses would be paid'. A little earlier than this, a collision at Penruddock had resulted in Jane Bell being injured. In June 1866 there was an accident involving a goods train and in early February the wife of David Johnstone, the gatekeeper at Rakefoot level crossing, lost her life in an accident there. It was reported that she had acted negligently and when Johnston asked the Directors for compensation he was told that had it not been for their sympathy for his severe loss, they would have dismissed him. Compensation was out of the question.

Mr Boulton, meanwhile, had not left the stage. He was still continuing to dispute the bank's payment to him and was looking for a larger sum in settlement.

On 30th March, Cawkwell, for the LNWR, decided the time was right to reply to the letters from the Directors about the Sheffield traffic. He wrote:

> Clearing House inform me you seek a division via Ingleton of traffic between Whitehaven District Leased Lines and Sheffield as the shortest route. In making the agreement with you, we never contemplated the sending of traffic off our line in the way you suggest by a division via Ingleton and the traffic from Workington if not sent via

Ulverstone would, of course be sent via Keswick, Shap and Preston. There is little difference in mileage between Ingleton and Shap routes and the difference to your company must be small and inconsiderable. Further, I do not wish it to be understood in the Clearing House that we agree to send traffic off our own line, as between your company and mine we are quite prepared to give you your full mileage proportion less working expenses it cannot therefore much affect your company whether we carry the traffic via Ingleton or Shap. I will be glad if you will instruct Mr Dawson to credit you on the mileage via the Furness Railway for your distance between Penrith and Cockermouth at 33⅓% less working expenses.

There was no way, given the problems between the LNWR and Midland during this period, that the LNWR was going to use the Ingleton branch for through traffic.

In August 1866 it was possible to declare a dividend of £1 15s. 0d. The latter part of 1866 saw a steady increase in traffic but after the turn of the year there was a decline. This was attributed to the stagnation of the iron trade and to make things worse, bad weather had adversely affected tourism.

1867-8

The dividend declared at the first shareholders' meeting for 1867, held in February, was a mere 1 per cent. The other bad news was that Boulton was pressing ahead with legal proceedings in spite of the fact that on 30th January the original claim had been dismissed. By August there had been an improvement in revenue and the dividend jumped to 2½ per cent. Even so, the Directors were far from complacent. They reminded the shareholders of the great depression in the iron trade and referred to 'financial calamities which had affected the tourist traffic'. There had, they reported, been a steady increase in general traffic. By this time Boulton's new legal proceedings were well underway and it was alleged that he was demanding money well in excess of what had been paid.

In September 1866, the NER had opened the Eamont-Redhills spur, so completing the East-West link and enabling traffic to flow directly from the CK&PR to the Eden Valley branch and vice versa. The Directors of the CK&PR, when they originally saw the potential for a line such as the one they had built, must have realised this final piece in the jig-saw was inevitable - and, of course, they had not had to go to the trouble of building it!

The fortunes of the company did not see a dramatic improvement, however. In April 1867 the Board, in an effort to improve the revenue situation attempted to get an extension of the tourist season but failed. An interesting appointment, given the period, was made in April when the crossing-keeper at Rakefoot crossing resigned. The job went to a woman, Mrs Dixon, who received 5s. per week and a house rent free. A fatal accident occurred on 20th May. Thomas Park, trespassing on the line between Embleton and Cockermouth, in a drunken, state, was knocked down and killed by a train.

In 1868, the revenue levels remained about the same and dividends of 2½ per cent and 2 per cent were declared for February and August respectively.

Boulton's action was continuing but no decisions could be reached. In fact this remained the situation during 1869. A minor adjustment in the accounting procedure, whereby it was decided in future to close the accounts on 31st December instead of 31st January, was partly held to be the reason why the first dividend declared was only 2¼ per cent but this was specious, to say the least. In the second half the dividend had dropped to 1½ per cent.

The 1870s were a period of mixed fortunes for the railway, tempered, not least, by the dramatic decline of the iron trade in Cumberland.

1870

The year opened with an agreement with W.H. Smith & Son for bookstalls and advertising on station walls at Cockermouth and Keswick. This agreement was in conjunction with the LNWR and Furness Railway (FR) and included Whitehaven and Workington. Relationships between the companies and the rights relating to the setting up of bookstalls fluctuated a great deal over the years and there was not always agreement about who should be given the contracts. This particular arrangement carried with it a first class pass for the bookstall inspector and one for the advertising manager with third class passes for the newsboys at 5s. per mile per annum between any stations on the line. In addition Smith's parcels would be carried from London to Whitehaven at current rates, but with the proviso that parcels could be opened at Penrith and then sent on from there without extra charge. Advertising boards would be carried free.

Spedding had been liaising with the bank over the matter of Boulton's claim but no settlement could be agreed. In February, the arbitrator appointed to try and settle the difference with the company and Boulton awarded Boulton £1,915 with interest. However, the Court of the Queen's Bench almost immediately set this aside, arguing that the arbitrator had exceeded his jurisdiction. Mr Boulton was a man with considerable tenacity; he was not prepared to let matters rest there!

During June an arrangement was made with the Post Office for the use of the company's telegraph and it was agreed with the Post Office that the Railway could carry Keswick mail. The existing agreement with the Electric Telegraph Company was cancelled and the whole apparatus handed over to the company. The Post Office paid the Railway £1,300 and the company then agreed to maintain the poles and fix any new wires needed in return for its use. In July a special Board meeting was held. This resulted from the decision of Henry Cattle to move on to pastures new and 'a more lucrative appointment'. It was decided Peter Thompson should succeed him.

On 2nd September an accident occurred involving three special trains. There had been a Volunteer Review at Penrith and after the event the trains left Penrith at 10 minute intervals. The first train, bound for Egremont, was made up of 15 coaches. A single engine was in charge of this and at Penruddock it was halted to allow the service passenger train from Cockermouth to pass. The latter was due in Penruddock at 7.51 pm. Meanwhile the second special, consisting of

COCKERMOUTH, KESWICK, & PENRITH.

SUNDAYS.

LEAVE	1 2 class a.m.	1 2 class p.m.	1 2 class p.m.	1 2 G class p.m.
Carlisle	7 20	1 5	5 0	
Penrith	8 50	1 50	5 40	5 0
Blencow	9 0	2 0	5 50	5 10
Penruddock	9 13	2 13	6 1	5 22
Troutbeck	9 19	2 19	6 7	5 28
Threlkeld	9 33	2 33	6 19	5 39
Keswick	9 45	2 45	6 30	5 50
Braithwaite	9 51	2 51	6 36	5 56
B'nth't' Lake	10 6	3 6	6 50	6 8
Embleton	10 12	3 12	6 58	6 14
Arr. at Ck'mth	10 20	3 20	7 10	6 25

SUNDAYS.

LEAVE	1 2 G class a.m.	1 2 class a.m.	1 2 class p.m.	1 2 G class a.m.
Cockermouth	7 0	11 50	†3 40	8 30
Embleton	7 8	11 58	3 47	8 38
B's'nth't' Lake	7 15	12 5	3 53	8 47
Braithwaite	7 30	12 20	4 5	8 58
Keswick	7 38	12 28	4 12	9 7
Threlkeld	7 48	12 38	4 21	9 17
Troutbeck	8 2	12 52	4 33	9 28
Penruddock	8 9	12 59	4 39	9 36
Blencow	8 20	1 10	4 50	9 46
Arr. at Penrith	8 30	1 20	5 0	10 0
,, Carlisle	9 35	5 30	5 45	

† Third class Tickets to London and Liverpool will be issued by this train.

MARKET TRAINS.

COCKERMOUTH MARKET.—On Mondays, Market Passengers will be conveyed to Cockermouth by the first Down Train. Tickets available for Return by any train during the day.

PENRITH MARKET.—On Tuesdays, Market Passengers will be conveyed to Penrith by the first Up Train. Tickets available for return by any train during the day.

KESWICK MARKET.—On Saturdays, Market Passengers will be conveyed to Keswick by the first train Up, and the first train Down. Tickets available for Return by any train during the day.

Cockermouth, Keswick & Penrith Railway Timetable, April 1870.

no less than 39 coaches, and heading for Whitehaven, arrived. This train, perhaps not surprisingly, was being banked at the rear and the last two vehicles were a brake van and a horse box. The first special was put into a siding and the second was being put into the loop. At this stage the third special, destined for Maryport, appeared. The driver, T. Smith, had ignored the down distant and, as a result, this train crashed into the banking engine of the second special. The impact projected the banking engine forward and it destroyed the horse box. The brake van, also propelled forward, smashed into the rear passenger coach. Up to 40 people were injured by the collision, one man dying in hospital later. Another man leapt out of the carriage in which he was travelling and fell over the viaduct where it was standing. He sustained serious injuries. It was suggested the accident might have been far worse but fortunately the last coaches of the second special were not occupied. This was attributed to the fact that rain was falling when the train left Penrith and people did not go for the rear coaches because they were beyond the covered platform. Medical aid was given on the spot by Drs I'Anson, Syme and Peat (from Whitehaven, Egremont and Workington respectively) and they were all thanked by the Directors for their help.

Someone, it appears had a grudge against the Railway and on 19th September tampered with the connecting rods of a pair of points at Penruddock station. A £50 reward was offered for information leading to a conviction but it was not claimed. On 21st September, Captain Tyler held an enquiry into the Penruddock accident and in October the LNWR agreed, without prejudice, to meet the claims. This, however, was not the end of the matter.

1871

The NER asked for an extension to be made to the engine shed at Penrith so that one of its engines could be stabled there overnight to avoid the need of taking it back to Kirkby Stephen. The Directors of the CK&PR considered this request when they met in February and decided they could not meet any expense which would be incurred by this. If the NER wished to build the extension it was welcome to do so - but at its own expense!

Another rather dramatic 'accident' occurred on 13th February. The No. 10 Up Goods was uncoupled at Troutbeck from the engine and after standing for about five minutes it ran back from the station and reached such a speed that it was not halted until after passing Braithwaite station. Fortunately no damage was done but it was clear the two people travelling in the brake van had been at risk. One, John McCormack, was a LNWR cleaner and the other, Adam Dodd, was an authorised passenger. Although the cause of the train running away was not discovered there was a strong suspicion someone had tampered with the brake. The outcome was a decision not to allow persons to travel on goods or mineral trains in future unless they were working them.

In March the LNWR paid out £4,329 in respect of the Penruddock accident and then came the sting. On 30th March, William Cawkwell wrote to the Directors of the CK&PR informing them their company must pay its share. The response was very predictable; the Directors repudiated any such liability and so another long wrangle was underway!

The number of items for cartage from Keswick station fell quite sharply and so one of the two horses used for this purpose was sold in April. In the same month there was a discussion about the possibility of converting part of Keswick refreshment room to a ladies' second class waiting room. This was prompted by the need to accommodate the increase in excursion traffic. It was proposed to reduce the rent from £50 to £45.

The Cumberland Union Bank remained keen to sort out the Boulton claim which was still unresolved and in July put forward another scheme for a settlement. This was promptly rejected by the Directors but they did say they would consider other ideas. They appeared to be almost paranoid about this matter and certainly demonstrated considerable intransigence about the whole affair. The bank, almost in despair about their stance, sent a letter in August asking 'have you *nothing* to offer?' It seemed they did not and all that was suggested was 'a frank discussion'. A meeting was arranged for 19th August. In the meantime the Penruddock settlement also remained in dispute. On a different front, the Directors decided to let the Keswick Hotel go and, in October, agreed to a conveyance to this effect in favour of the Keswick Hotel Company.

William Cawkwell wrote to the Directors again on 16th November. This time he pointed out that the underground passage planned for Penrith station had never been built. He asked the Directors whether they would be prepared to share the cost of doing the work and they agreed. At this stage the issues became rather confused, whether by accident or design it is not really possible to say. In December Cawkwell wrote again and now included in the Penrith scheme the extension of the station roof which it seemed the NER was happy to help fund. The CK&PR protested at this move by stealth, stating that only the underpass had been agreed. However, having made the point the Directors agreed to consider sharing the cost of the roof.

As the year ended, meetings with the bank proved fruitless and attempts to settle Boulton's claim were unsuccessful.

1872

A round of movements opened the year with John Scott at Bassenthwaite Lake resigning. William Reay moved up to take his place, leaving a vacancy at Penruddock which was filled by the appointment of Joseph Tinnion from Blencow. Another John Scott, from Redhills Junction box, took on Blencow.

Passengers using Penrith station could look forward to better protection from the rain; the Directors felt they could support the plan to extend the station roof. At the same time it was agreed to extend the siding at Bassenthwaite Lake station. Shared payment for the Penruddock accident remained in contention and in February a decision was made for it to go to arbitration. The date for the hearing was fixed for 11th, 12th and 13th May.

In a surprising move, through bookings from Cockermouth to Carlisle were discontinued and through fares from Keswick to Carlisle were advanced to allow a division to the CK&PR of local fares. In May a decision to allow bookings of third class passengers on all trains with the discontinuing of market trains was seen by many as a step in the right direction; the Directors, however, would soon regret having made this concession. At the shareholders' meeting in August, the Board commented on the death of one of its members, John Simpson, referring to it as 'a deplorable accident on your line of railway'. It was said at the time that a certain amount of mystery surrounded the accident. John Simpson, who lived at Beacon Side, Penrith, also had a property (described as 'a picturesque country residence') at Penruddock. On a day in July, he had gone down to Penruddock, travelling on the 10.10 am. It seems that on alighting he had set off down the track but shortly afterwards had been struck by a mineral train. The locomotive passed over his leg virtually severing it, the 'cinder box struck him violently on the chest and the whole train passed over the mutilated limb'. Simpson was nearly 70 years old and it is surprising he did not die as a result of these injuries or even from the shock he must have experienced. As it happened, he did not but was placed in the van of a luggage train coming from Keswick, conveyed to Penrith and taken to the Railway Tavern after which, and having been attended by Dr Taylor and Dr Robertson, he was taken home. The last part of this journey, about a mile, had to be by hand-cart which, fortunately, was fitted with springs. A large crowd followed and almost throughout Simpson was conscious and able to speak. Shortly after arriving home, he died. There was something of a puzzle because he appeared to have fallen on the track already before being hit by the train. At the first hearing of the inquest it was stated Simpson had been struck by lightning before the train hit him. An adjournment was called in order to hear evidence from the driver of the train, John Shildon (an interesting name for someone who was possibly an ex-S&DR man) and Thomas Wearmouth, the guard (of Shildon). Shildon said that as the train approached Simpson, he had already fallen on the track and twice attempted to get up, managing only to get the main part of his body clear of the line. Shildon confirmed that when he approached Simpson he had indeed claimed to have been struck by lightning. Simpson allegedly repeated this to Wearmouth. Wearmouth also pointed out that for some reason, which he was unable to explain, he had found Simpson's watch seven yards away from its owner. A verdict of 'Accidental Death' was recorded.

In August a decision was finally made to do away with the refreshment room at Keswick station altogether, but now it was necessary to get the agreement of the new hotel company. In addition there had been an offer from a Mr Atkinson to run it and he was prepared to pay £150 per annum to do so. This offer was turned down and in October the hotel company agreed to terminate its use of the area, but only on the understanding that if there was a decision to reinstate it, the existing agreement would be honoured.

At the end of August there was another accident to a mineral train. On the 26th of the month the east distant signal at Penruddock was not raised on the arrival of the No. 6 Down Goods and the facing points remained locked. These were then damaged by the No. 3 and No. 4 Up Minerals. The station master's proposed increase in wages was postponed for six weeks and the porter was reprimanded.

In October a proposal was approved to allow cattle trucks to be attached to passenger trains although there was a limit of five on any one train. Later, in November, as the cold weather arrived, thought was given to passengers' comfort and footwarmers were fitted to all first and second class carriages. There were problems with the lateness of the mails from London and on several occasions the 2 pm from Penrith had been held back. The Directors felt this was not acceptable and orders were issued not to hold this train if the mails were late.

1873

Wood and Thompson had been following through the matter of the NER request for shed accommodation at Penrith and in January were able to report that they agreed 'with the S&DR Company to allow them the annual sum of £25 in lieu of providing shed accommodation at Penrith for one of their engines working over this line'.

Following the moves at the beginning of the previous year, Edmund Porter had been appointed to the Redhills box as signalman but had resigned. The reason given was that he felt overworked given the long hours of duty and the Directors decided to modify the routine for the next person appointed. There would be two days off each week and every third Sunday.

What led to a change of mind it is not possible to say but in April the proposed ladies' second class waiting room, to be made out of the refreshment room at Keswick, was abandoned in favour of a gentlemen's first class waiting room!

A fatal accident occurred on 9th April at Troutbeck station. A S&DR fireman fell from the front of his engine and was run over.

On 4th April a meeting was held at the Farmers Club in Penrith. The purpose was to revive the possibility of promoting a railway from Penrith to Langwathby. The scheme was well received and the honorary secretary, Charles Farrier, approached the Directors of the CK&PR for their support. The Directors were uneasy about the group's plans but simply replied at this stage that they would give it serious attention. They did infer that perhaps they (the CK&PR) were better able to promote such a railway but went no further.

The introduction of third class places on all trains was not working to the company's benefit and so it was resolved to drop the practice after 1st June. To compensate a little there was a move to reduce first and second class fares, although the decision to reduce first class was later rescinded. After a second consideration of the projected Penrith-Langwathby Railway, the Directors decided to put their own scheme forward, consult the shareholders and prepare a Bill for Parliament. However it seems no further action was taken.

In spite of the rather precarious state of trade, mineral trains were getting longer, a fact which led to a decision to do away with the west-facing points at Penruddock station and move them to the west end of the long siding in order to provide passing room for these longer trains. Further improvement work was agreed in August. An 'underground bridge' was to be provided at Keswick and Cockermouth. In addition signalling was to be remodelled to meet Board of Trade requirements. Double arm semaphores would be used or platform signals with distant signals in each direction with repeaters, where necessary. Most of the main line facing points interlocked with distant signals, the exception being at Cockermouth where traffic was worked in both directions on the same line of the passing place making the method impracticable. Wood was wary. He pointed out that improvements had been carried out since the Railway opened and the plan would be costly. He had obtained quotations from Saxby and Farmer and the total was £4,648 19s. 5d. The Directors were rather taken aback and on Wood's suggestion decided to carry out modifications at Keswick, Bassenthwaite Lake, Troutbeck, Penruddock and Cockermouth, with the last being put to the Joint Station Committee (which later approved).

In December more steps were taken, this time to erect a block telegraph wire throughout the line with all the necessary equipment and to introduce absolute block in addition to the train staff system. Colonel Hutchinson, from The Board of Trade inspected and passed the new signal arrangements at Keswick, Penruddock and Bassenthwaite Lake. One piece of good news which the Directors received in 1873 was that the arbitrator for the Penruddock accident came down in the company's favour. The LNWR had to foot the bill.

Tourism in the Lake District continued to be very actively promoted by the LNWR , although the company seemed to lay more emphasis on Windermere as a destination rather than Keswick. Nevertheless, by this stage it was possible to book tickets to Keswick from over a hundred stations. The most expensive (first class) was from Richmond (in Surrey) at 97s. with the cheapest, 9s. 6d. from Workington. The Lake District circular tours were very popular. One started at Keswick (via Penrith) and then on by coach to Grasmere, Ambleside and Windermere, thereafter returning by rail from Windermere to Oxenholme and so back to the point of departure. The other was the same journey but in reverse. Ticket holders from south of Crewe could break their journey at Lancaster if they so wished.

1875-8

In 1875 the Directors seemed almost preoccupied with the purchase of rail. In 1873, 300 tons of steel rail had been laid and the relaying of the line progressed during 1874. In April the doubling of the line from Troutbeck to Threlkeld was mooted. However it was felt the time was not right for this but it should considered again in the not too distant future. In readiness, Wood was instructed to prepare detailed estimates. On the whole 1875 was a very quiet year the only other decision of note being the one to lengthen the platform at Bassenthwaite Lake station by 50 yards to the south.

In February 1876 the Boulton case was discussed again. There had been no settlement and a claim figure of £29,000 had been mentioned. This was totally unacceptable and eventually matters were to take a rather bizarre turn. In May, application was made to the LNWR for a carriage to be attached to the first down goods out of Penrith for passengers arriving on the 4.29 am from the South.

In May, also, Mr Farrier reappeared. He seemed to be getting rather short of patience with the CK&PR Directors who had not replied to his letters! He pointed out that he had been communicating with the Midland and wanted to know whether the CK&PR felt the time was right to advance the scheme. The Directors decided to hedge a little. They wrote back saying that at present they were not in a position to take steps for the formation of the proposed railway. However, they would be pleased to hear what the Midland felt about the scheme!

William Reay moved further up the scale in November when he was appointed station master at Keswick from Bassenthwaite Lake. He was replaced at Bassenthwaite Lake by Thomas Kidson. During the year discussions started about a proposal to erect a carriage shed at Cockermouth. On 3rd March, Thompson received a letter from Addison of the Maryport & Carlisle Railway. There was a problem because the sides of the engine pit which the CK&PR had made in the M&CR carriage siding had started to collapse. A request was made for these to be rebuilt. The letter then goes on, 'I find it will be necessary to erect a timber shed over our carriage siding . . . to protect our carriages from the weather. I can make the shed long enough to enclose our engine also. I assume there is nothing to prevent us doing this'. As far as the final remark was concerned, Addison, in principle, was right in his assumption although correspondence continued to flow until the following year between Thompson and Addison and Findlay. Plans were drawn up and it was eventually agreed that the shed could be erected and a nominal ground rent would be paid by the M&CR to the LNWR. There was, however, one momentary hiccough when it was suggested the CK&PR should make a contribution to the cost. Thompson was indignant and on 4th August, 1877 wrote to Findlay, 'I fail to see why we are called upon to join in the expense of providing the shed as it has not been necessary for the purposes of this line to keep carriages at Cockermouth, for which it is intended. West Cumberland Market Stock are kept there and these run on Mondays from Whitehaven to Cockermouth and back only - it is for your [LNWR] convenience they are kept there, because there is not enough space at Whitehaven . . .' Findlay, in reply, pointed out that Thompson was in error '. . . one of the trains that works over the Keswick line stands at Cockermouth every night. It would be in your interest to cover these'.

Towards the end of the year, the Directors decided on what must surely have been drastic action to resolve the Boulton case. They decided to take it to the House of Lords. At a meeting on 29th November it was agreed the advice of counsel should be sought on the best way to proceed.

At a meeting on 24th February, 1877 this possible course of action was discussed again. By this time the Directors seemed less keen on the proposal and they decided to adjourn the meeting to seek further advice. They reconvened on 28th February and on this occasion Waugh actually urged them to consider carefully the course of action they were proposing to take. Again, no decision was reached and it was agreed to meet again in March. When they did a vote was taken, Spedding and (Major) Thompson did not vote and it is reported nobody voted for an appeal. In April there was a meeting with the bank and a settlement of £5,214 4s. 6d. was accepted (less £400 for certain payments already made). The whole business had been a costly and acrimonious affair with considerable legal fees having been paid. Some disgruntled shareholders were later to take issue with the Directors over the way in which the matter had been handled.

In May another problem re-emerged. The Directors expressed concern about arrangements involving the FR and others which affected the CK&PR in relation to the 'shortest route' working clause in the LNWR and C&WR agreement. More legal advice was taken. The company was given the opinion it had no 'locus standi'. In a more positive vein, the tourist agents Messrs Cook and Sons were given permission to issue tickets for use on the line and retained 10 per cent of the fare as their portion. In December, the company was again in trouble with the LNWR because it was failing to honour the free tickets it issued to Whitehaven and certain other stations in West Cumberland. In the end the CK&PR agreed to fall in line with the other companies which had agreed to do so.

1878 was, on the whole, an uneventful year. On 22nd November, 1878 there was another accident at Penruddock involving a goods train whilst it was shunting. Wagons were thrown off the rails and there were resulting delays to passenger trains.

The 1870s Decline

The most significant aspect of the 1870s was the marked decline in the iron trade in West Cumberland. The consumption of iron ore decreased considerably and the railway's receipts in 1874 fell quite dramatically. It was reported that half the furnaces in West Cumberland had been shut down and the depression was severe. This decline, especially in the transport of minerals, continued in 1875, although towards the end of the year there was some improvement which gave rise to optimism and a view that the worst was over.

In the Summer of 1875 the first Keswick Convention was held. This brought together Christians sometimes referred to as 'evangelicals'. It is perhaps not surprising, given the enthusiasm and zeal displayed by these people, that from modest beginnings, the convention, an annual event, became a major one attracting Christians of all denominations on a global basis. The large numbers attending resulted in good business for the Railway and in later years were directly responsible for visits by locomotive types which probably would not otherwise have found their way onto the line.

There was more growth in 1876 but this was far from the improvement hoped for and in that year the Directors had to concede to the shareholders that in their view the iron trade was unlikely to pick up in the short term. 1877 saw the Directors vindicated in this view and the receipts were down again. By 1879 the depression in the iron trade had continued to deepen and further falls in revenue were reported. In this particular year the directors insisted another factor was to be held partly responsible for the falling revenue. Third class passengers had been catered for on all trains and 25 per cent of the drop was attributed to the loss in income as a result of this.

The August dividends declared during this period were:

1872	3¼%	1874	3½%	1876	3½%	1878	2¾%
1873	5½%	1875	5%	1877	3¾%		

What happened in 1879 was to incur the wrath of the shareholders in an unprecedented manner!

Crisis in 1879

In January 1879, Wood informed the Directors that re-modelling and renewal at Penrith Junction and station would be necessary to meet the requirements of The Board of Trade. The renewal of the cabin was particularly important. The work would cost £1,330. The Directors had no option but to approve it. The early months of 1879 saw the Lake District in the grips of a particularly cold Winter, described in some publications as 'the great frost'. It resulted in a lot of inconvenience for local people as water supplies froze and moving around became more and more difficult. However, the wintry beauty attracted visitors in their thousands and it was possible to report that 'the railway passenger traffic has greatly increased'. Much of this traffic no doubt conveyed those who wanted to skate on Windermere and Coniston, substantially frozen as the weather tightened its grip, but the CK&PR benefited as well as the crowds came in. Later in the same year, the Railway was to experience a freeze of a different form which would prove equally uncomfortable.

In February 1879, the men of the permanent way department were told their pay would be reduced . This, it was said, was necessary to effect a considerable saving to the company. Why this group was singled out is not clear but it spoke volumes about the financial predicament which was developing. The outcome resulted in a crisis at the August meeting of the shareholders. The Directors announced that compared with the same period in 1878 when revenue had been £18,390, that of the current year had been only £13,522. They felt the permanent way renewal must continue and in view of the financial commitments they could not recommend a dividend be paid. The second freeze of the year!

In spite of all the talk of recession over the previous years, this was one decision the shareholders found hard to stomach! Some of them had already been critical of the manner in which the Directors had been dealing with the Boulton case. They were particularly unhappy about the way in which the Board seemed determined to fight on in spite of the considerable cost involved in doing so. The legal costs were reckoned to be in the region of £7,500. It was Major Spedding who, as the newly appointed Chairman, and at his first meeting in this capacity, had to fend off the anger which came, to a large extent, from a group of Penrith shareholders, Mr Pattinson being one of the most vocal. The meeting, we are told, became 'animated'. Spedding had observed in his opening remarks that the large number of people present might well mean a storm was brewing and he was certainly right. The rail, recently purchased was too expensive and the purchase handled badly, it was alleged. Litigation had been unnecessarily costly. Further, there were wasteful traffic movements. In short the railway was being badly managed. After Pattinson's tirade, it was moved that the Directors should take a reduction in salary to £200 per annum.

There was another matter, although nothing to do with expense. This involved the proposal to appoint Edward Waugh (Senior) as a Director in succession to Isaac Fletcher and Edward Waugh (Junior) as the company solicitor in place of his father. Strangely, it seemed the former proposal was the one about which there was a lot of objection. A lengthy debate ensued and Spedding defended Waugh as one who had worked hard for the company, especially over the Boulton claims and also the very expensive arbitration claim involving the LNWR and the accident at Penruddock. A fortnight's adjournment was proposed but the meeting continued (it ran for six hours). Waugh's appointment was eventually approved (41 for; 28 against) but not before John Pattinson had been nominated in opposition. He pointed out in strong terms that the shareholders had seen the dividend drop from 6½ per cent to 0 per cent! A discussion also took place about the way proxies were organised in relation to support for Waugh . Pattinson even went so far as to suggest 'Mr Waugh has gone personally to all the ladies in the district and solicited their support as a personal favour and through friendship'. When the next item on the agenda, the reappointment of Mr Jameson came up, Pattinson immediately proposed Mr Altham as an alternative and at this point doubt was expressed about the wisdom of going on with the appointments of Directors. However, it was agreed a poll should be taken as to whether the retiring Directors should be reappointed or whether there should be an adjourned meeting to appoint new Directors. Mr Altham then moved the resolution should be rescinded as he felt it made the meeting nothing but 'a solemn farce'. A poll was taken and a move to adjourn the meeting was defeated. At this point Pattinson agreed not to pursue matters further. By this time it was 4.40 pm and a special meeting, scheduled to follow the main meeting to discuss the raising of a further sum of money, was abandoned. This seems to have been the longest and liveliest meeting in the company's history and one, the like of which, the Directors did not wish to see repeated!

The Cockermouth Joint Station Committee 1864-1880

During these opening years of the Railway, the Cockermouth Joint Station Committee had met on a regular basis to address the various issues which arose in the running of the station. In 1864 Harris was Chairman with the CK&PR represented by Messrs Bass, (William) Fletcher Hoskins and Thompson. In August of that year, the committee appointed Joseph Wales to be the station master at a salary of £100 per annum plus a house. In 1869 Mr Purssell was appointed joint Secretary to act with Henry Cattle.

The committee made a number of decisions relating to the actual structure of the building. In 1869 they decided amongst other things, to provide a gentlemen's first class waiting room. In 1870 Wales resigned and the committee expressed the view that because the goods and passenger stations were so far apart they should have separate men in charge of them. As a result, Robert

Mitchell, who had formerly been the booking clerk, was appointed station master and Joseph Bewsher was put in charge of the goods station.

The committee also had an eye to the general appearance of the station and in November 1871 resolved that fir trees should be planted on the waste land on the west side, the railings in front of the station should be removed and placed in a straight line from the corner of the approach road to the cattle loading place. The following Spring, on Wood's instigation, the station was repainted. There was a dispute over the LNWR claim for a toll over the portion of its main line between the Parliamentary point of junction and the boundary of the CK&PR line at Cockermouth. No agreement could be reached, initially, but eventually the insistence that this toll be levied was withdrawn.

In 1872 the signalman at the Junction signal box was working from 5.30 am to 10.00 pm each day, a period the committee rightly considered was far too long. A relief man was appointed. In 1873, the Board of the CK&PR recommended that an underground passage should be constructed between the platforms (referred to earlier) and, further, that a change be made to the pointwork at the station. The estimated costs were: subway £600; sidings £760; signals, with associated work, £1,840. These proposals were accepted at a meeting on 22nd February, 1875, subject to approval by the Board of the Maryport and Carlisle which was also using the station.

An irregularity was noted at a meeting held on 3rd December, 1875. The accountant, Peter Thompson reported that inconvenience had been caused because the goods agent, Bewsher, had allowed the accounts to get badly into arrears; the returns were being made late. This situation was clearly known before the meeting because Bewsher had been instructed to attend and give an explanation. At the meeting he pleaded ill-health because [he said] working conditions were poor in the dilapidated goods offices. He maintained other clerks had also been affected. Thompson and Fitzsimmons agreed to send assistance to work up the arrears and Bewsher was given a caution. Mitchell, at the passenger station, also found himself in trouble. There had been complaints from the travelling public about the delay to trains, brought about by the movement of cattle. Mitchell was cautioned and told punctuality must be maintained for passengers.

Mitchell seems to have come to grips with the situation but Bewsher did not. On 1st February, 1876 it was reported he had absconded - and there was a deficiency in the accounts of the CK&PR and the M&CR. In his absence he was dismissed and Patrickson, the chief goods clerk at Penrith, took his place. Perhaps this incident spurred the committee on because the members expressed the view that a new goods station should be built without delay. There was then the matter of where to build it. Two options, perhaps obvious, were considered namely the existing site or the passenger station, in the case of the latter, jointly owned land to be used.

Up to this point the minutes of the meetings are written by hand. The minutes for the meeting dated 24th August, 1877 are typewritten. This, it seems, was considered to be a significant meeting. The CK&PR was represented by Fletcher and Spedding; the LNWR by Cawkwell and (Major) Thompson. It was agreed desirable that a committee should immediately be appointed for the management of the Cockermouth Joint Station in terms of the Agreement between the two companies, and that the question of plans and the site of the proposed new goods station be referred to this committee together with all other matters under consideration. Further, any new works when agreed should be under the direction of the CK&PR Engineer but that the Engineers of both companies should make a joint report on siting in relation to cost. In addition, a committee be appointed to deal with matters relating to Penrith joint station and this committee should include the members of the Cockermouth Joint Station Committee and also two members of the Board of the North Eastern Railway.

The next meeting took place in the Chairman's room at Euston Station on 1st November, 1878. Those present included Moon, Fletcher, Spedding, Wood and Thompson. There were five other representatives of the LNWR. Alternative plans for the improvement of Cockermouth station were submitted by Worthington, the figure put on the work being £6,900, although it was reckoned this could be reduced by £1,000 if the old engine shed was converted to a goods shed. The scheme was generally approved and Wood, with Worthington, was instructed to look at the details. Moon, keen that the scheme should go ahead told Wood to complete the purchase of 2½ acres of land for which notice had already been served.

The Motive Power

The motive power during these first 15 years can be identified in part, although in a period when photographs are rare, there is little evidence of this sort available. The writer who described the opening journey regrettably made no mention of the motive power to give some clues about it. The LNWR, it will be recalled, had the responsibility for passenger traffic and the Ramsbottom 0-6-0 'DX' class first introduced in 1858 was available in large numbers and certainly had a role on the line. It is very likely a member of this class hauled the inaugural train. Some 943 'DX' class engines were built at Crewe between 1858 and 1874. Tuplin in *North Western Steam* describes the 'DX' as

. . . a plain straightforward engine spoiled in appearance by what must be regarded as attempts at decoration. The chimney had a wide flange with pieces cut out of it and the splashers over the leading and driving wheels had curved slots. The upper part of each rear wheel was hidden by a rectangular plate forming a foot-plate balustrade extended forward to hide the reversing screw and the lever that connected the nut to the reversing rod. This plate gave the enginemen waist high protection against side winds and there was a very small weather-board on the back of the boiler; otherwise, nothing.

These engines certainly did stalwart service and 86 of them were sold to the Lancashire and Yorkshire Railway. In 1874 Webb introduced a class of 0-6-0 tender engines referred to simply as the 'coal engines' and examples of this class were to be found on the line. The mineral traffic, which had to be hauled not only over the branch but also over the EVR and the gruelling Stainmore route, was in the charge of the S&DR and in these early days mineral trains were hauled by the 0-6-0 '1001' class; a group which continued to operate alongside others for many years.

Chapter Four

Changed Fortunes:
1880-1890

1880

Initially the situation in 1880 seemed little changed. At the February meeting of the shareholders it was announced that although revenues had fallen still further, the Directors proposed a dividend of 2½ per cent and this was accepted. It was also decided to raise a further £8,000 through debentures. In spite of the financial problems and the unwelcome action in the permanent way department, the company adopted a magnanimous stance in August when it helped to fund a new classroom at Thelkeld School! In August, also, the company decided to petition the LNWR for a through coach on the 10 am train from Euston. There had been complaints from passengers travelling through from Euston and stations on the route, who were destined for Keswick and Cockermouth, about the inconvenience suffered by having to change and transfer luggage at Penrith. It was suggested that this vehicle could be worked back as a through connection at mid-day. Rather in the vein of other petitions no reply was received to this one and the company found it necessary to take up the matter afresh. Another proposal which did bring a prompt response involved the retiming of the 9.55 am from Penrith to an hour earlier. This was quickly rejected by the LNWR because it would break the connection at Penrith with the 9.17 am from Carlisle and the 9.45 Eden Valley train which it was argued brought a considerable number of passengers onto the line.

During 1880 it was resolved to remove all remaining iron rails and replace them with new steel ones. However, in order to save money, it was resolved to fit these rails within the usual work routines so that no extra men would have to be employed.

On the operating side it was agreed, in response to a number of requests, that the 5.12 pm train should stop at Threlkeld for a trial period of one month and that during that time the number of passengers taking advantage of the facility would be monitored. In addition, an application was made to the NER and the Midland for through bookings via Appleby. The Threlkeld stopping train appears to have been a success because in February the practice was continued. The practice of attaching passenger carriages to the 6.20 goods train from Cockermouth to Keswick was extended to include Penrith with stops at all stations. This move came in response to a request for the LNWR to be petitioned to provide extra passenger trains; a request on which the Directors of the CK&PR felt unable to act. The NER then approached the CK&PR and asked to be allowed to run mineral trains at night. In spite of the doom and gloom with falling receipts, the NER felt these trains would be more helpful in coping with the heavy coal traffic. A further advantage, it was argued, was that there would be no need for running double trains. It seems the NER was becoming uneasy about these because the practice might prove dangerous as well as damaging the line and causing delays. The CK&PR Directors were not at all sure about this proposition and decided to defer making a decision. When they did so, on 14th February, they agreed but with the proviso that there would be a speed restriction of 15 mph.

Talks with the Midland having proved fruitful it was announced that a service would run between Penrith and Appleby (Midland) starting the following Spring. Threlkeld passengers seemed to have made use of the stopping facility by the 5.12 - the arrangement was made permanent, at least until the Summer timetable. What led to this decision being reversed is not clear but on 12th May the order was revoked. On 7th June, further improvements to train services were announced. An additional service on weekdays would operate from Penrith to Carlisle and vice versa. The former would connect with the arrival of the CK&PR train at Penrith at 10.35; the latter with the departure from Penrith at 5.12 pm. There had been no reply to the petition for a through coach from Euston and so another petition was sent. As in the previous case, the request was for a through coach on the 10.00 am from Euston which, in effect, would be complemented by a through coach being attached to the 1.25 pm at Penrith. The LNWR responded that a through coach could not be provided but did attempt a compromise. From 1st July, the 12.55 pm from Carlisle (arriving 1.35 pm at Penrith) would be extended to London (arriving 8.30 pm) to give what was described as 'an improved connection'. G.P. Neele, the Chief Superintendent of the LNWR, disclosed later that he had, in fact, been in favour of a through coach but on looking into the working of it had concluded with some reluctance that it was impractical.

In August it was agreed that the signal box at Penrith would have to be moved to the downside of the line to make it possible to extend the sidings on the up side. The 5.12 and Threlkeld entered the arena again when the Winter trains were discussed. A compromise was reached in that the train would stop 'under special circumstances' although these were not specified.

On 30th September, 1880, Wood presented the Directors with his rationale for relaying the track. He pointed out that it was laid at present with intermediate chairs of 20 lb. and joint chairs of 30 lb. with larch sleepers. There had been no accidents in 15 years which could be attributed to shortcomings in the permanent way and so it could be argued no change was necessary. However, on more recently built railways (he pointed out) heavier chairs had been used. The LNWR had recently installed chairs of 46 lb. on the L&CR section, replacing ones of 25 lb. Heavier traffic could well be on the line in future and so heavier chairs would be desirable. Then again it had been suggested only the chairs needing replacing. Wood made it clear he was not happy with that proposition. He wanted new chairs and new sleepers, the latter to be foreign and of the square cut creosoted type. All the recently replaced items (and it will be recalled there was a considerable quantity!) would have to be removed, although they could possibly be used in sidings. During the previous five years 3,600 new sleepers had been put down each half year, this out of a total of some 55,500 sleepers, excluding the sidings. Of these 24,360 had been on curves, usually of less than 50 chains radius. Wood pointed out that if 2,500 chairs were replaced every half year the work would take 11 years. The estimated cost additional to normal replacements was £250 each half year. Wood presented his rationale with conviction, but the Directors were hesitant to commit themselves to the outlay when revenue and prospects were not particularly buoyant. They opted to have replacement using the heavier chairs and the new sleepers but only on a 'when needed' principle.

In October 1880, Tennant of the NER wrote to the CK&PR asking for three engines from his company to be shedded at Cockermouth as this would facilitate working arrangements. There appears to be a veiled threat in the letter that if such an arrangement is not possible 'The traffic will be taken in another direction'. The Directors asked the Cockermouth Joint Station Committee to consider this request and possibly arrange for the erection of a suitable building.

(On 1st December it was agreed the 5.12 should stop at Threlkeld for the rest of the Winter !)

1881-4

In early January 1881 Euston became involved in the discussions. It was suggested that NER engines should run through to Workington and be provided with accommodation there. This was provisionally agreed to be a temporary measure *pro tem* but in February, Tennant wrote again to say that after careful consideration the NER had decided to decline the offer to work through to Workington and stabling facilities were required at Cockermouth 'with as little delay as possible'. There was disagreement amongst the members of the joint committee about the location of this shed. The CK&PR plan to build it in the field adjoining the high level station was opposed. In view of this it was decided to refer the matter to the Chairmen of the LNWR and CK&PR, Moon and Spedding. At about the same time, the committee did agree to accept a tender from Boltons to build a new goods warehouse. The problem relating to the NER shed remained unresolved until June when it was agreed to place it on the ground acquired for the extension of Cockermouth goods station. In July the NER decided that the proposal to build them a shed at Cockermouth be postponed!

During the year G.P. Neele wrote to the company asking whether it might be possible for the 1.40 pm from Penrith to be retimed to make a connection possible with the 7.15 am from Euston, arriving at Penrith at 2.30 pm. The Directors decided against any change. There might have been a little bit of 'tit for tat' in this!

The Buttermere Slate Quarry had been in discussions with the LNWR about procedures for constructing a line and had been told that if the line was to be passenger carrying a Bill would be needed. The quarry company did not wish to carry passengers and therefore, in November, approached the CK&PR to ask whether that company would build the line. Clearly there would be a certain amount of slate, flag and stone traffic created and , as well, the LNWR had offered some support. A meeting was arranged at Carnforth on 7th November, 1881 at which the CK&PR was represented by the Chairman and Captain Gandy. These two met a group from the Buttermere Company. The Buttermere group expressed a preference for a 'tramway' in the direction of Braithwaite but they had encountered problems in acquiring land. One landowner, Mr Marshall, had objected strongly to the line passing through one of his fields. The length of this tramway from Honister to Braithwaite would be about 8 miles. The proposal was for 'a narrow or 2 ft railway'. Wood had already costed the project at £1,300 per mile and the total cost, including land, was estimated at around £20,000. The Buttermere Company appeared to be quite desperate to get the line built, arguing that without it their enterprise might well fail. The company felt it could guarantee a revenue of £1,500. At this stage the CK&PR felt it could not undertake the construction but expressed the view that it might be able to subscribe towards it and all possible support was assured. The Chairman even agreed to write to the principal objector in an attempt to use his influence to make him change his mind! As it turned out, Mr Marshall was not to be easily swayed. He did not like the prospect of what he considered to be the disfigurement [his word] to the hillside it would cause and in its passage above the lower part of Borrowdale and Cat Bells along Derwentwater. Visitors, he felt, would not find it acceptable. 'Those who are interested in the beauty of the place have a strong feeling against the scheme' he wrote. Mr Marshall was not entirely negative. He went further and proposed another route which in his view was more in keeping with safeguarding the environment. Wood, however, did not feel the alternative was practical.

At the half-yearly meeting of shareholders in August, it was possible to report a slight increase in revenue and a resulting dividend of 5 per cent. £400 in revenue had been lost in March when traffic on the line had been stopped completely for several days by snow. Further occurrences of this type would prompt the Directors to examine for themselves ways of preventing such hold-ups.

The first half-yearly meeting in 1882 (25th February) saw an even better dividend of 6¾ per cent but it was down again in August to 5½ per cent.

On 22nd April the Directors received a letter from Findlay of the LNWR. It was about passenger receipts and must have sent a cold chill down a few spines. In the letter, Findlay pointed out

. . . the attention of my Directors has been called to the fact that the earnings of the passenger trains over the Cockermouth Keswick and Penrith Railway are unremunerative, whilst the number of trains run is in excess of that provided for in the Agreement of 20th February, 1864. Seeing that no extra payment has been made for these additional trains, I am requested to state that the Directors will require the Cockermouth Keswick and Penrith Railway, if they wish the running of these trains to be continued to guarantee a payment of not less that 1s. 6d. a train mile in respect of them.

The CK&PR Directors found this a bitter pill to swallow; in fact they did not want to swallow it at all! Spedding went off to see G.P. Neele to request that there might be terms more favourable to the CK&PR and the LNWR was ready to accept 6d. per mile for one train in each direction between Penrith and Cockermouth on weekdays and the service to be that of June, the previous year. Although he felt progress had been made, Spedding was still not fully satisfied and decided to see Moon. When this meeting eventually took place in November, Moon refused to be drawn on the issue and so no further understanding was reached.

In May of the same year there was a double accident near Bassenthwaite Lake station involving No. 6 and No. 7 down mineral trains. As a result, an NER engine ran away without anyone on it and reached Cockermouth where it 'smashed up' a Maryport and Carlisle passenger train standing at the down platform. Fortunately no passengers were on board. In the end the CK&PR agreed with the NER to meet the costs equally of the damage to the M&CR stock which totalled £334.

In early September it became known that the Mid Cumberland Railway was proposing to build a line between Hesket New Market and a point on the CK&PR. This caused consternation amongst the Directors and on 5th September a special meeting was called to discuss the situation. The general feeling of the meeting was that if a line was to be built, then the CK&PR should do the building. On 4th October the Mid Cumberland approached the CK&PR asking whether it would be prepared to subscribe but, for obvious reasons, the CK&PR declined to do so, giving as the excuse the fact that only a small amount had been forthcoming at that stage, anyway. However, this approach gave the CK&PR a greater sense of urgency and on 7th October the Directors held a meeting at which a proposal to promote a line between Troutbeck station and Hesket New Market was discussed. When a vote was taken, although four were for the proposal and three against (an eighth member had left before the vote was taken), it was decided the absence of unanimity must lead to the shareholders being consulted and it was agreed that an EGM should be held on 4th November. When this took place views were very much divided. The Chairman, seconded by Henry Howard, proposed that 'it is expedient to promote in the ensuing session of Parliament a Bill to enable this Company to make a branch from Troutbeck to Hesket New Market'. During the debate, there was speculation voiced about the possibility of the Midland taking over the Furness with a view to gaining access to Barrow. Waugh was convinced this would happen and also that the Windermere branch would be extended to Ambleside and eventually Keswick. He saw the Hesket New Market branch as having an important role to play in the scheme of things. However he was accused of wishful thinking and the whole project could turn into a white elephant if the other schemes did not materialise (as proved to be the case).

Waugh also attacked the LNWR suggesting the working agreement with them was a travesty and that the CK&PR had 'sold their birthright for a mess of pottage' An amendment was proposed by Mr Favier and seconded by Mr Glasson 'that consideration of such a vital matter [building the branch] be postponed in order to give the shareholders time to inform themselves of the desirability or otherwise of the proposed new undertaking'. This amendment was carried. In the event the scheme did not materialise.

By November another scheme involving the CK&PR was being discussed. On 3rd November, Spedding met with Mr Musgrave, the Chairman of the Solway Junction Company (SJCo.). Musgrave wanted to know whether the CK&PR would promote jointly with the SJCo. a line between Brayton Junction and Bassenthwaite Lake station. The CK&PR felt it could not go along with such a joint venture but would not oppose the scheme. It also indicated a willingness to enter into traffic arrangements.

At a meeting on 6th December, it was noted by the CK&PR Secretary that notices had appeared in the newspapers of the proposed Braithwaite and Butteremere Railway as well as the Solway Junction notices and at this meeting a letter was considered which had been received from the SJCo. It was resolved that they approved of the petition to introduce the Bill in 1883 but would not bear the cost of all or part of it and further they would not consent to running powers. The CK&PR would be given powers in the Bill to subscribe £30,000. The SJCo. went ahead but ignored the request of the CK&PR relating to running powers and in spite of the fact that the CK&PR asked again that this be withdrawn from the draft Bill, this was not heeded. The CK&PR was also anxious to make proper provision for the junction at Bassenthwaite Lake and the use of the station. It was proposed to replace the level-crossing with an overbridge.

In January 1883 William Dixon found himself in the spotlight for outstanding service to the company. On 29th there was a land-slip at the end of Briery tunnel and the line was blocked until the afternoon. However there was another slip the following morning and again the line was blocked for several hours. We are told that for his vigilance at the time of the slip and his exertions to prevent a further 'catastrophe' he was awarded £1. There was concern about the possibility of further slips but Wood was able to reassure the Board that steps had been taken to prevent this, although he recommended that the slopes over the tunnel and the wall beyond should be eased and land acquired for the purpose.

The NER decided to start the night service on 1st March. The Directors were dissatisfied with the way in which the Solway Junction was acting and on 24th February decided to oppose its Bill. In the event it did not get onto the Statute Book. In a period when the Board of Trade was becoming more and more concerned about safety, signalling and train operations generally, the company decided, on 25th August, to adopt the Tyer's Tablet system between Cockermouth Junction and Cockermouth passenger station for a trial period of one year. By this time the system was five years old and therefore somewhat still in its infancy. The charge to the company was £5 for the year and then £150 if it was retained. The Board of Trade approved its use but made it clear that it would reserve the right to insist that the train staff and ticket system be introduced if deemed desirable. In December, the following year, the system received a favourable report.

By October 1884, the Board had come to the conclusion that the platform accommodation at Penrith was inadequate especially for Summer trains and the LNWR was requested to improve it.

1885-1889

As the 1880s progressed the railway enjoyed a period of relative calm although dividends remained low in view of the continuing depression in the iron industry. In February 1884 the dividend was 5 per cent, in 1885 it dropped as low as 1¾ per cent although rising again in the second half of the decade and finishing at 5 per cent. The revenue receipts at February 1886 and 1887 compare as follows.

| | 1886 | 1887 |
	£	£
Coaching	8,692	8,629
Merchandise	4,172	4,292
Cattle	293	269
Minerals	7,595	11,073
Misc.	188	210

This shows an increase in revenue of £3,533, but expenditure increased from £12,334 in 1886 to £14,287 in 1887.

The sort of traffic which delighted the Directors of the CK&PR. The crew of '1001' class, No. 1083 on a mineral train exchange tokens at Embleton. The date is unknown, but notice the dress of the station master and also the form of the signals carried on a single post.

North Road Railway Museum

The following year income from mineral traffic fell whereas that from general merchandise increased. Significant improvements to the signals at Bassenthwaite Lake were carried out in 1888, two platelayer's cottages were built and two more planned. In that year also, Captain Gandy died. He had been on the Board for 21 years.

The decline in mineral traffic led a number of shareholders to press for ways in which passenger receipts might be increased. Greater publicity was one area in which it was felt improvements could be made. At the shareholders' meeting in August 1897, Mr Hudson, a Penrith shareholder (the Penrith shareholders always seemed to be the most vociferous), came up with a plan to provide a train of open-sided coaches which could be used for special trips between Threlkeld and Bassenthwaite Lake, the cost to be one shilling each. The suggestion was never taken up!

Mr Thompson's Circulars

As mentioned earlier, Henry Cattle was succeeded as Secretary and General Manager by Peter Thompson, who did not retire until 1913. For a time, after taking over from Cattle, Thompson issued a number of circulars in very much the same vein as his predecessor.

One, dated 27th August, 1875 appears to indicate his displeasure that passengers have found a way of getting round the CK&PR fare structure relating to third and second class fares. 'I find that a great number of passengers for Cockermouth are taking 3rd Class tickets to Brigham in preference to booking 2nd Class to Cockermouth. Cease 3rd Class through booking to Brigham from the end of this month'. In a more magnanimous frame of mind, on 22nd July, 1876 he issued the instruction: 'You can issue a 3rd Class ticket twice a week to Mr Moffatt to Keswick at a fare of 1s. 6d. for the double journey and endorse the ticket "Return"'. [Mr Moffatt was the Band Master at Penrith.]

The circular (numbered 80) of 1st December, 1877 gives details of a rule added to the Code.

> If a portion of a train becomes accidentally detached and runs back down an incline . . . call the attention of the station in the rear towards which the portion of the train may be running by giving 3 beats twice and placing the electric semaphore arm at Danger. The signalman who receives this signal must acknowledge with an exact repetition by pressing the plunger 6 times, pausing after the third stroke'.

Any approaching train was to be stopped and then an attempt made to get it into a siding.

Circular No. 89 (22nd March, 1880) 'Commercial travellers are now permitted to carry free of charge double the weight of luggage allowed to other passengers'. On 22nd June, 1880 he informs the station masters that H. Gaze & Son, tourist agents, will be issuing tickets over the line and these are to be accepted but checked. On 31st March, 1881, there is the important directive stating that after April, Parliamentary Tickets can be booked on all trains to West Cumberland (except the 5.12 pm from Penrith 'when 3rd Class must be booked'). The circular of 1st April, 1884 gives the information that a contract has been agreed with *The West Cumberland Times* for newspapers to be carried to 'local' stations. (Bundles will not carry news stamps.)

So to the end of another decade. Although growth did not appear to be as great as had been hoped, the condition of the railway was reckoned to be healthy and dividends, on the whole, steady. In spite of some misgivings, it was felt there was no particular cause for concern; far from it, as the next year would indicate.

Motive Power

Beginning in 1881, Webb rebuilt 500 of the Ramsbottom 'DX' class to form what was known as the 'Special DX' class. These engines were fitted for working automatic vacuum brakes and members of this class were used on the line. Another class to appear at about this time was the 'N10', an 0-6-0 designed by Webb and known as the 'Cauliflowers' (because the LNWR crest depicted on the splashers of the driving wheels resembled the vegetable). These locomotives which had the distinction of being the first to use the Joy Valve Gear were still in evidence on the line after nationalisation. Also in 1881, Webb introduced an 0-6-2 class called the 'coal tank' and members of this class were used on the line.

Minor accidents were not uncommon. Here a 'Cauliflower' has been derailed near Bassenthwaite Lake.   *Cumbrian Railways Association*

Chapter Five

Some Significant Decisions:
1890-1900

1890-1

In February 1890 the Board was able to report to the shareholders that during the previous half-year there had been the highest passenger traffic on record. In consequence, the dividend declared was 6½ per cent. The year passed without major event, although on 11th June William Peel was killed at Bassenthwaite and the company was served with a writ by his father. A settlement was agreed by the Secretary and the solicitor.

It was during this year that the first of a considerable number of annual dinners was held for the employees of the railway companies in the region. Men from the CK&PR were joined by those of the NER and LNWR for these events. It seems that initially the 'white-collar' workers were probably the only ones invited but certainly by 1894 all groups were present and about 100 attended the dinner held in Penrith. There was a considerable amount of raillery in the after-dinner speeches and it was, in fact, at the 1894 gathering that H.C. Howard caused outbursts of laughter and applause when he made the remark, quoted earlier, about the NER not holding trains for the CK&PR. By 1910 over 130 people sat down to a meal and the event was just as good humoured being, it was said, 'the most enjoyable to be held for some years'.

In April 1891, the death was reported of the man who had in many ways been the inspiration for the railway, namely, Edward Waugh. He was lamented by his fellow Directors as 'one of the chief promoters of the Railway and solicitor to the Company'. In May 1891 steps were taken to put in hand a significant development. Wood was asked to prepare plans and estimates for the doubling of the line between Troutbeck and Threlkeld. Over the next few years the Directors were to agonise a great deal over whether or not to implement the scheme. In the same month an application was received for a siding into Briery Bobbin Mill and later the same month it was approved, provided the proprietor Mr Philipson paid the cost of preparing the land. The company agreed to lay down a siding to accommodate 20 waggons but would retain the ownership of all the materials and rails. Philipson would pay all the carriage charges. On 30th May a goods engine was derailed at Bassenthwaite Lake station.

In August, Wood was ready to give a report on the proposed doubling. In it he asked that Threlkeld station should be extended. The Directors decided to reconsider the project. On another front, one group of workers who felt they had made progress in improving conditions of work were the platelayers. They had petitioned for better working times and were informed that in future they could leave work at 1 pm on Saturdays, provided one man remained until 4 pm. In addition, for overtime purposes, eight hours would be the norm for a working day. Further, a covered carriage would be provided for men working on the ballast trains. Station masters, too, in reply to a request they had made, were told they would have occasional relief, but it would not be practical to provide this on a daily basis.

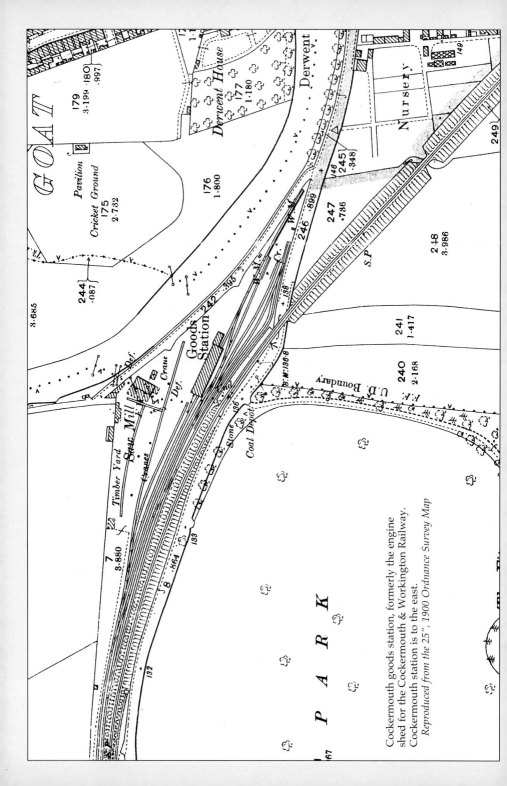

GOAT

179
3·199 ·180
·997

Pavilion

Cricket Ground
175
2·732

Derwent House

177
1·180

176
1·800

Derwent

Nursery

149

249

244
·087

3·685

242 ·395

246 ·899

247
·786

245
·348

248
3·986

S.P.

Goods Station

241
1·417

240
2·168

F.W.

B.M.186·8

U.D. Boundary

F.B.

Timber Yard

Star Mill

Crane

Coal Depot

Stone

Def.

7
3·880

8 ·664

183

132

67

P A R K

Cockermouth goods station, formerly the engine
shed for the Cockermouth & Workington Railway.
Cockermouth station is to the east.
Reproduced from the 25", 1900 Ordnance Survey Map

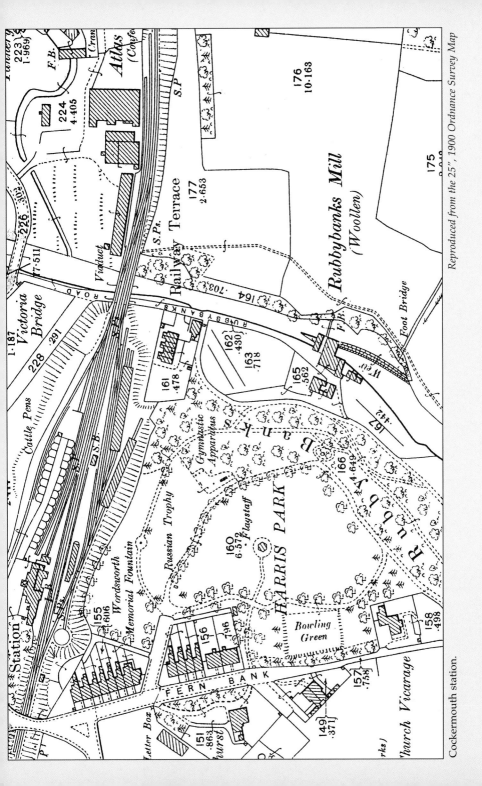

Cockermouth station.

Reproduced from the 25", 1900 Ordnance Survey Map

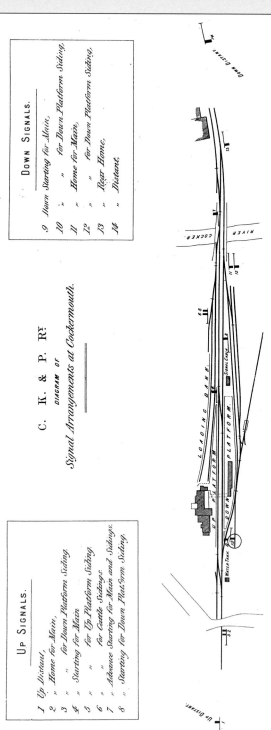

C. K. & P. Ry.

DIAGRAM OF

Signal Arrangements at Cockermouth.

Up Signals.

1   Up Distant,
2   "   Home for Main,
3   "   "   for Down Platform Siding,
4   "   Starting for Main,
5   "   "   for Up Platform Siding,
6   "   "   for Cattle Sidings,
7   "   Advance Starting for Main and Sidings,
8   "   Starting for Down Platform Siding,

Down Signals.

9   Down Starting for Main,
10   "   "   for Down Platform Siding,
11   "   Home for Main,
12   "   "   for Down Platform Siding,
13   "   Rear Home,
14   "   Distant,

An undated plan of signalling arrangements at Cockermouth.

In October the LNWR announced that it proposed to reduce the number of trains to four each day during the Winter months. The CK&PR felt this to be inadequate and asked that five should be provided.

Perhaps the long hours with only occasional relief began to take its toll on some station masters; J. Ewart, the station master at Embleton was removed from office for ' insobriety ' and was downgraded to being a porter at Keswick. Mr Blackburn replaced him. Less than two months later, Mr R.A. Holt was 'removed' as station master at Cockermouth and replaced by Mr Robert Little.

After June 1891, passengers on the line could avail themselves of refreshments in the form of ' sweetmeats '. An agreement with The Sweetmeat Automatic Delivery Company Ltd resulted in them placing machines on all the stations, including Cockermouth.

Plans moved ahead for doubling, as the year came to a close. Heskett was authorised to conclude the purchase of the land needed.

1892

In July 1892 matters were moved on further when the company came to consider the requirements of The Board of Trade Order [1890] in relation to small or non passing stations. General Hutchison had suggested that changes should be made between Threlkeld and Troutbeck where the system of working the block in what was referred to as the permissive form was used for the up direction. The permissive block system involved allowing more than one train into a section provided a train could be seen from the one behind. This system was in violation of the Board of Trade requirement that the absolute block system should be used. On 24th June the company was informed that the Board of Trade would give it three months to effect the change. The Permanent Way Committee met and recommended that a signal cabin should be erected about 2½ miles from Threlkeld station to divide the existing block section between Threlkeld and Troutbeck stations. It also recommended that home and distant signals should be provided but that no loop line should be made at the cabin at that stage. Threlkeld station should be converted to a passing station with an island platform. The members pointed out that these improvements would also facilitate the doubling of the line, so giving greater weight to the argument for carrying them out. In October, Wood was once again asked to press ahead with estimates for the doubling. The Permanent Way Committee, in the meantime, turned its attention to Keswick station and in October presented plans for enlarging it.

Excuses had to be made when the Board of Trade enquired in November if the absolute block system was soon to be introduced between Threlkeld and Troutbeck. Shades of Bouch; Wood reported that work on the cabin had been delayed by bad weather but he was optimistic the work would be finished on time. The cabin came into operation on 9th November which meant the absolute block system was in use throughout the line. Plans were also approved to extend the back loop at Keswick station and to provide an additional long siding behind this loop. Wood proposed the installation of a new signal and siding at Braithwaite station, an additional length of siding at Threlkeld station and put forward a scheme to extend siding facilities for the Threlkeld Granite Company and the Directors approved all these items.

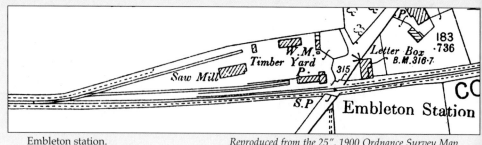

Embleton station.

Reproduced from the 25", 1900 Ordnance Survey Map

Bassenthwaite Lake station.

Reproduced from the 25", 1900 Ordnance Survey Map

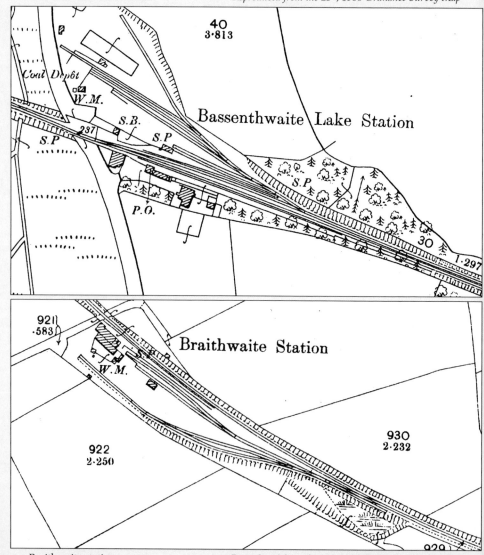

Braithwaite station.

Reproduced from the 25", 1900 Ordnance Survey Map

CK&PR advert in The Official Guide to the LNWR for 1892.

By this time, Wood had also prepared the plans for the doubling of the track from Troutbeck to Threlkeld and presented them to the Directors at the end of November. The Board seemed hesitant, presumably wanting to be sure that given the existing trade climate, the work would be justified. The Permanent Way Committee was asked to produce further information to enable a decision to be taken and the members reported on 17th December. The committee made the following observations:

There had always been difficulty operating trains over the section under consideration because there was a rising gradient. The distance between Threlkeld and Troutbeck Stations is 4 miles and 59 chains all of which consists of heavy ascent gradients; 1 in 68 for ¾ mile from Threlkeld and beyond this, 1 in 62½.
The usual time allowed for trains in this section:

	Passenger	Goods	Mineral	
Down	10	13	15	minutes
Up	14	18 to 20	20	minutes

However, the weather can affect these. In fact the 'Up' times are nominal and can be up to 30 minutes for some trains. If the normal loads are exceeded this can increase to 40 minutes.
During the last Summer, there had been 15 ordinary trains in each direction on four days each week and 16 for two days; eight passenger, four mineral, three goods and one ballast.

KESWICK STATION
Elevation from platform
Approach side
Ground Floor Plan
Booking
General
Stationery
Platform side

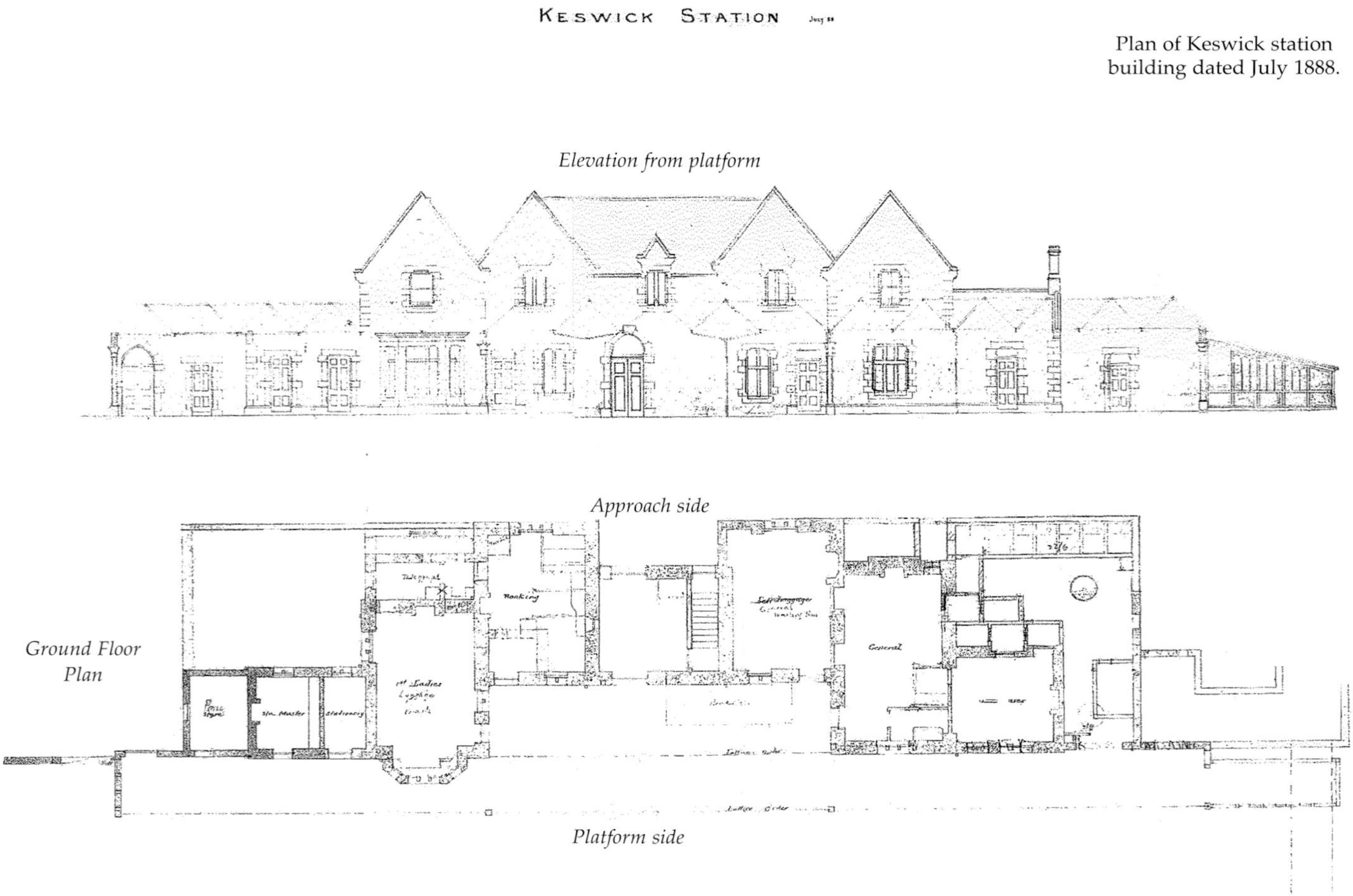

Plan of Keswick station building dated July 1888.

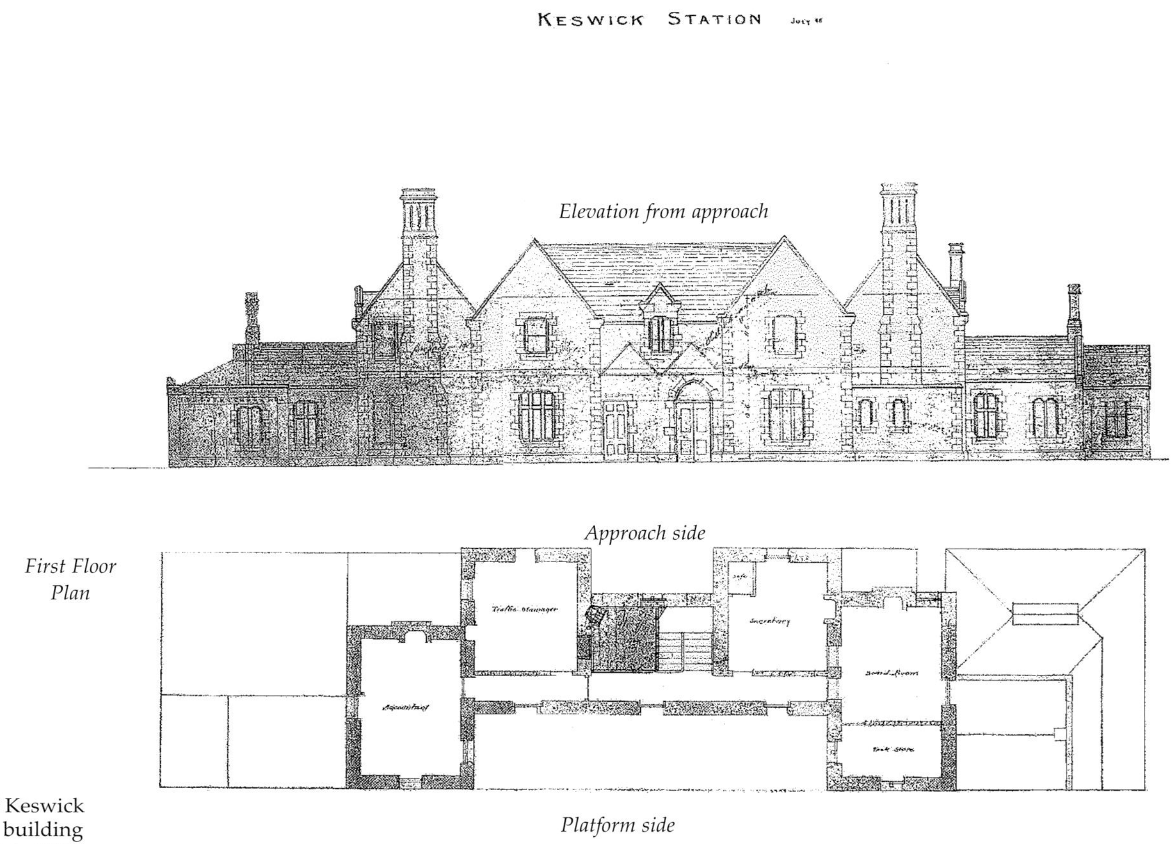

KESWICK STATION
Elevation from approach
Approach side
First Floor Plan
Traffic Manager
Secretary
Board Room
Accountant
Platform side

Plan of Keswick station building dated July 1888.

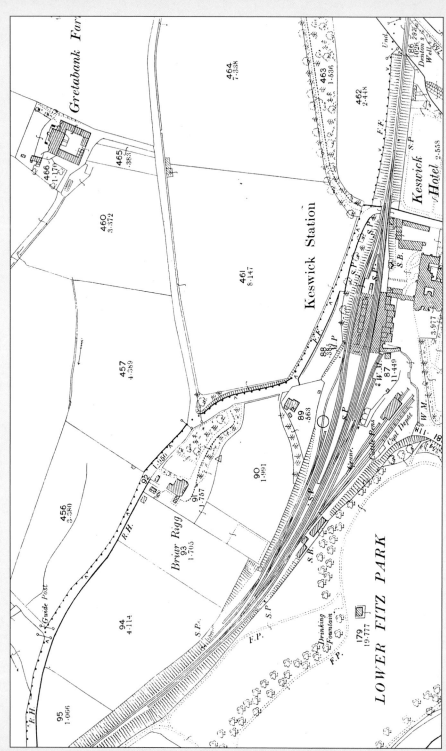

Keswick station.

Reproduced from the 25", 1900 Ordnance Survey Map

In addition to these there were special excursions, some relief passenger and some relief goods. Sometimes there were six to eight extra trains each day. The greater part of the excursion trains to Keswick pass in the morning and return in the evening. At times the line becomes crowded so that they have to be worked in quick succession. Some excursion trains are heavy and slow and their progress up to Troutbeck affects other trains (in both directions). The result is that ordinary passenger trains become unduly delayed or to avoid this these excursion trains are detained in loops or sidings. This causes annoyance to the 'excursionists' [*sic*] who frequently get out of the carriages so exposing themselves to danger.

Often this crowded state in the excursion season results in a heavy train being required to shunt twice from one main line to the other to allow of one or more following trains to overtake, as well as get past others going in the opposite direction. Also extra goods trains to Penrith are needed to meet the developing business of the granite quarry at Threlkeld. Delays to goods are becoming more serious and the situation is made worse 'by the limited hours of working for the men on the trains'.

The committee then commented on the effect the introduction of the absolute block system had had on operations.

The section between Threlkeld and Troutbeck stations, which till recently has been worked in the up direction by the permissive block is now, on orders from the Board of Trade, divided into two block sections worked in absolute form. The result is that not more than two trains and these only when separated by the New Block Cabin can travel between those stations at the same time. On the old system three or four trains, if necessary, could follow each other on the Up journey.

The Board of Trade also require that means be provided for obviating the dangers existing on heavy gradients from the possibility of sections of trains breaking away and for this purpose, a passing loop with attendant signalling facilities should be made at the New Block Cabin, with safety points to turn off the main line any runaway vehicles. The doubling of the track would avoid the cost of this and also would permit the inclusion of safety points, not only at the New Block Cabin, but also other points [places] in particular Troutbeck and Threlkeld stations. The estimated cost of redoubling is £22,000.

Land has already been purchased (with the exception of one or two small sections). No Act of Parliament would be required. The work could be started at once.

It was no surprise that the Permanent Way Committee strongly recommended the work should be put in hand.

The images presented in some sections of this survey are alarming to say the least. Trains queuing along the line, irate excursionists jumping in and out of trains whilst this was taking place, delays and the ensuing problems, not least angry passengers no doubt accosting station staff. It is perhaps a tribute to the signalmen that no real catastrophes occurred! The Directors needed no further convincing. They immediately approved the scheme.

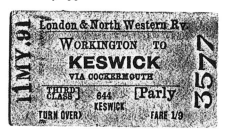

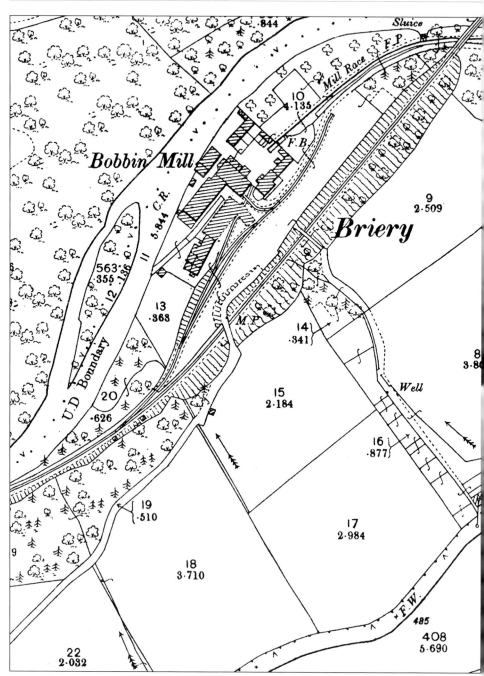

Bobbin Mill.   *Reproduced from the 25", 1900 Ordnance Survey Map*

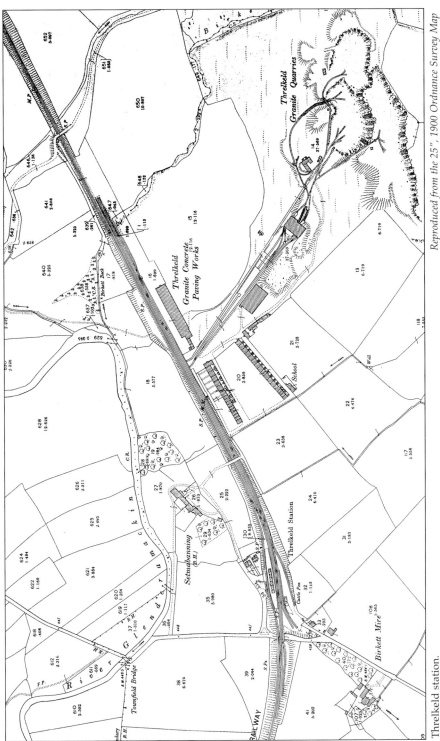

Reproduced from the 25", 1900 Ordnance Survey Map

Threlkeld station.

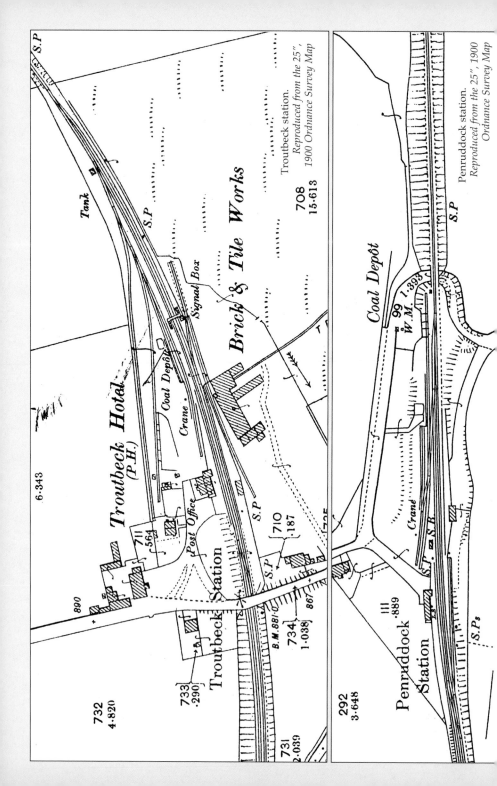

Troutbeck station.
*Reproduced from the 25",
1900 Ordnance Survey Map*

Penruddock station.
*Reproduced from the 25", 1900
Ordnance Survey Map*

1893-4

In April 1893, Wood invited tenders for the work of doubling the section between Troutbeck and Threlkeld and these were opened by the Board on 17th June:

	£	s.	d.
R.H. Hodgson of Workington	14,889	2	6
G. Grisenthwaite of Penrith	15,573	16	10 ½
Watt & Wilson of Glasgow	16,084	19	8
Morrison & Mason of Glasgow	16,334	5	9
James Young of Glasgow	18,153	10	5

These figures show considerable variation although all but the one from Watt & Wilson contain an element for six months' maintenance; Hodgson £400, Grisenthwaite £100, Morrison & Mason, £50 and Young £150. There is almost a suggestion that the higher the initial outlay, the lower would be the cost of maintenance. The contract was awarded to R.H. Hodgson and Waugh [jnr] was asked to prepare a contract.

The condition of Walthwaite viaduct started to give some cause for concern and in October it was felt the best remedy would be to fill in two arches at the eastern end.

The Permanent Way Committee had stated in its report that no Act of Parliament would be required for the doubling but the company did put a Bill before Parliament for this purpose. The Act is dated 1894 and simply formalises what had already been or was being done, stating 'the Company has acquired by agreement the whole of the land therefor and have partly constructed the said widening and it is expedient that the same be confirmed and the Company be authorised to complete and maintain the same; to acquire additional lands and retain what they have and to raise additional capital. The section to be widened passed through the Parishes of Crosthwaite, Greystoke S. Johns, Castlerigg and Wythburn, Threlkeld, Matterdale, Mungrisedale and Hutton Soil'.

The construction carried out was sanctioned and confirmed. Further, 'No more than two roods [sic] sixteen perches of Threlkeld Common can be purchased or acquired or three roods twenty-four perches of Guard House Rigg Common'. Other areas are mentioned and in Section 13 it is stated that 'for the better prevention of trespass . . . there shall be a penalty not exceeding 40 shillings for trespass . . . but notices shall be posted and must be renewed if for any reason obliterated or destroyed'. (If there was no warning, there could be no penalty.)

By August, Major Yorke was able to inspect the work. He made certain recommendations and said he would be back in a month to reassess the situation but the line could be used. In fact the inspector did not return until 24th November and his comments on that occasion related to certain interlocking arrangements at Keswick which needed minor modification. A further plan to double the track as far as Penrith was initially abandoned in view of falling receipts.

The Variety Automatic Supply Stores realised that there was potential for sales on the CK&PR stations and so made an application to install machines. The company was not viewed in the same favourable light as the purveyors of sweetmeats and on 10th September, the request was refused.

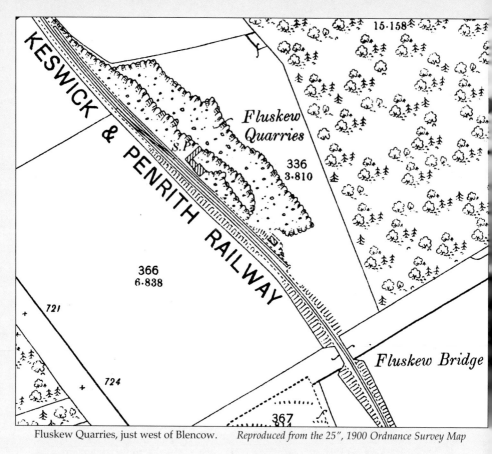

Fluskew Quarries, just west of Blencow.   *Reproduced from the 25", 1900 Ordnance Survey Map*

Blencow station.   *Reproduced from the 25", 1900 Ordnance Survey Map*

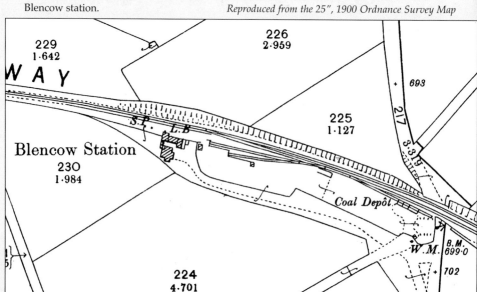

1897-9

Once again there were problems involving Lord Leconfield. This time it was alleged that when land was acquired during the early stages of construction some land he had sold to the Railway had not been properly conveyanced and another protracted dispute ensued. Waugh, as solicitor was asked to act and resolve the problem.

On 2nd July, 1897 the Directors approved a new rule book. This was introduced on 1st November of that year and 33 years on from the first rule book. It is a very different document. In effect it is the LNWR rule book with sections such as that relating to 'Regulations for Slip Carriages' being blocked out as 'Not applicable to the Cockermouth, Keswick and Penrith Railway'! The small print and tightly packed sections must have made it a more daunting prospect for those whose reading skills were little more than elementary, but railways and railway procedures had moved on and become more sophisticated. There are some 280 rules in over 170 pages. The general regulations now take up Rules 1-27, with Signalling Rules 28 to 86.

On 3rd December, it was agreed that in line with the decision made by the LNWR and M&CR, second class fares should be reduced to 10 per cent above the corresponding first class single. Silloth Convalescent Home benefited to the value of £2 2s. from the Directors' goodwill.

Public demand for the earlier conveyance of mail to Keswick, in the morning, together with a late dispatch in the evening resulted in the Chairman and Secretary visiting Euston on 17th March, 1898 and meeting Harrison to make a case for this facility. The Post Office entered the discussions on 29th March and the matter was kept under review.

During April another scheme came up for building a light railway; this time from Caldbeck to Penruddock. After carefully considering the project, the Directors decided to support it and offer any help they could. Another area in which they felt able to offer financial assistance involved the improvement of the road between Troutbeck station and Patterdale. They agreed to donate £50 in two £25 payments towards the cost of this. In line with their customary benevolence, £5 was donated towards Threlkeld Day School expenses; this turned out to be one of many donations to this particular cause. It was agreed during May that the passing loop at Bassenthwaite Lake station should be extended at the westward end by extending the facing points a few yards beyond the crossing gates; the cost to be £120.

During the latter part of the decade and more so in the next and beyond, the Directors had to devote more and more time in dealing with claims for better wages and improved conditions by the work-force. In August it was the turn of the signalmen and permanent way staff to make a submission and in October the platelayers were awarded an increase of 2s. per week (23s. to 25s.) and the gangers 1s. (22s. to 23s.). In addition a shilling was allowed for Sunday inspection. Others also received improved wages; carpenters, masons, smiths and painters from 25s. to 26s., signal fitters from 25s. to 27s., telegraph inspectors from 28s. to 32s. and permanent way inspectors from 37s. 6d. to 40s. Signalmen with over five years experience received 1s. increase (giving senior signalmen 24s. and junior 21s. and the relief men received 20s. instead of 19s).

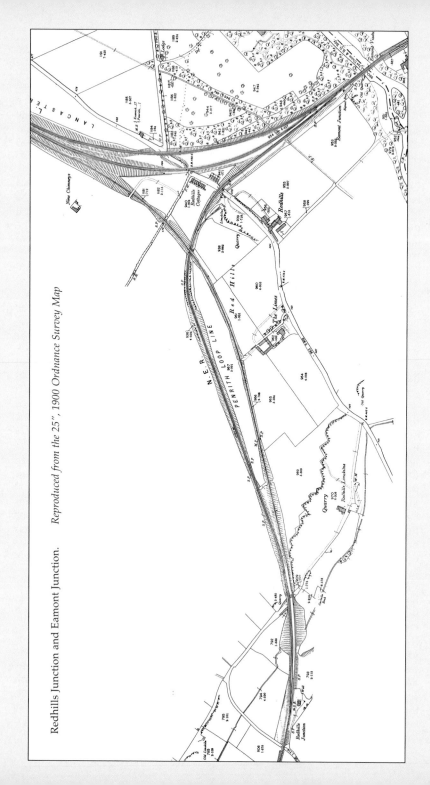

Redhills Junction and Eamont Junction. *Reproduced from the 25", 1900 Ordnance Survey Map*

The box at Redhills would have two ordinary signalmen dividing the work equally between them, giving 8½ hours working per day for each man but no overtime would be allowed for extra work or night duty. At Penruddock the large box was being manned 17¼ hours each day and the small one 15¾ hours with both men being relieved by a man from permanent way. In future there would be three signalmen with the time divided as nearly as possible equally between them with their times of working alternated week by week. The signalman in the large box would get 22s. per week with the junior and relief getting 20s. No overtime would be given unless more than 12 hours had been worked. At Troutbeck the same conditions would apply as those at Penruddock but relief would be provided by a porter rather than the permanent way staff. The same would also apply at Bassenthwaite Lake but the relief man would no longer come from the permanent way staff but a man who would work on the station platform when not acting as relief. Station masters also received higher salaries: at Keswick £100 per annum (from £95) Threlkeld 23s. per week to 30s., Bassenthwaite Lake, Troutbeck and Penruddock 23s. to 25s. per week and Embleton, Braithwaite and Blencow 21s. to 23s. per week. The result of all this was the employment of three extra men; platelayers at Blencow, Troutbeck and Bassenthwaite Lake all at 18s. per week.

Improvements of a different type were put in hand. In November, Wood was instructed to obtain the necessary apparatus to illuminate Penruddock station with acetylene gas. However, some members of the travelling public were not happy with the level of lighting at Penrith station and Harrison had occasion to write from Euston pointing out that there had been complaints about this. The gas superintendent was asked to give a report and did so. It was noted that 14 of the lamps were of an 'old' design and should be replaced by ones of the standard LNWR pattern, namely bell-bottom suspension lamps. Further, at the south end of the station two additional two-flame pillar lamps should be installed together with a bracket light in the lavatories and a bell-bottom light in the gentlemen's urinals. These improvements were carried out at a cost of £46.

The Directors decided to ask the shareholders to approve £10,000 to be subscribed towards the proposed Mid-Cumberland Light Railway between Caldbeck and Hesket New Market and Troutbeck and Penruddock stations provided the promoters could show that all other capital required would be taken up.

The year was not without accidents. A fatal one occurred on 14th November when Gilbert Howard, a fireman, slipped and fell from an engine working a train of empty carriages as he was exchanging the train tablet at Bassenthwaite Lake station.

The Directors had second thoughts about the proposal concerning the Mid-Cumberland Light Railway and in February 1899 rescinded their previous proposal to be put before the shareholders. The revised proposal was that the company should provide £10,000 in capital.

In April, following Thompson's outlining of the Summer services, it was decided to petition the LNWR to extend the short train which ran the previous year from Penrith to Keswick to Workington with an additional late train from Workington at 7.07 pm arriving at Keswick at 8.10 pm and Penrith at 9.05 pm. The Chairman and Secretary met Mr Sifton of the GPO on 24th March to reopen the matter of the company carrying the mail and it was agreed that further thought was needed. The problem with Lord Leconfield rumbled on! In June it was agreed there should be an experiment to run a through train to Workington.

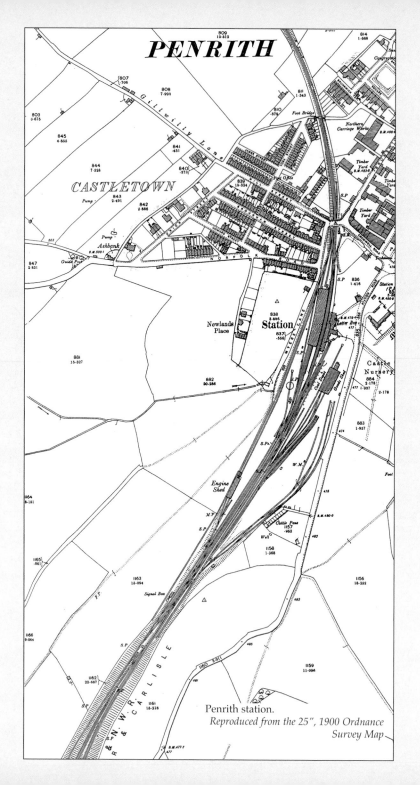

Penrith station.
*Reproduced from the 25", 1900 Ordnance
Survey Map*

The acetylene lighting at Penruddock was a success, so much so that Wood was instructed to remove it to Blencow and then install another larger generator at Penruddock.

Plans to double further sections of the line now received careful consideration and in August, Wood was instructed to purchase a strip of land between Troutbeck and Penruddock which belonged to Mr Howard, for this purpose. Plans were also to be prepared. By October it was resolved to double the line between Redhills Junction and Blencow station and Penruddock and Troutbeck stations and negotiations started with the appropriate landowners to obtain the land required. Messrs Pattinson, Riley and Glasson were appointed as a sub-committee to confer with Heskett to further this aim. In addition, Wood arranged the purchase of land from Sir Henry Vane in order to lengthen the up platform at Bassenthwaite Lake station and it was resolved to remove the siding points on the up loop line. With a view to their community responsibilities, the Directors decided to subscribe £1 1s. per annum for the support of a parish nurse appointed for the Saint John's Keswick District.

Although the acetylene lighting had proved successful, a new form of energy was coming into use and on 17th October, the Windermere and District Electricity Supply Company Limited put in a tender for what was described as an extended installation of 'the Electric Light' throughout Keswick station. Another sub-committee was formed to consider this proposal and this consisted of Messrs Spedding, Marshall and Pattinson. On 14th December a detailed specification was placed before the Directors by Mr Fowkes and the cost put on the work was £303. The Directors baulked at this and their initial reaction was to ask how the cost could be reduced. Mr Fowkes assured them no reduction could be made and the Directors decided to accept the tender. The deliberations about the early morning trains carrying mails came up again and it was felt no alterations could be made without the consent of the Postmaster General.

So to the end not only of the decade but of the century. By this time Keswick was well and truly on the tourist map and tourists could travel there on through coaches from Liverpool, Manchester, London and York. However, there had been drastic reductions in mineral traffic and the problems in this respect were by no means over. In addition a new century, indeed the next two decades, would bring challenges of a different form and from an unexpected quarter.

Motive Power in This Decade

During this period, the LNWR continued to use the 'Special DXs' and 'Cauliflowers' as its mainstay for motive power. An additional class which came onto the line in the late 1890s was the 2-4-2 tank, first built by Webb in 1890.

As far as NER mineral trains were concerned the motive power was much as before although Fletcher's '398' class started to appear along with the '1001s'. Locomotives of the '398' class lasted well into the 20th century. There were restrictions imposed by the load limitations and discussions with subsequent decisions about the use of heavier engines were yet to take place.

Cockermouth at the turn of a new century, when the trains saw considerable numbers of passengers.   *H.C. Casserley Collection*

A view from the same period of Bassenthwaite Lake station.   *J. Alsop Collection*

Chapter Six

The End of an Era:
1900-1923

At the turn of the century, James Spedding was Chairman and Peter Thompson, the Secretary. The other Directors listed were Sir Henry Ralph Vane, Bart, John Pattinson, Reginald Dykes Marshall, Henry Charles Howard, Hamlet Riley, Thomas Glasson [of the McGlasson family - it is not clear why he dropped the prefix 'Mc'] John Watson Nelson, Charles James Cropper, Miles MacInnes, The Honourable Cecil Duncombe and Sir David Dale, Bart.

1900-1

The new century brought with it business as usual and the first matter that had to addressed by the Directors involved plans to install a hydraulic lift on the up passenger platform at Keswick station. This move had come about following the decision to put such a lift in the Keswick Hotel. Negotiations had been progressing between the hotel company and Spedding for the supply of water for this lift and the supply was to come from the Greta Bank Estate. A lift of the same type could be used at the station to convey passengers' luggage from the entrance on the north side of the station. In March, the decision was made to install such a lift at the end of an underground passage to be made at the side of the existing one. The water supply came from a source on the side of Latrigg at about 600 ft. It was piped across in a 3 in. bore pipe to near Greta Bank Farm where there was a small reservoir and thence to the hotel. On another front, the Directors were approached in January by a deputation from Messrs Hasell (of Dalemain, who had been very much involved in the construction of the Lancaster and Carlisle and, later, the Ingleton branch) Harding (Penrith), Phelps (Birmingham) and Wilson (Manchester) to ask whether the company would be well disposed to a scheme for a line from Troutbeck to the neighbourhood of Carrock Fell with a view to opening out quarries and mines there. The Directors were a little cautious and agreed to consider the proposal. Later, in February, they decided they could not comment until a detailed plan was provided. Progress in the purchase of land for the doubling continued and at the shareholders' meeting in February, a dividend of 6¼ per cent was announced.

On 12th March a special Board meeting was convened; the subject to consider the tenders for doubling the track. Two tenders were received :

Section 1	Redhills Junction to Blencow station			
	W. Grisenthwaite	£4820	11s.	3d.
	R.H. Hodgson	£4873	18s.	6d.
Section 2	Troutbeck to Penruddock stations			
	W. Grisenthwaite	£5203	19s.	6d.
	R.H. Hodgson	£5614	3s.	6d.

It was agreed that Grisenthwaite should carry out the work on Section 1 but the Directors could not reach a decision on Section 2 and they asked Wood to have further discussions with both contractors, presumably with a view to bringing down the cost. In April, Wood recommended that Grisenthwaite should be awarded the contract for Section 2 and the Directors did so: 16th September was agreed as the completion date for the work. The Directors had now considered the proposal to construct a line to Carrock Fell but were not convinced the scheme was financially viable and so decided not to support it. A letter was received from a Dr Knight, requesting that two trains each day be stopped at Highgate cabin to pick up and set down schoolchildren (between 6 and 8 were involved) but this was not seen as practical and the request was declined.

Grisenthwaite started the work but made only slow progress. In August the Directors expressed disappointment when they met on 9th of the month and a letter was sent to the contractor conveying this disappointment. In October, the members of the Permanent Way Committee were asked to inspect the work, touring Section 1 on 15th October and Section 2 on 12th November. By this time, of course, the completion date had passed. It should have come as no surprise when Grisenthwaite pleaded poor weather as the reason for the lack of progress! He held out the hope that the job would be finished by the end of the year.

Grisenthwaite's optimism was ill founded, however, and on 7th January, 1901 with the work still unfinished, the Permanent Way Committee met him again at Troutbeck. It was felt progress was still far from satisfactory but they were reassured by the contractor that both sections would be finished by the end of the month, weather (of course) permitting.

What was described as a 'slight accident' occurred to a mineral train on 7th January between Troutbeck and Penruddock stations. Flagman Henry Walker, who was sent to protect platelayers on the main line 'having withdrawn his signals . . . allowed a mineral train to proceed beyond him without first receiving intimation from the gang that the line was clear'. He was fined 5s. and two others, John Robinson and Henry Walker jnr, whose actions it was alleged had led to the misunderstanding by the flagman, were reprimanded and cautioned.

The shareholders sanctioned the issuing of £25,000 of new stock at the half-yearly meeting in February. These were all taken up by June. Another vending company approached the company during May. This had the rather unusual name of the North Lancashire Mutoscope Company. They gained the Directors' favour and were told machines could be placed on all stations on the line. The cost would be £1 per annum in rent plus 20 per cent of all money received in excess of £5 in any one machine in one year.

It was June before the work on doubling the track was complete. On 2nd June the section between Penruddock and Troutbeck stations was brought into use, having been approved by the Board of Trade Inspector, Colonel Yorke. Notice of the completion of the other section was given by 18th June. More offerings of a benevolent nature were made in July when the Directors agreed to subscribe £50 towards the cost of enlarging Embleton and Wythrop schools. Although this was made with the proviso that the full cost could be met by ordinary contributions, it was not an insignificant amount to be giving away. On the other hand, when asked to make a subscription to support the Crosthwaite

Parish Nurse Fund, in August, the Directors declined because, they reasoned, it would mean that to be fair handed they would have to help all the districts along the line! However, they did say that they would consider any claims relating to treatment of any of the company's workmen. On a welfare front, the Directors did decide, following a request from the LNWR, to join a scheme to pay pensions to widows and families of company employees.

Something of a cliff-hanger happened to two trains on 5th August. The driver of the 6.05 pm from Cockermouth took his train into Bassenthwaite station against the signals. At the same time, a train was entering the station at the opposite end and the facing points were set for the down line. It over-ran the facing points for 80 yards and the two trains halted with only 150 yards between them.

By November, Grisenthwaite had disposed of or removed his equipment with one notable exception, namely the small locomotive he had been using. Someone had the bright idea that the company could well make use of it for ballasting and permanent way purposes and so it was purchased. It was also felt a suitable van should be bought for use with the ballast train. In addition it seemed sensible to build a shed to house the locomotive. Flusco Quarry was suggested but other sites would be considered. When the LNWR became aware of the company's action, which they did later the same month, an objection was immediately lodged with the Directors. It was argued that such a move, namely in the company acquiring a locomotive, was in breach of the agreement. Clearly the Directors were not at all happy about the prospect of giving up their new acquisition, which was, after all, the only locomotive they had ever really owned and so they decided to try and resolve the matter in a manner which would enable them to keep it. The saga was to be a long one!

The only known photograph of the locomotive which led to the Directors of the CK&PR taking issue with Euston. It seemed to them a good idea to acquire this engine, when the opportunity arose, for lighter duties. Euston thought otherwise!

1902

At their first meeting of the New Year on 9th January, the Directors' discussions soon turned to their new acquisition. They did have to consider an accident to a goods train, on 23rd December (1901) when three wagons were derailed between Penruddock and Troutbeck, after the train had left Penrith at 7.20 pm, and the resulting delay to the last passenger train of the day brought to a halt at Gill Head Cutting after part of it left the rails (there were no injuries). However, they were keen to find a solution to the impasse with the LNWR and so they did the only obvious thing, given the circumstances; they formed a sub-committee. The LNWR was petitioned again. By the February meeting, no reply had been received.

The Directors asked Wood to get estimates for installing acetylene lighting at Braithwaite and Threlkeld and on receiving these, in April, the work was put in hand. On 12th February Harrison, at Euston, sent a letter to the company about the locomotive. In it he suggested a deputation should join him at Euston on 6th March to consider the situation. Messrs Marshall, Cropper and Glasson agreed to go.

In the meantime there were problems with the hydraulic lifts at Keswick. Although, perhaps, it is difficult to imagine problems with drought conditions, there had been those resulting from a lack of water caused by frost. A pump seemed to be the answer and the cost of this was put at £150; but there was also the matter of how much water Spedding would be prepared to have moved in this way. The business was resolved to the satisfaction of all parties and the pumps were installed in April; one third of the cost to the Railway, the rest to the hotel.

The CK&PR delegation went to Euston on 6th March. The principle was accepted that the LNWR had the responsibility for providing engine power for maintenance - but the debate did not rest there. In May it rumbled on, the issue being who was actually responsible for power for permanent way work and ballasting. Thompson entered the discussions and on 25th March, he explained to the LNWR that the CK&PR had always, in effect, provided engines for the work. In the absence of any engines of their own, they had used NER engines in the early days but this practice had long ceased. During this period they had paid the NER the same rate as they had paid the LNWR but had never raised the question of costs, thinking them to be their responsibility. For the last 20-25 years the company had used the goods trains for the conveyance of ballast and when the Grisenthwaite engine came on the market it seemed a good opportunity to effect an economy by purchasing it. The use of this engine would also be manpower efficient. In spite of this, the LNWR was adamant and the CK&PR had to concede defeat. The company promised to sell the locomotive but pointed out that it expected easier terms than usual for the use of an LNWR engine. Thompson, supported by Wood, then negotiated terms for the future. The company would give the LNWR a day's notice for the use of an engine but shorter notice might be necessary in emergencies. An engine would probably be needed once a week but sometimes more. After a further, lengthy, discussion it was agreed that for permanent way works between Keswick and Penrith, Thompson would apply to the station master at Penrith for an engine and for the Keswick to Cockermouth section he would apply to the station master at

Workington. A day's notice should be given whenever possible and the present charge of 7s. per hour for an engine would be reduced to 6s. per hour. This would include the use of a brakevan and brakeman. The charge would be calculated from the time the engine passed onto the CK&PR at Penrith or Cockermouth until the time it passed off again. The CK&PR agreed to discontinue the use of goods trains for carrying ballast and, therefore, stopping them between stations for the purpose of unloading.

There was a more relaxed mood on 26th June when most of the staff were given a day's holiday to celebrate the Coronation of King Edward VII and for those who were required to be at work for essential purposes, there was to be a day off in lieu. John Wood also received a pleasant surprise; the Directors awarded him £800 for the extra work involved in the doubling of the track.

After the celebrations, it was back to business. It had already been decided not to make Braithwaite a passing station after all and then Mr Philipson of the Briery Bobbin Mill asked that the charges levied for the use of his siding should be dropped. The best the Directors felt they could offer was a reduction from 1s. to 6d. per ton. They acknowledged the downward trend in the bobbin industry and took this into account but were keen to point out that any improvement must result in the old rate being brought back. In August, it was decided an auxiliary frame should be put in at Bassenthwaite Lake station, with the cabin, to meet what was seen as likely requirements by the Board of Trade, following a report which had been received from Captain Druitt concerning the placing of a new crossover road between the main lines. Also in that month there was another petition from the signalmen asking that duty be 'equalised' throughout the line and also be made to compare favourably with the routines of other companies. The Directors felt they could not meet this demand but they did ask Thompson to use his discretion in making adjustments where he felt it would be appropriate.

Mr Bewsher, of Embleton, was the next to approach the Directors with plans. He had acquired land to extend his timber business and needed siding facilities. Wood reckoned the cost to be £300, and this would include a long siding of 300 yards with two connections in the centre forming a loop for shunting and a connection from the back siding to the goods yard. Mr Bewsher did not want to put the sidings in at his own expense and wondered what the company's terms would be. He made it clear that he still wished to continue using the station sidings and the yard and was at pains to point out that the increase in capacity had resulted not from further development, but from the fact that he had decided to move part of his business from Penrith. The Permanent Way Committee, as it happened, had become concerned about Brewsher's timber being on station premises other than in the normal course of transit and the move seemed a good one. The company decided to go ahead with laying down a siding and then to charge a tonnage in and out in addition to the ordinary rates for carriage and the use of station terminals.

As the year closed, the Directors no doubt felt their hunch regarding Bassenthwaite Lake station had been correct; the Board of Trade Inspector approved the work.

The crossing at Bassenthwaite station in a photograph taken in 1905. Problems with this crossing are referred to in the the text (see page 111 and 113). *John Alsop Collection*

The impressive island platform at Keswick. *Lens of Sutton*

1903-6

Trade in 1902 had proved fair and at the shareholders' meeting on 28 February a dividend of 5½ per cent was announced. In the previous year payment for services to the two operating companies had amounted to £6,489 10s. 0d. to the LNWR and £3,147 4s. 5d. to the NER. The total expenditure had been £17,054 14s. 8d. This was soon to change dramatically. Mineral and goods mileage was 62,956 and passenger, 73,892, reckoned to be a satisfactory state of affairs and everybody, not least the shareholders, seemed happy. John Pattinson, who had served the company as a Director since 1881, died. His place was taken by his son J.W. Pattinson. We have cause to be grateful to the Pattinsons. They carefully preserved most of the letters they received on company business together with a variety of documents; all are now available for posterity.

During the course of the year a number of developments occurred and Mr Brewsher gave further thought to his need for a siding. A letter was received from Canon Rawnsley (of the National Trust). The letter was sent to Spedding and expressed some dissatisfaction with 'northern connections'. He asked that these might be improved bearing in mind there was nothing North (or South) connecting with the 6.35 pm from Keswick. Further an additional ('reliable') train was needed to connect with the Limited Mail to London which left Carlisle at 8.41 pm. Rawnsley was a man of some standing and Spedding instructed Thompson to make enquiries. More automatic machines made their appearance in April when the Sweetmeat Automatic Delivery Company Limited were allowed to place machines on the stations at Keswick and Cockermouth for a rent of £3 per annum plus 5 per cent on any amount over £30 being taken in either machine. In an aesthetic vein, the NER agreed to place 'photographic views of Keswick and other places of attraction' which were of the area served by the CK&PR, in some of their carriages. The CK&PR were to provide the prints and 500 had been suggested. A Mr Robinson who was already supplying the NER with similar views had been approached and asked to act. The cost was to be £16 for 100 copies and the Directors found this acceptable. Troutbeck station was given the advantage of acetylene lighting, following a decision in October. In November, Brewsher informed the Directors that he had decided to build his own siding and only wanted a connection. The previous proposals were withdrawn and the Directors were only too happy to oblige. There had been some representation for day excursion tickets from Cockermouth and Keswick to Liverpool and Manchester on one day each week to start on 1st January, 1904 and in November the LNWR finally approved this, the tickets to be 11s. from Cockermouth and 10s. from Keswick.

News on another front was not good. By the end of December there had been a noticeable decline in mineral traffic, again ascribed to the state of the iron and steel trade. The result was an inevitable fall in the dividend to 4¼ per cent.

The Working Timetable for the Summer showed 30 up trains and 32 down trains, with two passenger workings on Sundays [*see Appendix Three for details*].

It is well known that many of the railway builders of the 19th century built structures, not least bridges, which have more than met the demands placed upon them by later generations of locomotives and trains. When Bouch designed the bridges of the CK&PR he seemed to have rather less of an eye to anything more than the fairly immediate future. It was inevitable, with the development of the locomotive, that the day would come when heavier locomotives would be planned which it was hoped could be run on the line. The day came, in fact , on 4th February, 1904, when Worsdell, Chief Mechanical Engineer of the NER wrote to the Directors of the CK&PR. He referred to a meeting held between his assistant Vincent Raven and John Wood. The matter under discussion was the intention of the NER to introduce the new, heavier class 'T' (0-8-0) engines and whether it would be possible to use these engines on coke trains over the CK&PR. Wood had said that such a move would almost certainly result in the necessity to strengthen some of the bridges and enquired whether the NER would be prepared to meet some of the cost of this work, either directly or by effecting a reduction of working expenses. Worsdell considered this and replied on 17th May, following a proposal from the CK&PR that 30 per cent instead of 35 per cent of the gross receipts should be paid to help offset any costs. This virtually coincided with a decision by the NER during May to give a rebate of 10 per cent off through coke traffic to help the plight of the iron industry. Some surprise was expressed at the CK&PR suggestion. Worsdell made it very clear that in his view the CK&PR should be strengthening its bridges as a matter of course! If the company was to earn revenue under 'modern conditions' this was essential. He stressed that 'lines built a long time ago must be up graded'. He went further and suggested that '35 per cent in today's terms could be unrealistic and if challenged and an adjustment deemed necessary, it might prove cheaper to strengthen the bridges!' The Directors decided to defer making a decision when they met on 9th June. The decline in trade continued and in August a dividend of 2¾ per cent was proposed.

In November, the Directors received a letter from Robert Pearson of Penrith. He was a coal merchant and along with others of his trade felt it was unfair that the station masters could act as agents for the sale of coal from the station yards, thereby disadvantaging the merchants. It was hoped a stop would be put to this practice but the Board felt it did not wish to change the existing arrangement. The members had not heard the last of Robert Pearson.

The Directors' *bête noire* struck again from 21st to 24th November in the form of snow blocks, although there were only 24 hours without trains, between the 22nd and 23rd November.

An unusual sight was witnessed by travellers and others using Keswick station on 2nd January. Two men, Joseph Little and Thomas Gibson, had been employed from 6 am to 6 pm to hold a chain across the station road between the two posts indicating the railway's property. (There must have been an easier way to do this!) It was agreed to hold the coke rate rebate until 31st March in order to give further assistance to the iron industry.

At their meeting on 9th February, the Directors were asked to consider a letter which had been written to Sir Henry Vane. The letter, dated 30th January, had been written by Colonel Hoskins, the son of the railway's first Chairman. It read

Dear Sir Henry,

I should be very glad if you could kindly place before the Chairman and Directors of the C.K. & P. Rly for their favourable consideration that I should like to give them the Wheelbarrow and Spade given to my Father on the occasion of cutting the first sod of the C.K. & P. Rly to be kept by them in their Boardroom.

I should be very glad if they could accept them and would have them sent to the Boardroom.

Yours sincerely,

R. Hoskins.

What a splendid gesture, allowing these artefacts to be preserved for posterity. The Directors readily accepted them and said they would certainly find a suitable place. The items were delivered in early February from Higham.

In May another 'artefact' came to the fore again. Quite what prompted him to do so remains a mystery, but Cropper reminded his fellow Directors that the locomotive they had purchased over three years ago was still unsold. It was felt anything over £300 would be a fair price if a suitable buyer could be found.

Although the 10 per cent rebate had been further extended, this time to 30th June, at the meeting on 8th June it was felt there could be no further extensions and Euston was in agreement with this. However it was resolved to investigate other ways in which the iron masters might be helped. Later it was decided to make an allowance on a permanent basis: on rates of 5s. or under 5d.; over 5s., 6d.

With a view to promoting the railway, the Directors were asked to consider subscribing £5 towards the expense of producing a large poster containing views of Keswick scenery. Some 3,000 copies had been obtained by the Urban District Council for £43 10s. In an attempt to make their publicity items more attractive, Cropper pointed out that Mrs Rawnsley had supplied a painting, done by her, of Derwentwater and Bassenthwaite lakes for the purpose of embellishing the company's timetable handbills.

On 12th October, John Wood announced his intention to retire. He was highly praised by the Directors, having been with the railway since its inception and was given a presentation costing £25 2s., not an inconsiderable sum of money. In November, A.M. Bristow was appointed to succeed him from 1st December.

Canon Rawnsley, forging ahead with his plans to acquire properties and land for the National Trust felt the Directors might be prepared to help out. In December he invited them to subscribe towards the purchase of Gowbarrow Estate for public use. They politely turned him down.

The matter of using heavier engines was raised again in June 1906, this time by Smeddle, the NER District Locomotive Superintendent at Darlington. He wrote regarding the use of the class 'C1' engines and in particular some experimental runs. He wanted to start 'soon' but the Directors, still rather anxious about the prospect deferred, again, to October. At this point they decided to face up to the matter and asked Bristow to prepare a report including estimates for strengthening the bridges which would be affected by the NER so-called 'heavy engines' and also to prepare the bridges for a double line of rails. In July the Engineer presented his report including a cost of £80 for the work and was told to proceed. In August he prepared an additional report which gave details of strengthening the bridges for the class 'T' engines. The Directors decided to stick with the work for the class 'C1'!

In October, Joseph Tinnion resigned as station master at Penruddock and was presented with £25 for long service. There was the usual move up the ranks; John Blackburn, station master at Embleton took his place and J.W. Ewart, the booking clerk at Keswick, became station master at Embleton. In 1906, Sir Henry Vane resigned as Deputy Chairman and his place was taken by H.C. Howard.

1907

Throughout this period there continued to be a growing movement, generally, for improved conditions in a variety of work places and the CK&PR was no exception. The improvements for platelayers and, in a modest way, for station masters, has been referred to already. On 11th July, the Board considered a plea put in by the signalmen for their hours and conditions to be reviewed and improved. By this time, they were working 11 hours each day on weekdays with porter/reliefmen covering for the rest of the time. The working day at Blencow provides an example.

Signalman Bewley
    1st Week   5.00 am to 4.00 pm
    2nd Week   10.30 am to 9.15 pm

A. Watson, Reliefman and Porter

	Platform	Signal box	
1st Week	10.00 am to 4.00 pm	4.00 pm to 9.15 pm	
2nd Week	10.30 am to 4.30 pm	5.00 am to 10.30 am	(1 hour off during the day)

The men at Redhills Junction, Keswick, Cockermouth and Cockermouth Junction did not join this particular 'memorial' (petition). At Redhills, for example, where two men shared the duties they followed complementary routines based on 8 hours one week and 8¼ hours the next. At Keswick with two boxes and four men there was satisfaction with the routine in spite of the fact that some shifts ran to 11 hours. All four were on an equal footing but acted as main and relief alternately, with the relief taking the early shift and then the early shift man doing other work, for example on the platform, later. At Cockermouth station the signalman worked 10 hours one week and 10¼ hours the next, with the reliefman on duty 11¼ hours (but given 2 hours off for meals) one week and the next a remarkable 12 hours, with 2 hours off for meals. It was argued that the maximum working period should be 10 hours and the committee recommended changes. At Blencow, the box opened from 5.00 am to 9.15 pm and the routine would become:

Signalman Bewley
    1st Week   5.00 am to 3.00 pm
    2nd Week   11.15 am to 9.15 pm

A. Watson, Reliefman and Porter

	Platform	Signal box	
1st Week	11.00 am to 3.00 pm	3.00 pm to 9.15 pm	(1¼ hours off)
2nd Week	11.15 am to 4.00 pm	5.00 am to 11.15 am	(1 hour off)

The one hour lost by the signalman was made up by the relief being one hour less on the platform.
During this period the boxes opened as follows

Penruddock	5.30 am	to	9.00 pm
Troutbeck	5.30 am	to	9.15 pm
Threlkeld	5.45 am	to	9.30 pm
Keswick A and B	6.00 am	to	9.30 pm
Bassenthwaite	6.45 am	to	9.45 pm
Cockermouth Station	6.30 am	to	9.50 pm

The variation in these times reflected to some extent the pattern of services. Those who found difficulty getting up in the mornings would find it more conducive to work as far West as possible! It was recognised that at Bassenthwaite it would be necessary to employ an extra man to take the entire duty at the small box at the eastern end of the passing loop and it was proposed this man would alternate his duties week by week with the reliefman in the large box. This would mean the hours in the small box would be from 7.00 am to 7.00 pm with a break from 3.30 pm to 6.00 pm plus meal intervals. The Board agreed these arrangements should be implemented.

During this year combined rail and coach tours were introduced from Cockermouth and Keswick. These commenced on 20th May and were continued to 28th September. Tour 1 (Mondays, Wednesdays and Saturdays) was to Penrith by rail and thence by coach via Eamont Bridge, Brougham Hall, Clifton, Lowther Park, Lowther Castle Askham, Tirril Moor to Pooley Bridge and returning by way of Dalemain Park to Penrith; a total of 20 miles. Tour 2 (Wednesdays, Thursdays and Saturdays) also started by going to Penrith by rail and then by coach via Carleton Hills, Eden Hall, Great Salkeld, Lazonby and Kirkoswald to Nunnery Walks (where two hours were allowed) thence back to Penrith via Eden Hall; some 24 miles. Timings were:

From:	*May, June*	*July, August, September*
	am	*am*
Cockermouth	8.58	9.03
Keswick	9.32	9.40

Armstrongs Coaches helped to operate these tours.

On 11th October the Board received a further request for a morning and an evening train to stop at the Highgate box in order to take up and set down schoolchildren who travelled long distances to and from school and whose journeys would be considerably eased by this facility. This time the Board acknowledged the advantages of this but pointed out that the Board of Trade would have to be consulted. Following such a consultation, the Board of Trade agreed, provided certain work was carried out. The cost of this was estimated at £170 and the Board felt it proper to ask the Education Committee to pay.

Meantime, in May, Canon Rawnsley agreed to write the text for a 'Guide to the Lake District' to be issued jointly by the company and the LNWR. There was a complaint, in June, from Mr Hartley of Armathwaite Hall about the state of the up platform at Bassenthwaite Lake station. It seems all sorts of goods were

A local freight passes through Highgate Halt. The Halt was made only for use by schoolchildren.
It did not have a nameboard. The locomotive is a Webb 'Coal Tank'.   *Lens of Sutton*

Penruddock in 1910. Who is the little girl, keen to be in the picture?   *J. Alsop Collection*

being left around and so the Directors decided to build a goods shed thereby releasing the waiting room from being used as a repository for goods in transit. Mr Hartley appears to have had some influence because it was also resolved to 'put the Waiting Room in order and make it comfortable'. The discussions may have led, also, to the decision, in June, to install acetylene gas lighting at the station. In December, approval was given to build two cottages at Blencow station for the signalmen.

1908

The beginning of 1908 saw a resolution to construct an additional room at Keswick station in front of what was referred to as the Paper Room, over the platform, the cost to be £50. The Blencow cottages, it was agreed, should have three bedrooms. The facilities for the school children at Highgate were discussed again at a meeting on 13th February and arrangements for stopping the trains were approved. A tender from Grisenthwaite of £485 for building the Blencow cottages was accepted and 3,000 creosoted sleepers were bought from Messrs Christie & Co. for 3s. 11½d. each.

On 22nd and 29th February there was a snow block on the line and the Directors approved the spending of additional payments to clear the line. Blockage by snow continued to be a more than usually sensitive issue with the Board who regularly discussed ways in which it could be avoided. However, some may have seen this particular block as a blessing in disguise. It prevented a number of shareholders from Penrith getting to the first half-yearly meeting. Certain Penrith shareholders had been getting a reputation for giving the Directors a hard time either by being contentious and argumentative or asking awkward questions. It seemed there would not be a quorum and it is reported that some ladies who lived in the Keswick district and were shareholders, were exhorted to attend in order to make the meeting possible. Receipts continued to fall markedly. A dividend of 3 per cent was announced at the shareholders' meeting.

Mr Glossop asked the Board to provide a siding for his quarry near Embleton and the Board considered this request on 11th June. Mr Glossop was finding transportation to the railway very expensive and had investigated the possibility of building an aerial way. The conditions imposed by the County Council for this made the cost prohibitive and Glossop could see an end to his business if the siding was not built. The Directors made it clear that the company could not build the siding; it would have to be a private siding. However it would meet the cost of connecting it provided this did not exceed £200.

About this time a problem arose which in some ways was a foretaste of things to come. The motor car had arrived on the scene ! However it was not, as yet, posing a threat in terms of a significant alternative means of transport but, rather, difficulties at crossings; in particular, the one at Bassenthwaite Lake station. The problem arose because the view of the road from the box was obscured and so it was virtually impossible to see cars approaching. A radical solution would be mooted eventually but for the moment it was agreed a caution board should be erected.

Back at Highgate, on 16th June, Colonel Druitt inspected the work that had been carried out. Platforms had been built 150 feet long and 6 feet wide but only 2 feet 6 inches above the rails. This was because only schoolchildren were meant to use them and, further, because of this it was agreed no name boards should be put up, so making the point that the platforms were not for public use.

In August, John Wood was offered a directorship but had to turn it down on grounds of ill health. Other changes occurred; Mr Reay, the station master at Keswick died and Mr Allison moved from Bassenthwaite to take his place. Mr Hutchinson at Blencow moved, in turn, to Bassenthwaite Lake and the post at Blencow was advertised. At the shareholders' meeting a suggestion was made that railmotors should be used between Keswick and Penrith but this was not followed through. A minor altercation occurred following an accident to a young child who was sitting on its mother's knee in a third class compartment on a train which was about to leave Bassenthwaite station. The ticket collector closed the door and trapped the child's big toe. Damages of £2 11s. 6d. had to be paid!

By October, the cottages at Blencow were completed and a weekly rent of 3s. 6d. was set for them. There had been complaints about the possible risk of accidents to platelayers not being given proper warning of approaching trains and so five dozen whistles were purchased for use by this group of workers.

On a domestic front, the company, via Pattinson, received another letter from Robert Pearson who continued to be aggrieved about the arrangement, described earlier, whereby the station masters were able, as a sideline, to act as coal and coke dealers, so enhancing their incomes. This was quite in order and no malpractice was involved. He wrote:

> I am venturing to address you, along with the other Directors of the Cockermouth, Keswick and Penrith Railway on a matter which is of very great importance to me and other traders in this district.
> You are doubtless aware that the station masters on the Keswick line are allowed to act as coal and coke dealers and also as agents for the sale of the same on behalf of other people. I have for many years been a tenant of the Railway Company in respect of depots on their line and I find that the official position which the station masters hold (apart from the advantage of having a weekly wage) gives them such an advantage with farmers and others coming to your stations that my trade is completely ruined in their districts. I and others consider that the competition is quite unfair.
> I venture to draw your attention to the very first rule of your company which commences as follows
> > Rule 1. All persons employed by the Company must devote themselves exclusively to the Company's service.
> > Rule 11. No servant of the Company is allowed to trade either directly or indirectly for himself or others.

Pearson goes on to insist that the practice be stopped. Once again the Directors saw no reason to take any action.

1909-13

The need to continue to provide passengers with newspapers and other reading materials was addressed on 11th February, 1909 when Wymans were given permission to run the bookstall on Keswick station, W.H. Smith having declined. At the same time, Kershaws were afforded advertising privileges.

Accidents continued to happen, in spite of all the precautions taken by the Railway. On 20th April a boy named Walter Russell Scott was killed on the line. An interesting insight into certain practices of the day, before the advent of the National Health Service, is provided by an incident at Blencow station, when one of the company's masons, Mr S. Bewley, was taken very ill. Dr Johnstone was called and after treating Mr Bewley put in a bill for 10s. 6d. Sadly, Mr Bewley died and the matter of who should settle the doctor's bill had to be resolved. In a magnanimous gesture, the company accepted the responsibility to do this rather than pass it to his widow.

At Bassenthwaite station all was not well. In spite of the caution board, the unthinkable had happened. On 23rd July one of those newfangled motor cars had been damaged on the crossing. The company, in what must have been something of a test case, refused to accept responsibility. On the other hand the owner of the car insisted it was the fault of the company. On 28th August, rather surprisingly, the company backed down a little. The Directors agreed to settle damages but without accepting liability. It was also decided the situation at the crossing gates should be reviewed. On 14th October, the Permanent Way Committee reported that the signal box, as it stood, did not give the signalman a clear view of the road in the direction of The Pheasant Hotel. The members of the committee suggested the box should be moved a few yards nearer to the gates, so giving a better view. After careful consideration it was felt that a new box should be built. However, at this juncture, what must surely have been a novel suggestion was made. This was to provide a signal on the road with a single arm 10-12 feet above the ground for the purpose of indicating to approaching motors from both sides, when the gates were closed. This signal, it was argued, should be connected to the block lever of the existing gates hence ensuring that the signal would act with the gate block. The Permanent Way Committee went away to consider this. When it reported again on 6th October it stated that moving the box would be the only effective solution. The Directors accepted neither. They felt the best way forward was to leave things as they were but to put a larger wheel in the cabin for greater leverage when opening and closing the gates. This was not the end of the story.

At a meeting on 11th November, it was decided that Embleton station should be lit with acetylene gas and on 24th November, a sum of £21 was allocated for 20 lamps and equipment. On 8th December, Major Spedding died. He had been Chairman for 30 years and was the last surviving member of the original Board. He had survived the ordeal of his first meeting in the chair, when it was proposed no dividend should be paid; he had steered the company through both difficult and rewarding times. The new Chairman was H.C. Howard, with R.D. Marshall being made Vice-Chairman. For four days in January 1910 (28th-31st) the line was again blocked by snow. The Directors urged the Permanent Way Committee to do its utmost to take steps to prevent this happening by investigating possible solutions to the problem. Another insight on the day to day misdemeanours of some staff is provided by a report that the relief signalman at Penruddock, Mr Todhunter, had been fined 3s. 0d. (1s. 0d. each week for three weeks) for his neglect in tablet working procedures.

The desirability of through workings from the Midland during the Summer was expressed on 14th April and the company agreed to consult the LNWR. Through carriages from Leeds to Keswick were introduced as a result. At this meeting, the Directors also considered a number of demands for compensation from passengers who had been inconvenienced as a result of a train delay at Penruddock. Fearing a precedent might be created, they decided to refuse to meet these claims. On 12th May the Board joined the many others in sending a message of condolence on the occasion of the death of King Edward VII.

Discussions followed about the standing of the station master at Bassenthwaite Lake who also had the role of sub-post master. It was resolved to pay £6 per annum for additional office accommodation for the Post Office work and, the following month, to build this sub-post office at the end of the existing booking office, adjoining the platform. In July there was a change of plan and it was felt better to site it immediately behind the booking office.

There were still problems at the Bassenthwaite signal box! The provision of the larger wheel did not appear to be the solution. On 9th June, it was agreed to review the matter yet again and a committee was set up consisting of Messrs Marshall, Glasson and Pattinson. It only took one week for them to propose that the box should be moved after all and this time the Board agreed. A letter was sent to the Board of Trade seeking authorisation for this work.

The members were still concerned about the stoppage of traffic in the Winter by snow. It will be recalled they had made various requests that the problem be given serious consideration and if at all possible, solved. There had been no effective response to this request and so the Board decided to meet on 11th August at Penrith and travel the length of the line in an attempt to work out how blockages could be prevented. No definite decisions seem to have been made as a result of this trip except to consult the Caledonian Railway (CR), which was happy to offer advice on the preventative measures it used. Following this, there was a decision to convene a joint meeting with the NER; the latter had more than a little experience in this aspect of operations.

A petition that the 1.15 pm from Whitehaven on Saturdays, which formed the 2.02 pm from Cockermouth to Keswick and which had only run during the Spring and Summer should be continued throughout the year, was viewed favourably by the CK&PR and it was agreed, in turn to petition the LNWR. A letter was received on 28th July, following a visit by the Board of Trade Inspector authorising the change of location for the Bassenthwaite box.

It is rare to find recorded in minutes the details of engine numbers but such is the case on 27th August when it is reported that LNWR engine No. 3069 had sustained a broken spring of the leading pair of tender wheels. This engine was working the passenger train which departed from Keswick at 9.38 am. Some wheels left the rails causing damage but fortunately nobody was injured. The incident occurred on 22nd August.

In October, no doubt having in mind the onset of Winter and the prospect of snow blocks, the Directors decided to follow up their decision to seek advice from the NER. There had been some discussion with the CR but on 28th October a group of the Directors met Vincent Raven. He explained that the NER ploughs were wooden, weighed 26 tons and were 11 ft high, although they had acquired some recent additions which were made of steel and at the same height weighed 27 tons. The NER reckoned two or more engines were needed for the wooden ploughs when used on Stainmore, the steel ones might need more. The Directors were interested and enquired about the cost. They were told a wooden plough would cost £428 to make so they could expect to pay around £500; steel, £590 to make and selling at around £725. The recommendation was to place a plough at Penrith which was always in readiness and the NER would be prepared to provide engine power at the usual rate. The Directors were clearly taken aback somewhat by the cost and asked whether there would be the possibility of hiring a plough, say for a fixed period. They felt that the demands they would face would be nothing like those posed by Stainmore and the number of times a plough would be needed, far less. The NER felt it could not enter into an arrangement for hiring. The times of greatest demand would take all the ploughs it possessed. The Directors decided not pursue this approach but to consider, instead, putting up some sleeper fences. In December the Permanent Way Committee suggested putting a sleeper snow fence at Penruddock station against 'Green's Field' and a stone wall 40 yards long at Highgate Wood, next to the wood, together with a sleeper fence from the west end of the wall for about 160 yards.

Canon Rawnsley appeared on the scene again in December, this time to ask whether a notice could be put up at Troutbeck station indicating the nearby National Trust Property of Gowbarrow. This was agreed in principle and the Company's station board at Troutbeck thereafter became 'Troutbeck for Ullswater, Patterdale Gowbarrow and Aira Force'.

Another facet of railway staff activity emerged in January 1911 when it was decided station and permanent way staff should start ambulance instruction. In fact this was to develop a strong and enthusiastic following as time would tell. During February an extension to the Briery Bobbin Mill was approved and Mr Philipson agreed to pay for its use; the rate to be up 3d. per ton to 9d. (although this was later reduced back to 6d.). Cockermouth UDC asked that the through service with the Midland operated the previous Summer be extended to Cockermouth (from Keswick) but the company did not feel it could recommend this. On another front, the LNWR was asked to allow passengers holding half-day excursion tickets to Carlisle to return at times other than 7.40 pm.

Foreman porter Cutts was presented with a week's wages in April for his work as an ambulance instructor. The enthusiasm for this particular activity was growing rapidly. Perhaps he was lucky to get the money when he did! In May the Directors felt it necessary to examine all expenditure in detail. The revenue was described as being 'in a low condition'. The fall in revenue seemed irreversible. There was a very considerable decline in the coke traffic from Durham. To some extent this resulted from a new type of manufacturing process which made it possible to use the West Cumberland coal, with its high phosphoric content, for producing coke which could be used effectively in the

A fine view of LNWR 0-6-0 No. 87 waiting to leave Penrith with a passenger train for Workington.

William Nash Collection

blast furnaces. The Directors conceded that traffic of this type was so low that it had virtually disappeared. The payment to the NER for traffic services was £502 1s. 2d., half the amount for the previous year (£1,159 12s. 7d.) and down to one-sixth of the amount paid in the early 1900s.

Payment to the LNWR more than held up during the same period; there was a slight increase to £6,734 13s. 7d. Whatever the reasons, it was perhaps optimistic to the point of being naive to believe matters could substantially improve. The dividend for June was to be only 1¼ per cent. A number of measures were put forward to combat the situation. The Directors would accept a £100 deduction in their annual fees, there would be no further increase in salaries at head office beyond 20s. per week unless approved by the Board, platelayers would take full responsibility for their sections and the 'junior fencers' would be laid off, Mr Black at Flusco Quarry would be given one month's notice and the gardeners' pay would be limited to £40 per annum. In addition only one painter and an assistant would be kept on and substantial amounts of work would be contracted out. Some 'trimmings' must go as well. The half-yearly luncheon held in conjunction with the half-yearly meeting would be discontinued except for press representatives. The one bit of good news was that everybody would get a day off, or equivalent, for the Coronation of King George V on 22nd June.

The fall in trade was certainly beginning to bite although in spite of the difficulties the traffic did revive a little, later in the year and the dividend went up to 3½ per cent for the period ending 31st December. In August the LNWR announced that it intended to abolish second class from 1st January, 1912 (except in the London Districts) and so all second class fares would have to be cancelled. The CK&PR Directors were far from happy with this move and stated emphatically that they wished to retain second class. On 26th August Frank Ree wrote from Euston pointing out that if the LNWR agreed to this they would, in effect, have to run trains with empty carriages between Cockermouth and Whitehaven which would not make sense. He urged the CK&PR to come in line with the proposals and in the end the CK&PR did so. From 1st January, first class fares would be reduced from 2½d. to 2d. per mile for a single and remain at 3d. for a return. Third class would remain at the existing rate except fractions under ¼ mile would be dropped, ¼ mile up to ¾ mile would be charged as ½ mile and greater than ¾ mile as for a mile.

During August there was a 2-day national strike by railway workers and as a result, the CK&PR had to hire conveyances between Keswick and Penrith. The cost for carrying some 525 passengers had been £106 9s. 6d. and as usual when this sort of situation occurred the question of who should pay was raised. The CK&PR felt that as the normal conveyor, the LNWR should foot the bill. The LNWR was not so sure! In the end the matter was resolved by the two companies sharing the cost. One decision which did come out of this situation was that in the event of a future strike the CK&PR could provide a driver and fireman to work a train.

By the 12th October the new sub-post office was finished at Bassenthwaite Lake station and the Directors went along to inspect it. In spite of some predictions to the contrary, coke traffic did pick up a little towards the end of the year £1,088 5s. 8d. being paid to the NER. The result was a rather higher dividend of 3½ per cent.

During February 1912 an attempt was made to frame rules under which the representatives of the hotels in Keswick would be permitted on the station platform to meet the trains. It seems some of these people had, in the view of the company, been over-reaching their duties. In January, Mr Messenger representing the hotels had offered the company £40 per annum to have staff representation on the platforms; the Directors put the price at £12 10s. for each of the four hotels. It was agreed that hotel representatives, but not hotel porters, would be allowed to bring luggage from the hotels to the trains, that hotel representatives could only attend passengers on inward-coming trains (not passengers departing) that no-one other that railway porters could open carriage doors, that only one representative could be sent from each hotel and that they must in no circumstances cross the line. Further, each must wear the uniform provided by the hotel and each hotel must have its own distinctive uniform. Each representative would be allocated a place on the platform and none must ever be present whilst under the influence of alcohol.

By now the ambulance classes had developed to the point where a Dr Burnett was taking them and such was the level of competence that a team was entered for a national competition open to all railway companies, to compete for the Challenge Shield. The Directors agreed to pay 15s. for the expenses for each man whilst away in London. (Foreman porter Cutts reported that during the competition on 1st, 2nd and 3rd May, the team had scored 103¾ marks out of a possible 300.)

Perhaps the Directors saw the small upturn in trade as a sign for optimism; at their meeting on 8th February they decided to keep their fee level at £300 per annum, in spite of the recommendation of the Expenditure Committee the previous year!

The strike by coal miners lead to a special meeting being called on 6th March to plan how best to meet the demands of the situation. Some passenger trains had been taken off at the start of the strike: 3.15 pm Penrith to Cockermouth and 7.41 pm Cockermouth to Penrith. To these were added the 9.03 am Cockermouth to Penrith and the 8.30 am Penrith to Cockermouth

The permanent way staff were put on half-time working. The station staffs likewise but they would be paid two-thirds of their salaries.

By the 11th April, when the Directors next met, the strike was over, and it was anticipated that by 15th April normal services and working would be resumed with the exception of the 3.15 pm and 7.41 pm trains. At this meeting the Board considered a request to put down a siding for the Cumberland Granite Company, between Bassenthwaite Lake and Embleton stations. This was approved at a cost of £200 on the understanding it was not to be a private siding. During June, British Petroleum asked to place a small store in Keswick station coal yard. In fact The Anglo American Oil Company had already applied successfully to do this and so the Directors agreed to afford BP the same facilities.

In August William Glasson died and, in November, to replace him, the Directors felt it appropriate to offer a directorship to Peter Thompson for his long service to the railway. He accepted on the understanding that when he joined the Board on 1st January, 1913 he would cease to be Secretary and Manager. However, in December, the Directors asked Peter Thompson to continue in his role of Secretary and Manager until 28th February, the following year, and then take up a place on the Board on 1st March and this he agreed to do.

When the signalmen, platelayers and gangers all petitioned for increases in wages during the latter half of the year they were told that the poor revenue levels which were persisting would mean only small increases would be possible. However, the signalmen were told that as a concession they would get a full week's holiday each year (instead of six days!). Foreman porter Cutts received his due deserts in November for all the good work he had done. The station master of Troutbeck retired and he was appointed to succeed him.

It would appear there were some problems with the appointment of a successor for Peter Thompson.

On 23rd January, 1913 a meeting was called at Euston with representatives of LNWR, the NER and CK&PR to discuss this prospective vacancy in the management of the CK&PR. In February Thompson was asked, again, to continue in his current post until the end of March and to join the Board on the 1st April. Eventually Mr Entwistle was appointed to succeed him at that time.

A number of other matters had needed attention. Yet again there had been snow blocks and trains were stopped on 11th and 12th January. It seemed important to press ahead with the snow fences and obtain the necessary pieces of land. Later in the year (July) a sleeper fence was installed along the cutting near Blencow west distant signal. It appears the Threlkeld Granite Company had the use of the company's Boardroom and when this came up for consideration it was felt the arrangement should be allowed to continue and in view of the amount of traffic they passed over the line, the fee of £10 10s. per annum would continue. The Permanent Way Committee raised the issue of the general condition of the track and it was agreed that Mr Thurstan, the Northern District Engineer of the LNWR be asked to report and advise. When he did so in August, for the section between Cockermouth and Keswick, the Board was undecided on how to act and so deferred any decisions. The Directors did, however, place the rest of an order for steel rails initiated in January 1912, with the Workington Iron and Steel Company. In September the matter was raised again and it was agreed 2¾ miles should be relaid to cover the section described in the report as most in need of urgent attention. The estimated cost was £3,500 and the Directors asked for further estimates. A large number of 'white collar' workers received increases in wages during June and the list carries the intriguing footnote 'Parcels Carter B. Thompson - to be allowed an overcoat'.

In July it was reported that the company's locomotive had at last been sold! It had stood in the carriage shed at Cockermouth passenger station for the whole of this period. The buyer paid £100. Concern about the condition of some of the screw pile bridges was growing and costs for renewing these between Keswick and Braithwaite were sought. Bristow came up with the figures in November for strengthening these bridges and Entwistle was asked to approach the Board of Trade to ascertain whether the proposals would be sanctioned. It was also decided that the speed of trains must be restricted to 40 mph along the whole of the line. It may have been that the Directors were not too confident in Bristow's figures because after another look at them, in December, they decided to submit them to Thurstan for further scrutiny.

At the end of the year Hamlet Riley became Vice-Chairman, following the death of Marshall. There had been further growth in 1913, with £1,476 paid to the NER and £13,619 to the LNWR.

1914

The so-called Great War, brought about changes in many aspects of the nation's life, which would never be reversed. Included in these were Britain's railways. As the year opened no significant change was apparent. The matter of the screw bridges was raised again at the January meeting. The Directors seemed loathe to make any decisions but did resolve to consult the NER Engineer to find whether it might be practicable to fill up some of the bridges. Bristow was to investigate.

Station masters' pay was also on the agenda and the classification of stations was clarified. Cockermouth and Keswick were class 3 and all the rest, class 5. Class 3 posts attracted a salary of between £120 and £150 per annum; class 5 between £60 and £90. For both groups these figures included house rent, light, coal and water. The ambulance training was discussed again. Mr Allison, the station master at Keswick suggested attendance at classes should be encouraged by the provision of a small shield by the Directors which could be presented to the winners of a competition held between teams along the line. The Directors said they would present such a shield provided it did not cost more that £5. Turnbill, the Superintendent of the LNWR complained that the point locking bars on the CK&PR were too short and Bristow submitted an estimate of £66 for lengthening 18 of them from 18 ft to 33 ft and this was accepted.

At the end of January the first decision about the screw pile bridges was made and No. 41 would be strengthened. One piece of information which seemed to augur well in this connection was that Manchester Corporation intended to take more water from Thirlmere. From this it was concluded there would be a reduction in the likelihood of flooding occurring ! Further thought was given in February to the matter of the bridges, when a committee was formed consisting of Messrs Riley, Pattinson, Thompson, Mark and Sir J.S.Randles to investigate the prospect of strengthening them. This group reported in April, having spent the day on 16th February inspecting them. At least three of the five bridges should be filled up and four if two proprietors, Hodgson and Stewart, could be persuaded to use the same occupation bridge. Their recomendations were as follows:

Bridge

No. 40   Three or four of the eight spans filled; heavier waybeams for the remainder.

No. 42   All three spans to be filled as none were required to deal with flood water.

No. 43   Two or three out of the seven spans to be filled. Four were needed for flood water.

No. 44   Five spans. The filling of these would be expensive because of a deep embankment and therefore extra columns and stronger waybeams would be the solution.

No. 45   Three out of the six spans could be filled as the proprietor had no right of way under the bridge in spite of having property on both sides. The embankment was as steep as No. 44 but the cost would be less because steel girders were already provided on the spans to be left open.

No. 48   The five spans would have to be left open as they adjoined the River Derwent and would carry a lot of flood water.

No. 49   At least three of the spans were needed for accommodation bridges and the remainder were needed to take flood water above that which passes through Nos. 47 and 48. Stronger waybeams would be needed.

No. 50   All 10 spans could be filled up provided a small severance of about one-third of an acre was purchased on the north side of the line and culverts made for field drainage.

There was a further suggestion that the main girders should be strengthened by the insertion of intermediate columns on broad concrete bases. The last recommendation was made with a view to enabling heavier locomotives to use the line.

The Directors wasted no time in putting this work in hand. No. 41, which had been considered in January, was finished by April and work was to commence on No. 42 immediately, the materials to be acquired from Threlkeld Granite Company. This was finished by May. Bristow was all for taking out the bridge structure but the Board would not sanction this action until the embankment became properly firm. Bristow was able to report, at the same time, that the land required for replacing the screwpile bridges Nos. 42, 44 and 45 had been purchased.

The Bridge Committee, having proved its worth was turned into the Bridge and Finance Committee so giving it wider powers. Its remit now became:

(i)   consideration of proposals to fill further screw pile bridges
(ii)   relaying of further sections of permanent way with new or second-hand materials
(iii)   tenders for new permanent way materials
(iv)   the financing of these items
(v)   pensions

In late June, Entwistle decided to 'withdraw' from his post. John Clark was appointed to succeed him from 1st July at a salary of £250. He was also given a £25 bonus for the extra work he had done during the previous year. At the same time, John Robinson became traffic superintendent. He also received a bonus (£10) for the additional work he had done during the previous year.

Estimates and proposals by Bristow were considered by the Bridge Committee which also put forward some proposals:

No. 45   A safer and stronger bridge by using steel girders on stone abutments over the road and river with the rest of the spans filled in.

No 44.   Either fill two spans and put steel girders over the other three or fill in the whole and provide a large culvert. The latter was agreed and this was allocated as the next piece of work.

The Engineer was authorised to proceed with the relaying of further sections of the line, 85 lb. rails for about five miles and others with 80 lb., as recommended by Thurstan. He was also instructed to get estimates for the erection of a new bridge to replace screw pile No. 45.

After 38 years as a Director, with four of these as Chairman, H.C. Howard died. He was succeeded by Hamlet Riley and John W. Pattinson became Vice-Chairman.

At the outbreak of war, the shareholders were informed that under 'The Regulation of Forces Act (1871)' the Railway, along with all others, would be under Government control from midnight on 4th August, 1914. There would be an Executive Committee consisting of General Managers of certain companies with the President of the Board of Trade as its Chairman. Dividends would be paid according to calculations under the terms of the Government's policy and these were based on performance in 1913.

Connecting services at Penrith. *Above*: LNWR 4-6-2T No. 2273 is seen with an up local. *Below*: Tennant '1463' class 2-4-0 attracts admiring glances as it stands at the platform with a Darlington train.   *(Both) William Nash Collection*

As a result, during the war, these were usually 2 per cent. During August the first men to be called up for active service left the railway. They were Cutts, Wood (a clerk) and Thompson (an assistant linesman). All were unmarried and the company agreed to continue to pay contributions for them to the Railway Superannuation Fund.

It was decided to withdraw the through carriage to Carlisle for the winter.

1915-7

The war impeded much of the planned progress in 1915. Some of the work on the bridges was deferred although certain sections went ahead slowly.

An appraisal was carried out during June 1916 of the situation regarding the state of the track.

	m.	*c.*
Total length of main line and passing sections	41	30
84 lb. rails (purchased since 1898)	17	60
85 lb. rails ([purchased since 1913 and before 1916)	3	2
80 lb. rails (purchased since 1914 and before 1916)	4	44
Total heavy rail	25	26
76 lb. rails (purchased between 1888 and 1895)	9	40
76 lb. rails (purchased between 1872 and 1876)	6	44
Total length of main line and passing sections	*41*	*30*

In November 1916 the first casualties of the war were reported. Sergeant W. Notman, formerly a yardsman at Threlkeld, and Private William Hetherington, formerly a porter at Cockermouth, had been killed in action; Sergeant Wood, a clerk at Keswick, Private S. Atkinson, formerly a summer porter at Keswick, and Private Gibson, formerly a platelayer on No. 3 length, had all been injured.

A number of accidents albeit minor ones, involving goods trains occurred during the year including one on 16th October and another on 28th of the same month. Perhaps the war was taking its toll on the standard of the line.

The Directors decided that from 4th November the 'rebooking office' at Penrith would close. The NER would issue through tickets from their stations to stations on the CK&PR to minimise the need for rebookings. There is an interesting 'cameo' provided at the other end of the line, in Cockermouth, when James Batt, a newly appointed booking clerk of the M&CR who was allocated the task of issuing tickets on hiring days and given a special room for the purpose, decided to write a report on his working conditions on these occasions. In doing so he sparked off a long running debate. Batt was rather aggrieved by the fact that because the room he was allocated was used only twice each year as a booking office, at other times it was used to store yeast and poultry. Mr Batt objected to the resulting smell in such a small space! Furthermore, he had to deal with over 1,000 passengers on these occasions, most of whom travelled on the last few trains. The obvious consequence was that trains were delayed. In addition, the size of the room meant that the desk he used could only be 36 in. by 12 in. and the window space was such that anyone could easily reach in and take money from the desk. It was not unusual for there to be in excess of £50 in copper and silver. What made matters worse was that the rack with the most frequently required tickets (Aspatria and Bullgill) was situated behind him as he stood at the desk and, as a result, whilst he was turning round to reach for tickets, there was more opportunity for theft. The lighting was poor, being provided by old carriage lamps which gave only a low light and took up a lot of room. One of the lamps was placed on the floor to act as a heater and sent up a considerable quantity of smoke which made the room unpleasant to be in. Batt points out that additional light could be provided by opening the door but then the room became cold! It was also damp. In conclusion Batt states that he would like new accommodation with gas and a fireplace.

This carefully handwritten report is, in some ways, remarkable for the period. The obvious solution at the time might well have been to look for a new clerk. Not so. The report was received by the Traffic Superintendent of the M&CR who brought it to the attention of Thomas Blain. Blain promptly wrote to John Clark at the CK&PR requesting that better provision be made. Clark acknowledged Blain's letter but possibly feeling the issue was not urgent took no further action, only to be faced with another letter from Blain some two weeks later asking what action would be taken. At this stage Clark decided to raise the issue of making Cockermouth a closed station and suggested that if this were to happen it would be necessary to have a new cattle booking office. This, in turn, might mean some sort of dual purpose building could be erected. Blain seemed satisfied with this and Clark then wrote to Stones, of the LNWR, at Lancaster, asking advice for his Directors. In the meantime plans were drawn up and further correspondence between the three followed. In the end it was agreed the whole matter should 'stand over' until a decision could be made about whether or not Cockermouth should be a closed station. James Batt is not heard of again!

During December the Board was asked to consider the removal of some track for use in France but had to reply that none could be spared without considerable inconvenience to traffic. During 1916, the Directors felt they should make a number of donations to hospital and railway linked charities: £4 to the Cumberland Infirmary, £2 2s. 0d. to the Railway Benevolent Institution, £5 5s. 0d. to the Railway Executive Committee for Comforts for R.E. Railway Troops and £5 to the Mary Hewitson Hospital in Keswick.

By January 1917 it was possible to report that filling up of bridge No. 39 was complete, No. 41 had had steel girders installed and at No. 42 the timbers had been taken out and the girders were to remain. Nothing had been done to bridges 40, 43, 49, 50 and 51 whereas No. 44 needed several further trainloads of filling, No. 45 had five spans partly filled, No. 48 was to be left and the engineer's report was awaited on No. 52.

Eight allotments had been purchased at Briar Riggs Field and these would be let out to employees at 5s. per annum. It was suggested a screen of trees should be planted at Gillhead and Gibson Cuttings to assist further with preventing snow blocks. On and after 15th April there would be no Sunday trains.

In June the LNWR requested the use of heavier engines on the line but the Directors had to point out that the Board of Trade would not permit this. Over the night of 1st/2nd August a rather unusual occurrence halted the trains. The timbers of the west end arch of bridge 78 near Threlkeld, were destroyed by fire. Passenger trains were run to each side of the bridge and normal working was resumed by 2.45 pm.

There were clearly problems with Penruddock viaduct and Thurstan was asked to investigate and prepare a report. His findings proved rather alarming. He was of the opinion that the viaduct was very much in need of repair. Three piers were badly cracked and shaken and needed immediate temporary support. In addition he recommended a watchman should be employed until this could be done. The speed of trains over the viaduct should be limited to 10 mph. Numbering from the Keswick end, piers 1, 5 and 8 needed propping. Thurstan goes so far as to state the problems had arisen as a result of inferior workmanship during construction and comments that the foundations of the piers were 'not so well built as they might have been' (in one case the projected footings on the original drawings are missing). There was some distortion in other piers and attempts seemed to have been made to correct these using old rails and tie bolts. He concluded that the repairs would be costly and once the urgently needed work was done might be spread over the next year or two. The work, which would involve some risk and would need to be carefully monitored, was costed at £3,284. Cropper asked for alternatives, if possible, and this first proposal became Scheme A. Scheme B would cost £2,872 and Scheme C, £2,807. All involved a figure of £1,163 for attention to the arches and spandrils with different solutions thereafter. Scheme C involving filling the viaduct to a height of 1 ft above springing level with Arch 6 left open as an occupation road. Thurstan expressed his dislike for Scheme C saying that he was not convinced it would prove a long term solution. Any filling, in his view, should be to the full height of the viaduct (but would be more costly). Scheme B involved encasing the piers in concrete and Thurstan said he was happy with this 'if appearance is of no importance'!

In December Waugh (jnr) died so ending a family association with the Railway which had lasted over 50 years.

The Post War Period 1918-1923

Whatever had been the expectation, once the war had ended, there was no returning, it seemed, to the former state of affairs. The railways remained under Government control. Railway companies were informed that to restore their pre-war status would need a period of transition, such had been the upheavals and so Government control would remain for two years. During the war the costs of running the railways had increased sharply and linked with this, charges, especially fares, increased accordingly. The Government may well have wanted the opportunity to try and balance the books by gaining further revenue before handing back the companies to the control of their respective Directors. However there were other reasons which would become apparent within a short time.

April 1918 saw the reduction of services by one train each way each day. The problem of Penruddock viaduct was further discussed and it was agreed infilling would be the solution.

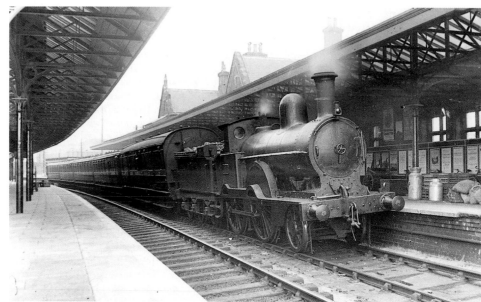

Main line trains at Penrith. *Above:* LNWR 'Precedent' class 2-4-0 No. 1678 *Airey* pauses at Penrith with an up slow train. *Below:* Bowen-Cooke 'Prince of Wales' class 4-6-0 No. 233 *Suvla Bay* is seen on an up fast. *(Both) William Nash Collection*

It was towards the end of 1918 that certain developments took an unexpected turn. A letter from G.M. Saunders & Son (of London) solicitors for Lord Ormathwaite's Cumberland Estate spelled out the problem. The letter alleged that the infilling of the screw pile bridges the previous February had resulted in considerable flooding of estate land. Grassland was of no use and crops had been ruined. The tenant had given notice to quit and a local lane was flooded and impassable. The letter referred to discussions which had taken place between Mr Broatch and the Secretary but in view of the fact that nothing had been done, threatened action within 14 days if the matter was not addressed. The Bridge Committee called a meeting; nothing hurried, it met at Braithwaite station 14 days after the arrival of the letter. Having considered the situation, any responsibility was denied. It was argued there was ample free run for the water but continued bad weather was the real cause of the problem. The members must have felt their case was helped by the fact that one of the sections flooded belonged to Bog Farm and the lane which was awash was called Watery Lane! They went further, however, and pointed out that the landowner had failed to keep the water courses clear and, worse, in places the water courses had been dammed, in effect, to allow carts to pass into the fields. It was also pointed out that some of the water causing the flooding overflowed these fields before reaching the Railway. More correspondence followed and in the end the committee agreed, without prejudice, to open one arch of bridge 43. It was not long before there were others complaints about flooding; one from the agents representing the estate of the late J.S. Harker and the other from the Braithwaite Drainage Board. This time it was agreed one span of screw pile Bridge 46 would be opened, again without prejudice and in complete settlement. The Board refused to accept any liability for Watery Lane. The altercations were to go on into 1919 with the Board trying to hold out against any further concessions.

On a less dramatic note, there was a petition at the end of the year for the use of Highgate platforms by the general public but this was declined on the grounds that the Board of Trade was not in favour and it was deemed impracticable.

1919

In 1919 alarm bells were sounding as the immediate prospect of returning the railways to the full control of their Boards seemed to be receding. During this period, rumours had also started to circulate about other motives the Government might have for holding on to the control it was exercising. By the end of the year, Hamlet Riley felt he must acquaint the shareholders with the situation as he and the other Directors, not only of the CK&PR but other companies, perceived it. Hamlet Riley felt the situation to be a matter of such concern that he did this by way of a memorandum and did not wait for the next half-yearly meeting. The memorandum sent out covered three pages of paper and spelled out a set of circumstances which gave more than a little cause for disquiet. It informed the shareholders of the Government's declaration in the

Autumn of 1918 to make transport very much a part of future policy in its plans in rebuilding the country's economy. A Bill, 'The Ways and Communications Bill', had been mooted at first but was replaced by 'The Ministry of Transport Bill'. Hamlet Riley pointed out that the announcement of this Bill was the first time the Directors - any Directors, for that matter, of the Nation's railways - had been made aware the Government had such plans. There had been no consultation either with the companies or the Railway Companies' Association. The Bill contained what they saw as a number of rather disturbing clauses. Control for two years (not considered to be unreasonable), the power to increase rates and fares but, alarmingly, a clause enabling the Minister of Transport to acquire railway undertakings on terms, failing agreement, to be determined by arbitration; this to be made possible under the authority of an Order in Council. These proposals had been opposed by the Directors who maintained there was a violation of the Railway Regulation Act of 1844. It was claimed that on the strength of this Act, capital had been subscribed to build and maintain the railway system. It was alleged that financial opinion, including that of the great bankers, the committee of the Stock Exchange and important financial houses in the City of London supported the railway companies in opposing the Government's plans. An understandable reaction! Further, it was argued many people had made investments to make the railway system possible; such people were still investing and legislation, if care was not exercised, could result in the sort of financial damage that would 'discredit or paralyse railway enterprise'.

However, history shows that usually when a Government begins to make this type of move there is almost an inevitability of the outcome and the juggernaut begins to move forward! The Government had plans, at that stage not too clear, but it was up to something. As a result it was considered advisable to make provisions and avoid being disadvantaged! The matter of compensation was addressed by the Railway Companies' Association (to which the CK&PR was admitted during April) in case the unthinkable happened. Representation was made by the Association and protracted discussions with the Government followed as the Bill progressed. It eventually became 'The Ministry of Transport Act' on 15th August, 1919. This was closely followed by the setting up of the Ministry of Transport with a brief to review the various transport systems, including railways. By this time the wind of change was considerably more that a gentle breeze, as time would tell.

Perhaps with these developments, matters relating to flooding could well have palled into insignificance - but it was still necessary to deal with them. Armison & Co, solicitors of Penrith, put in a claim for £50 on behalf of Mr T. Gibson who, until shortly before, had been one of Lord Ormathwaite's tenants affected by the flooding. The claim, accompanied by the threat of legal action, was for loss of crops. The Chairman, Vice-Chairman and Sir John Randle agreed to meet with Lord Ormathwaite to try and resolve the problems. This they did on 14th April and informed him the offer to open one span still stood. It was not until the beginning of December that it was finally settled this should be done. As far as the Gibson claim was concerned, the Board decided to take Counsel's opinion and the advice was to settle on the best terms (which turned out to be 20 guineas). There was also a settlement with the Harker Estate for damage to be put right. In the meantime the Bridge Committee had met at Penruddock station on 14th March and it had authorised the work of filling up the viaduct to continue but not to go beyond arches 5 and 6.

With the war over, the matter of commemorating the fallen was discussed and the first proposal which came under consideration was a war memorial at Cockermouth. The Chairman, Vice-Chairman with Messrs Highton, Mark and Holdsworth were to form a committee to help with the plans. The company offered a site of 30-40 ft in diameter and the LNWR agreed to this provided the War Memorial Committee met the costs of alterations to the station approach. The company then offered to carry out the work if the War Memorial Committee paid £400 and were responsible for having the foundations put in. To commemorate the fallen of the CK&PR it was agreed a brass or copper tablet should be put up at Keswick station, the cost to be £32-£34.

In July it was felt the company could offer free delivery of parcels up to one mile from the station at Keswick and the possibility of getting a motor for light goods was considered. In August the company donated £10 towards the extension of Threlkeld Churchyard and Cockermouth was to become a closed station.

At the end of September and early in October, the National Union of Railwaymen held a strike and no services ran after 26th September and until Monday 6th October when one passenger train ran in each direction. A full service was resumed the following day. During this period trade still remained at a low level. This was reflected in dividends of around 2½ per cent.

1920

The revenue level in the latter part of 1919 resulted in a 2 per cent dividend at the beginning of the year; in this way there was little change. Momentum for another sort of change was, however, gathering, as the Government pushed ahead with its plans to reorganise the country's railways. In January the Board approved the appointment of Lord Anslow as the representative for the smaller companies on the Future of Railways Committee.

The day to day business had to be attended to in spite of the fact that by now the future was uncertain. Signalman Joseph Dowthwaite found himself with a very uncertain future, as it happened, when he was convicted and given a one month prison sentence for stealing timber from a wagon at Cockermouth Junction. He was dismissed from the company's service.

During February further consideration was given to making Cockermouth a closed station and it was concluded the expense would be too great and so the plan was dropped. New tenders were sought for Keswick goods shed and the Board decided to buy 1,000 tons of building stone from the old Tweed Mill at Cockermouth to be divided between Embleton, Braithwaite and Keswick station. The material for the renewal of a further three miles of permanent way was to be purchased. On 1st May a special ceremony took place at Keswick station when, at 10.45 am, the Chairman unveiled the plaque commemorating those who had fallen in the war. The plaque had been engraved by Keswick School of Industrial Arts.

Penrith station. A medley of transport, horse and trap, possibly a taxi and the charabancs.

Former 'Samson' class No. 773 *Centaur* stands at Penrith Shed, 2-4-0s became much used on the line.

There was concern about the high ages of some of the Railway's employees and two members of the permanent way staff, William Lamb and John Greenhow were laid off. In this period such action could result in great hardship if there was no further financial support and so a gratuity of 8s. per week, with an additional 2s., was given to each man. The Board decided to rename the Bridge Committee the General Purposes Committee as it was felt this better suited its function.

The LNWR announced that it did not propose to put on any Sunday trains between Workington and Cockermouth but that the M&CR would run one from Maryport and one from Carlisle to Cockermouth. They hoped the CK&PR would approve an agreement for the M&CR engine and coach to run through to Keswick but initially the Directors were not too sure about this. Later, and after giving the proposal more thought, they asked that the LNWR should run a train from Whitehaven to Keswick and back on Sundays at least during July, August and September. At the same time a request was submitted that the LNWR consult the Midland with a view to reintroducing the Leeds to Keswick summer service as it had been before the war. The LNWR declined the request for the Sunday trains and also stated that it and the Midland could not see its way to reintroducing a Leeds Summer service. The CK&PR was not prepared to take 'No' for an answer and pressed the LNWR further but the LNWR was equally insistent and by August was still holding out. This service did not reappear. During July, Bristow expressed concern about the state of his health and indicated that he may not be able to hold his appointment for much longer. This was a matter the Directors were going to have to consider carefully at a later date.

At the end of 1920 advertising rights for Kershaws at Cockermouth and Keswick were to expire and the company decided to find a list of all existing advertisers to see whether they would consider all stations. In addition, Wymans bookstall contract at the two stations would also expire and it was agreed W.H. Smith should be asked to tender. Redmaynes of Penrith were to continue providing the uniforms.

During August the company received a letter from the Secretary of the Railway Companies' Association outlining a proposal by the Ministry of Transport that railway workers be included in the boards of management of the grouped railways. The Directors were not in favour of such a move and registered their disapproval.

Bristow's indication that he wished to step down on the grounds of ill health had prompted the Board to look for a replacement, and by 25th August a short list had been considered and a special meeting was held to review the situation. It would seem that either the Directors were unhappy to part with Bristow completely, or they were unsure about a new appointee, but it was agreed that the Chairman and the Vice-Chairman should interview Bristow and a possible replacement called Boyd to find whether a satisfactory temporary arrangement could be agreed. On 31st August, Riley and Pattinson explained to Bristow that the Directors proposed to appoint Boyd as the Engineer if arrangements could be made for him (Bristow) to do the inside work, and Boyd to do the rest with the responsibility as Chief Engineer. This was agreed and so, in effect, Bristow became Boyd's assistant.

The bookstall rights at Keswick station were eventually awarded to A. Chaplin of Keswick for £50 per annum with 5 per cent of receipts over £500. In the meantime the LNWR had transferred the advertising contracts to Frank Mason & Co. in The Strand. Advertising rights were, in turn, sought by them for Keswick station for a minimum of £50 per annum and this was accepted.

An innovation, introduced on 4th October, 1920, meant that compartments on trains could be reserved for 5 shillings. This amount had to be paid in advance and must involve either four first or eight third class tickets The booking could apply to through coaches working on the LNWR. Train services were affected from 25th October by the coal miners' strike; the 8.54 am and 7.09 pm up trains and the 3.00 pm and 8.31 pm down trains being cancelled. These were restored on 8th November. An adjustment to running schedules was made at this time when the practice of running an engine and an empty coach from Cockermouth to Keswick to form the 9.45 am was run as a service train reaching Keswick at 8.48 am; an improvement on running it empty! The head of Keswick School then petitioned the Board asking that the extra train be continued as it enabled children to arrive at school nearer the opening time (the alternative being one arriving at 9.27 am) and this was agreed.

Mr Saunders of Abingdon Street, Westminster, approached the company with a view to it joining the Association of Smaller Railways but the Directors decided not to do so. In December, the Directors decided to invite tenders for the materials for completely relaying the line. Wymans won the contract for the station bookstall at Cockermouth, awarded by the LNWR.

More discussions were held about the future, this time with the Cleator & Workington Junction, the Furness and the Maryport & Carlisle. It was agreed that the institution of a West Cumberland Group as a self contained unit would be inconsistent with the declared policy of the Government to have seven large groups. It was still more inconsistent with the policy of the majority of the Railway Companies' Association meeting (16th November) which was to reduce the number of groups to five. It was felt, however, that the Furness and West Cumberland areas should form a single administrative unit within its group.

On 29th August, Peter Thompson died. What a contribution he had made to the railway! He had given 49 years of service with an additional period of six years as a Director. The changing times, however, were reflected in the following announcement, made by the Directors on the occasion of his death: 'Having regard to the future arrangements under The Ministry of Transport Acts, it has been decided not to fill the vacancy for the time being'. The Directors added that they were carefully watching the developments regarding the Government's White Paper. Britain's railways were soon to face a radical restructuring

1921-1923

In spite of the considerable state of flux in railway circles, in January 1921 the Board went ahead in awarding tenders for the materials needed for relaying the line; from the United Steel Company at Workington, 400 tons of steel rails (85 lb.) British Standard Section (£23 per ton) with 12 tons of fish plates to suit; from the Anderson Foundry Company, Middlesbrough, 200 tons of cast-iron chairs and from Ibbotson Brothers of the Globe steel Works, Sheffield, two tons of cross slit hook nuts and fish bolts.

In April there was a special Board meeting to discuss the Railway Bill and in May the Directors stated they were prepared to accept the principle of the transfer of their undertaking as outlined in the Bill. There was a proposal that passenger services should be reduced: up trains from Cockermouth at 7.09, 11.20 am and 6.00 pm; down trains from Penrith at 7.30 am, 1.30 and 6.25 pm with the Maryport & Carlisle train leaving Cockermouth at 8.20 am and returning from Keswick at 9.45 pm.

The Board did consider calling a meeting of the shareholders at this time, but decided against doing so after the LNWR pointed out that it did not appear opportune for the moment to seek expert advice on the value of the undertaking and as a result there would be little to impart.

On 15th August, 1921 the Railways Act came into being. This was the next stage as the Government moved its policies forward. It was resisting any move to nationalise the railways (a decision based to some degree on wanting to avoid the financial liabilities with which it would have landed itself had nationalisation been the way forward) but seemed to be going for a middle road between this and the *status quo*; it was to be, in effect, the State regulation of privately owned monopolies. There would be a period of interregnum between the Government control and a new system the Act would make possible. For the moment, however, the CK&PR, along with the other companies passed back to the full control of the Directors. But not for long. The 1st January, 1923 would see the beginning of the restructuring of Britain's railways into four groups, the London, Midland & Scottish Railway (LMSR), the London & North Eatsern Railway (LNER), the Southern Railway (SR) and the Great Western Railway (GWR). The CK&PR would be absorbed into the first named of these. Possibly it goes without saying that the CK&PR Directors were, in spite if their former deliberations, still far from satisfied.

More movement of station masters took place in August and September. Robert Little resigned from Cockermouth and was replaced by William Ewart from Bassenthwaite Lake. Joseph Todhunter went to Bassenthwaite Lake from Penruddock and was succeeded there by John Clapham, a parcels clerk at Keswick. On 22nd November what might have been a very serious accident was averted by the prompt action of porter Bewley. The 2.05 pm Workington to Penrith was, according to accounts, being driven at 'excessive speed' between Penruddock and Blencow. A four-wheeled vehicle with two fixed gas tanks left the rails causing considerable damage to the track. The tanks caught fire and Bewley swiftly uncoupled the vehicle from the train which was then drawn into the station. The line was blocked from 3.50 pm to 8.17 pm but nobody was injured and Bewley was awarded £5 for his bravery.

The company had been having discussions, during the year, with a number of groups because some decisions seemed necessary with possible take-over looming. The company had control over Dubwath water supply and there had been protracted discussions about future arrangements for this. It was agreed in principle that the company would pass this over to Cockermouth Rural District Council, with the proviso that the CK&PR should have unlimited supply free of charge for Bassenthwaite Lake station and houses although this would not include a supply for the engine tank. On another front, in October, Mr Harrison asked whether the company would sell Flusco Quarry and in November it was agreed to ask £550 for the land and stone but not the present sidings and what land might be needed for doubling the track on that section. At the end of the year the company was informed that of the £24 million being allocated for the mergers, it would receive £6,209 although this figure was later revised and increased.

During the latter part of the year the Working Timetable showed 31 up workings and 33 down workings, although these included the ones running into and out of Cockermouth only [*see Appendix Three for details*].

The first shareholders' meeting of the year was held on Saturday 25th February, 1922 and was, it is said, 'not of a long duration'. In reporting it, *The Herald* used the sub-heading 'A Depressing Year' (in bold type) followed by 'Amalgamation with The L&NW Company'. The language of the report is colourful, if nothing else. It describes prospects, whereby the company (that is, the CK&PR) 'will be absorbed into the capacious maw of the great North Western group'. Although not strictly true, of course, as it turned out, nevertheless it put across the main message. The end was nigh! The Chairman, Hamlet Riley, put on a brave face and explained to those present the situation as it had evolved after the war. He felt their railway was in good form in readiness for the hand-over and hoped to get good terms for the shareholders. This, it must be said, was in spite of a decrease in returns in all departments! Since 1920 there had been a decrease in coke traffic of 49,200 tons, iron ore, 4,115 tons, road stone, 18,082 tons, livestock by 3,030 animals, general merchandise, 2,362 tons, limestone, 3,434 tons and timber, 8,630 tons. Of rather more concern was the fall in passenger traffic. In 1920 there had been 6,135 first class passengers and this number was down to 4,159 in the following year. In a similar way, there were 288,575 third class passengers in 1920 and 235,276 in 1921 and workmen passengers fell from 66,816 in 1920 to 34,728 in 1921. This resulted in an overall fall of 87,363.

A dividend of 1½ per cent was proposed. Some of the shareholders were far from satisfied. Their disatisfaction was voiced by Mr H.T. Pape of Keswick. He pointed out that had it not been for the Government subsidy of £6,000 there would not have been a dividend at all. He criticised the company for running half-empty trains when there might have been cheap excursions to football matches, for example. Mr Isaac Hodgson, also of Keswick was another critic. His complaint related to economic factors and he maintained the Directors must introduce some economies. He argued that the CK&PR was paying 91 per cent of income on expenses whilst the M&CR was spending 84.6 per cent and the Cleator and Workington only 76.1 per cent. There must be room for improvement. The Secretary, in reply, disputed the figures saying that it was impossible at the present time with the Government's involvement to reach such conclusions. In this respect he was certainly correct but Hodgson's insistence that expenses were too high brought him a round of applause. Mr Pape then took the floor again this time to question the wisdom of the company for opting to go in with the LNWR. In his view it should be joining up with the NER because the latter provided passengers for Keswick whereas the LNWR was more disposed, in his view, to take them to Windermere! He moved a resolution should be passed and sent to the Ministry of Transport petitioning for the CK&PR to be included in the same group as the NER. He found himself a lone voice in this plea; no seconder came forward. In April, the company was informed that the amount to be allocated in compensation would be £6,469 'now' plus £6,469 at the beginning of the following year and this was accepted. These figures would vary slightly but not by a significant amount.

There were still day to day issues to be dealt with. Boyd reported that there were problems at Bridge 81 east of Threlkeld station because the loads being taken over it were getting too heavy. A weight limit of 300 cwt was imposed. Crosthwaite Parochial Church Council (PCC) petitioned the General Purposes Committee on 30th September for the provision of a bridge over the railway, and this was agreed in principle, provided the PCC in turn agreed to sell to the company enough land to double the line in that section with the price to be the same paid for it. There was also an understanding that the path under the railway on the north-west side would be closed when the new bridge was opened. However, this decision was later deferred. On 31st October the Maryport & Carlisle train on the 9.45 from Keswick ran through the crossing gates at Embleton.

Hamlet Riley did not see the railway through the final stages before the amalgamation. Perhaps the pressures on him took their toll; he died in office during November after 31 years on the Board, eight of which he had been Chairman. John Pattinson was called upon to take his place. Clearly his period of office was going to be a short one. C.J. Parker became the Vice-Chairman. Another death during the year had been that of Bristow, on 23rd October.

The few remaining months of the company's existence were ones when the last essential items of business were carried out.

On 10th March, 1923 one detail requiring the Directors' attention was the disposal of the barrow and spade. They decided to offer them to the trustees of The Fitz Museum in Keswick, so safeguarding them for the future. (They remain there to this day.)

In spite of their promise to make every effort to get 'a good deal' for the shareholders, the economic position of the railway (along with others) gave the Directors very little bargaining power. Any hopes some of the shareholders might have had for making a 'killing' when the line passed into the control of the LMSR were quickly dashed when the reality of the situation became clear. The final shareholders' meeting was held on 10th March and the Chairman took some time reminiscing and outlining the history of the company. There were many notable achievements. John Clark, the present Manager, had been with the company for 56 years and he was celebrating his 71st birthday that very day. Two members of the staff had served for 51 years and 16 others for between 40 and 50 years. Mr Robinson, the traffic manager had been with the company 49 years and Mr Stanley, the accountant, for forty-two. Mr Cropper was the longest serving Director at 22 years. It seems to have been something of an emotional occasion, and this was heightened when the Chairman finished with the remark: 'It is difficult to forecast the fate of this little railway but I hope that whatever happens it will be to the financial benefit of the shareholders and for the good of the public and district and the country at large' (Cheers). At a special meeting which followed, the Directors were awarded £2,000 each in compensation.

Before the last meeting of the Board, a final feast was planned. This took place on Friday, 23rd March and was held in the Keswick Hotel for officials and staff. The purpose, it was said, was not to mark so much the demise of the Board but 'the taking over of the Railway by the London Midland and Scottish Company'. On the menu there was the choice of tomato or clear soup, followed by boiled turbot with egg sauce then roast beef with mashed potatoes and brussels sprouts, soufflé pudding and jelly, cheese and biscuits and coffee. That was not all; between the toasts there was entertainment as well! The first toast was appropriately 'The King' (proposed by the Chairman). This was followed by the song 'John Peel' rendered by Mr Robin Hodgson and 'Neptune' by Mr E. Harrison. The Chairman and Sir J.S. Randles then proposed the toast 'The Officials and Staff' and Mr J. Tange played a cello solo and the song 'Wigan Pier' was sung by Mr G. Bainbridge. Messrs Ewart and Clerk replied to the previous toast and then Mr E. Harrison sang 'The Windmill'. Messrs F. Stanley and T. Allinson proposed the toast 'The Directors' and Mr J. Tange played a selection of tunes on the musical glasses (made famous, the assembled company was informed, by being played by the Richardson family before the late Queen Victoria in 1845!). E.R. Turton and R.E. Higham replied to the 'Directors' toast and then Mr Bainbridge sang 'Dooleys Farm'. The accompanist throughout was Mr J.E. Moore. The evening's events concluded with the singing of 'Auld Lang Syne' and the National Anthem. No doubt there were many good (and perhaps not so good) reasons why it was a night to be remembered!

The last meeting of the Board was held the next day, on 24th March. The Chairman made it clear it was 'no seeking of theirs to be taken over by the new company but it was under an Act of Parliament and they had to bow down to it'. The company made the gesture of resigning its membership of the Railway Companies' Association and Mr Wivall, for the Keswick Hotel, thanked the CK&PR for its help over the years and expressed the hope the LMSR would be as satisfactory to deal with. At the end of its life, £100 worth of stock was worth only £32 (in spite of a bid for £35 and the refusal of £31), not a great return for all energy that had been expended in actually keeping the railway going during what had become a difficult economic climate. The much hoped-for economic growth had never really happened even from the earliest days, although there had been some high points, and in the light of the problems they had to contend with, many not of their own making, the Directors had done well for the company. Now their reign had come to an end. The 'little railway' would be controlled from afar. It was the end of an era.

'The Lakes Express' and Motive Power

In spite of the original reticence, the LNWR did introduce through coaches to Euston on a regular basis from the turn of the century. These included through coaches from Euston to Workington and this service became, in effect, the 'Lakes Express' which apart from certain periods (for example the war years) continued to run until the railway closed west of Keswick. The 'Cauliflowers' continued to give excellent service on the line and were joined from the LNWR fleet by members of the 2-4-0 classes, many of which had seen earlier service on the main lines but which had gradually been displaced by the newer and more powerful engines. The 2-4-0s became very commonplace in the area and were to be found in many parts of West Cumbria, the Workington contingent frequently finding its way onto the CK&PR, in addition to the members based at Penrith and Cockermouth. Exactly when these engines first appeared on the CK&PR seems to be a matter for some debate but certainly by World War I they were present in comparatively large numbers. These 2-4-0s came originally from four groups. The 'Newtons' were designed by Ramsbottom and entered service in 1866 hauling expresses on the Crewe to Carlisle section of the West Coast Main Line. They were all renewed or rebuilt (the distinction seems rather academic) by Webb as 'Precedents'. The 'Samsons' were also Ramsbottom's engines and these, likewise, were 'transformed' by Webb between 1889 and 1896 as 'Whitworths' or 'Jumbos'. Webb added to these 2-4-0 classes the 'Precursors' and 'Precedents'. By 1896 new, renewed or rebuilt, the LNWR had 236 2-4-0s with no significant difference other than some had driving wheels of 6 ft 9 in. (the 'Precedents') and others, 6 ft 3 in. (the 'Whitworths'). All the engines carried names but there seems no rhyme or reason about how these names were chosen and whilst many are familiar there is no apparent pattern and are quite haphazard in this respect. 2-4-0s mentioned as being associated or seen on the CK&PR include 'Samsons' which later became 'Jumbos': 486 *Skiddaw*, 628 *Tartarus*, 1168 *Cuckoo*, 642 *Bee*, 124 *Marquis Douro*, 793 *Martin*, 1166 *Wyre*, 632 *Ostrich*, 2158 *Sister Dora* (formerly *Serpent* but renamed in 1878) 424 *Sirius* and 794 *Woodlark*; a 'Newton' which became a 'Precedent': 1213 *The Queen* and Webb's 'Precedents': 890 *Sir Hardman Earle*, 850 *Merrie Carlisle*, 2191 *Snowden*. '(The numbers are those allocated by the LNWR.) A number of these engines saw service well beyond the demise of the CK&PR.

In 1886, Thomas Worsdell, of the NER, introduced the 'C' and 'C1' 0-6-0 class (later to be designated the 'J21' class). These engines appeared on the CK&PR in 1906, following the discussions with the NER described previously, and did sterling work over Stainmore and the EVR. Some of them hauled the last mineral trains on the line, some, indeed, surviving almost until the closure of the EVR in 1962. The 'C' and 'C1' classes were joined by the equally distinguished 'P1' (0-6-0) class. This group was designed by Wilson Worsdell, brother of Thomas, and introduced on the NER in 1898. The 'P1' locomotives were later designated 'J25s'. Along with the 'J21s' they hauled what few mineral trains were still being run (usually no more than four each day during the 1920s) and, again, were still in charge when the mineral traffic came to an end, some years later. The engines themselves lasted well into the 1950s.

LNWR 'Jumbo' 2-4-0 No. 794 *Penrith* has a tender full of coal in readiness for its next working. LNWR 4-6-2T No. 2273 can be seen in the background.   *William Nash Collection*

An unidentified 'Jumbo' storms away from Penrith with a local passenger train for the CK&PR line.

Chapter Seven

Interlude
A Journey down the Line in the Summer of 1921

It is a hot day in late July. Apart from a few wisps of high white cloud, the sky is clear and the sun is strong. In this kind of weather the scenery in the Lake District is at its most awe inspiring (although some Winter visitors might disagree!). At Penrith station, the 9.55 am for the Keswick branch will soon depart. An LNWR 'Jumbo' 2-4-0 simmers gently at the head of the train. The driver and fireman are quietly chatting, relaxing for a moment as they enjoy the sunshine. There are few people about but a number of holidaymakers have already boarded. A traveller finds an empty compartment in one of the four 6-wheel carriages, climbs in and sits facing the engine. The interior is clean and reasonably comfortable but there is the smell of fabric which, over the years, has acquired a dustiness which can no longer be removed, not even by thorough cleaning and the material has certainly seen better days. Carriage doors are slammed, the sound of escaping steam is heard and the train sets out on its journey.

It climbs slowly out of the station and up the incline as the line turns from a south-westerly direction to a more westerly one. As it does so, the traveller, looking out of the window on the left side, sees the West Coast Main Line veering away to the south. Now the line turns north-westerly and with luck there may be a glimpse of the hills beyond Ullswater but not of the lake itself at this distance. Shortly afterwards, the Eamont to Redhills link line can be seen on the right, even though it is coming in from the south. It is hardly used these days and is showing distinct signs of neglect. Eventually, after a little more than 3½ miles and eight minutes from Penrith, the train halts for the first time. This is Blencow station. Here there are passing facilities and the 8.54 am from Cockermouth passes on the last leg of its journey to Penrith where it will arrive at 10.12 am. The motive power is a 'Cauliflower'. Once clear of Blencow station, the train for Cockermouth follows a line which sweeps round almost 180 degrees before passing Flusco Quarries and then, for a while, travels south. The line now turns, yet again, to a more westerly direction, crossing Penruddock viaduct, before the second stop; this time at Penruddock station with its staggered platforms. The time is 10.14 and the train is now some 7½ miles from Penrith. Just beyond Penruddock, the line passes under the main road to Greystoke and Penrith and then, almost immediately, passes over the same road. After a short distance, the climb from Penrith is over and a height of 889 feet has been reached.

Troutbeck is the next station, almost 10 miles and 25 minutes from Penrith and is situated by the main road. After this stop the journey continues in a westerly direction, passing over the Trout Beck before heading south-west and entering a cutting, following which it turns westwards again. Soon the train passes over the largest viaduct on the line, Mosedale viaduct, with its 12 arches over Mosedale Beck. To the north are fine views of Bannerdale Crags and Scales Fell.

Experience of the journey so far may well prompt the traveller to reflect that it is easy to understand why there was not a lot of opposition by the 19th century 'environmentalists' to the building of this line. The scenery has been pleasant but not outstanding. From here on, however, opinion will almost certainly change. In the meantime, after passing through a series of small cuttings, the train has arrived at Threlkeld having travelled 14½ miles from Penrith. The ease with which it tackled this part of the journey, after leaving Troutbeck, may have escaped the notice of the traveller; the gradient is steep and it was problems with trains toiling in the other direction and often causing delays along this piece of line which led the Directors of the CK&PR to the decision to double the track here in the last century. The time is 10.29 am. After Threlkeld the train passes over the River Glenderamackin and on into the Greta Gorge. The scenery here is superb. The line crosses and recrosses the River Greta on bow string girder bridges and the river, sparkling in the sun, with the backdrop of the wooded hillsides creates a dramatic effect.

Whilst the traveller is enjoying all this and has possibly caught a fleeting glimpse of Briery Bobbin Mill, the train, perhaps unexpectedly, enters the tunnel just to the east of Keswick and in a few moments, after re-emerging and crossing the main road, has come to a halt in Keswick station, some 45 minutes after setting out. This is the headquarters of the railway, 18 miles from Penrith, and there is a lot of bustle here as porters and hotel staff in their various liveries hurry to and fro, dealing with the holidaymakers who are arriving. The station is light and feels spacious and the impressive Keswick Hotel stands adjoining it. It will not be possible to see them from the train but various conveyances are arriving and departing from the station and hotel precinct. The good weather is doing much to lift people's spirits. What a relief that the war is well and truly over and it is possible to get away on holiday again. What a joy to have this excellent little railway which takes people to the very heart of the Lake District, enabling them to benefit from the clean air

The short tunnel just east of Keswick. This is still open for those using the footpath which now follows the track bed, the longer tunnel is closed. *Cumbrian Railways Association*

This was a view of Bassenthwaite Lake possible from the train as the track approached the lake shore.   *H.C. Casserley*

and wonderful scenery. Three minutes later, doors are slammed again, a whistle is heard and the train moves slowly away, now to pass through an area where the countryside becomes more open. Heading westwards and over a long embankment and the River Derwent, the train steams into Braithwaite station, a distance of 20½ miles from Penrith. The journey so far has taken just over 50 minutes. There is a brief stop and the train is on its way again.

The line next turns in a north-westerly direction and after passing into a cutting and beneath Combs Beck, carried by Thornthwaite aqueduct, soon reaches the very shores of Bassenthwaite Lake. Surely here is part of the very essence of the Lake District experience! On the right the mountains and the lake combine to provide a magnificent vista. The water, almost still on this calm day, reflects the sky and looks quite blue. On the left, Wythop Woods rise steeply. It is easy to believe that nowhere else in England does a railway present the passengers with such inspiring views. They are breathtaking. It seems that all too soon the train reaches Bassenthwaite Lake station, 25 miles from the start of the journey, and comes to a halt. A few people alight. Perhaps they are holidaymakers or possibly shoppers returning from Keswick. Whilst waiting, the traveller notices a train heading towards Penrith; only the second one during the journey. It is a goods train, headed by another 'Cauliflower' and passes slowly through. At 10.56 am and on the move again, beyond Bassenthwaite Lake station, the line turns westwards once more and at this stage the terrain is no longer hilly and the track, as a result, is almost level. The penultimate stop on the journey is Embleton station at 11.02 am; nearly 28 miles from Penrith, and soon afterwards the passenger station at Cockermouth is reached. As the train arrives, one for Penrith is about to depart. The journey, a total of nearly 31 miles, has taken about an hour and 20 minutes but the pleasure and enjoyment of seeing the scenery on this Summer's day have more than compensated for what some would describe as slow progress. Indeed, the speed has made it possible for the traveller to savour the many delights the journey has to offer . . .

'Cauliflower' No. 8372, in LMS days, at Penrith on a CK&PR train.
P. Ransome-Wallis/National Railway Museum

Chapter Eight

Life in the LMSR: 1923-1948

Suddenly Keswick must have seemed a long way from Euston. In the days of the CK&PR, when there was a local base for the Railway in the form of a Board of Directors, it was possible to maintain a dialogue and champion the cause of the line with the doyens of the LNWR at its headquarters in Euston. The two parties did not always see eye to eye but Keswick had clout and used it as much as possible to the benefit of the Railway. Now all that had gone. To the new lords of the LMSR the line must have seemed just a very small part of a substantial empire and an empire which first and foremost needed urgent attention in its major elements. The result was that by all accounts this 'little railway' suffered a certain amount of neglect! It would be intriguing to know how the ex-Directors really felt. Did they feel a sense of relief that they no longer had to cope with the growing problems of falling trade or not having to deal with awkward shareholders from Penrith - or did they feel remorse that the railway they had nurtured seemed to lose the significance it once had? We shall probably never know unless one day a forgotten diary or journal comes to light.

The minutes of the LMSR Directors meetings from 1923 to 1947 contain only four references to the CK&PR by name. All refer to various proposals to strengthen bridges. This move was part of a wider one to enable all locomotive classes to use more lines on the system. The Works Committee minutes are more explicit and deal with a range of matters.

The programme to strengthen certain of the bridges was arguably the most significant one undertaken during the period when the LMSR was in control of the line; the bridges involved were mainly east of Keswick. In 1924 the Works Committee recommended that bridges 73 and 74 should be strengthened and on 24th October the Butterley Company was given the contract to supply girderwork. The engineer's estimate for the work had been £1,500 but the actual cost was £1656 13s. 9d. This work was reported as being complete by 1928.

Although there were no new bridge projects put in hand in 1926, Cumberland County Council agreed to relieve the LMSR of the responsibility for the upkeep of bridges associated with roads. The company made a payment of £11,292 10s. for this. There were 40 bridges involved although the County Council was already maintaining 12 of them under an Agreement of 29th December, 1922.

On 5th November 15 ft of railway embankment slipped into the River Greta causing problems by leaving an almost vertical face of earth with the upper edge only 6 ft from the rails. Prompt protective work had to be carried out and it was agreed the associated culvert should be rebuilt in concrete

On 22nd February, 1928 the chief civil engineer pointed out that between Threlkeld and Keswick there were 12 bow string girder bridges. Two had already been dealt with but more needed attention. Bridges 58, 67 and 71 were the next ones on his list. The estimated cost of these was No. 58, £1,000, No. 67, £2,300 and No. 71, £2,700. The Board approved that the work be put in hand and in June the contract for the steelwork was given to John Butler & Co. Ltd. The

'Cauliflower' No. 8492 takes the local freight through Keswick in 1938.   *Pamlin Prints*

A cattle train is headed by a 'Cauliflower'. This up train is seen at Troutbeck.
Cumbrian Railways Association

work on these bridges was reported to be complete by June 1931. The final cost was £5,118.

In December 1929 the reconstruction of bridge 49 between Braithwaite and Keswick was approved. The work, which involved reconstruction to culverts and an embankment, was estimated at £1,616. This work was reported as being complete in January 1932 at a cost of £1,511.

In 1930 bridges 65, 66 and 75 were on the agenda. The estimated cost of strengthening these was put at £4,551 and the work was approved by the Board. A contract was placed with the Widnes Foundry in January 1931 for the steel work for Nos. 65 and 66. By the time of completion in October 1933, the cost for 65 and 66 had increased by £1,055. Bridge 75 was completed in January 1934, the final cost being £2,667.

Approval was given by the Board in 1932 for underbridges 59 and 60 to be strengthened at a cost estimated as being £3,231. A tender from the Teeside Bridge and Engineering Work was accepted. The work was completed in March 1934. The cost was under estimate, at £3,034. In June 1933, Pearson and Knowles Engineering Co. Ltd was awarded the contract for the reconstruction of underbridge 55 at a cost of £219 12s. This work was completed by November 1934. On 25th October approval was given for the reconstruction of the Thornthwaite aqueduct (bridge 32) at an estimated cost of £1,560.

In May 1934, the contract for the steelwork for Thornthwaite aqueduct was awarded to Dorman Long and Co. Ltd. Approval was given to reconstruct underbridge 45 at Keswick by rebuilding the superstructure and abutments and the contract for the steel work went to J. Tildesley Ltd at a cost of £261 13s. 6d. In October, approval was given for work to be carried out on bridge 78, which took the line over the River Glenderamackin at Threlkeld. The chief civil engineer proposed that the superstructure should be reconstructed in concrete and steel and that new abutments should be built; further that the total length of openings should be reduced from about 120 ft to a clear span of 77 ft. The estimate put on the work was £5,056. The contract for the work was given to Thomas Varley and Son Ltd, in June 1935, at a tender price of £4,098 9s. 9d. The work was completed in July 1938, by which time the cost had risen to £4,634. Also in October an improved cattle dock at Penrith was completed.

The signal and telegraph engineer expressed concern in June 1935 about the telegraph route between Blencow and Penruddock, recommending that shorter spans and additional staying were needed to conform to modern standards. He reckoned the cost would be £640 and it was agreed the work should be put in hand. All the telegraph poles and wires had been renewed by March 1937. Bridge 2 over Crown Street at Cockermouth was seen to be in need of attention and, again, reconstruction using steel and concrete was the course of action, together with the southern abutment being rebuilt at a total estimated cost of £3,485. Thomas Varley and Son tendered successfully for this work in 1938 at a cost of £5,352 7s. 7d. Some eyebrows were raised at the discrepancy between the two figures, but it was pointed out that since the original survey it had been decided thicker abutments were needed and stronger girders and the work was eventually approved. Thomas Varley and Son won a further contract in 1937, this time for the reconstruction of bridge 41 over Newlands Beck; the tendered

The 'Cauliflowers' saw service in the LNWR, the LMS and then BR. Here No. 28589, in LMS days, takes a local train out of Keswick.

P. Ransome-Wallis/National Railway Museum

price being £1,549 18s. (against the estimate of £1,406). In March 1938 a new siding for the Blencow Lime Company was in place. The cost of this was £823.
(In 1939, World War II started. Thereafter there are no Works Committee Minutes extant until 1945.)

An idea of the length of service under the old CK&PR is indicated in the retirements listed. In October 1924, J. Little, an underman at Keswick, retired after 50 years on the Railway, J. Nicholson, a subganger, also finished, having worked 35 years and W.S. Sewell retired after 40 years. All had reached the age of 70 and all received a gratuity of 8s. per week. Others who retired during the next few years were awarded the same level of gratuity.

There seem to have been few incidents of note during this period although under the 'Mishaps' section it is reported that on 9th November, 1925 a goods train ran into a platelayers' lorry between Bassenthwaite Lake and Braithwaite and as a result, a ganger named Stamper was suspended for one week with loss of pay!

Changing Circumstances

During the early years of the LMSR the pattern of public transport was starting to change radically and the new bus companies formed in the early 1920s went from strength to strength. The company was keenly aware of this and realised the need to respond to it. The first reaction was to try and contain the development and this was done by attempting to block Bills for wider powers for operating motor buses in competition with the railways. The intention was to try and force a Royal Commission on transport. Initially there was some success in this blocking tactic but it was soon obvious this was a very short term approach. As a result it was decided to gain some measure of control in the bus companies and, not least thereby, some of the growing profits. The LMSR had more than a foot in the door with a substantial number of companies and in the area of the CK&PR they had interests in Cumberland Motor Services, with £68,750 invested in 1929, and Ribble Buses, £24,7841 invested in the same year.

In contrast to the growing revenues from the bus companies the LMSR experienced a drop in passenger receipts from £26,013,800 in 1923 to £21,763,617 in 1929. The development of road transport was clearly identified as the cause and Sir Josiah Stamp, Chairman of the LMSR, not only made this point to his fellow Directors but went on to say that in his view this trade would never return to the railways. The scene was set for cutting back on lines which were no longer economical and soon branch line closures to passenger traffic became quite regular occurrences. Six such closures to passenger traffic were sanctioned in July 1929, including the Skipton to Grassington branch. In addition to these moves, branch lines in Cumberland which had once served the iron industry were removed, being deemed of no further use, as revival of the industry was seen as out of the question. The Eskett branch went in 1930 and part of the Gilgarron branch between Parton and Distington, together with sidings at Mealsgate serving United Steels All Hallows Colliery, went in the same year. Passenger services between Whitehaven and Workington via Rowah and

During the LMS era the 'Cauliflowers' continued to give good service. No. 23583 heads a local passenger train.
P. Ransome-Wallis/National Railway Museum

between Moor Row and Siddick Junction were also discontinued because 'passenger traffic has seriously decreased because there has been the development of competitive road traffic'. Other closures to passenger traffic followed.

Much of this was happening around the CK&PR but at this stage there were no suggestions that the railway should restrict its operations. Nevertheless there must have been some concern about the way things were moving; the LMSR had bought motor buses - 18 Leyland Lions and 22 Albions in 1928 and purchases did not stop there.

In December 1936 the removal of the Redhill link was sanctioned, along with the abolition of the Redhills and Eamont signal boxes. The cost for the work, which was effected during 1938, was £4,048 but it was reckoned the cost justified the savings which would follow. In effect, the 'through route' from East to West became a thing of the past. In addition the track east of Blencow was singled again.

World War I certainly did not turn out to be the war to end all wars and conflict in Europe started again in 1939. As previously, the Government took control of the railways, this control coming into effect on 1st September, 1939. Shareholders in the LMSR received a 2 per cent dividend in 1940, much as the shareholders of the CK&PR had done back in 1914. The LMSR produced an emergency timetable that year and the Penrith - Whitehaven service consisted of four down trains (the first at 7.25 am; the last at 6.47 pm) with a Keswick to Workington service and these were complemented by four up trains (the first ex-Cockermouth at 7.11 am; the last at 6.31 pm) with a reciprocal working from Whitehaven to Keswick.

In January 1940 the area was affected by particularly heavy falls of snow and the line became blocked west of Blencow station. On Wednesday 1st February there was a serious accident when a group of men were at work attempting to clear the line. The railway staff were assisted by a party of soldiers. Three empty wagons were pushed into the cutting where the men were working but no warning appears to have been given or, if it was, it was not heard. The wagons ran into the workers and two men, Robert Watson and Joseph Hugill, together with one of the soldiers were killed. Several of the party were reported injured, including some of the soldiers; different accounts put the number between seven and nine.

A Gracious Interlude

Following the outbreak of war in 1939 and the realisation that the South of England would be the target of enemy bombing, many schools removed to safer havens in more remote places. Certain independent boarding schools removed *in toto* with pupils and staff going together. The West Country was an obvious choice. Miss (later Dame) Emmeline Tanner, the headmistress of Roedean (the famous Girls' Public School) was, by all accounts, a very remarkable lady with a strong personality. Initially, she was not in favour of 'giving in' lightly and decided her school would stay put (even though it was perched close to the top

PENRITH, KESWICK, WORKINGTON, and WHITEHAVEN

Mls from Penrith	Down	Week Days only. mrn	mrn	mrn	aft S	aft	aft E	aft
	436London(Euston)dep.	..	10N55	12K2	..	12N2	..	10L40
	Penrith ....dep.	..	7 25	9 45	..	1 10	..	6 47
3¾	Blencow A...........	..	7 36	9 56	..	1 21	..	6 58
7¾	Penruddock A	..	7 45	10 5	..	1 30	..	7 7
10	Troutbeck B..........	..	7 50	10 10	..	1 35	..	7 12
14¼	Threlkeld	..	7 59	10 19	..	1 45	..	7 22
18½	Keswick, for Derwentwater arr.	..	8 8	10 28	..	1 53	..	7 31
	dep.	..	8 15	10 35	1 5	1 58	5 45	7 40
20½	Braithwaite...........	..	8 19	10 39	1 9	2 2	5 49	7 44
25¼	Bassenthwaite Lake....	..	8 28	10 48	1 18	2 11	5 59	7 58
28	Embleton	..	8 34	10 54	1 24	2 17	6 5	8 4
30½	Cockermouth D arr.	..	8 40	11 0	1 30	2 23	6 11	8 10
	624 dep.	7 25	8 42	11 2	1 35	2 25	6 15	8 12
33	Brigham	7 30	8 47	11 7	1 40	2 30	6 20	8 17
33¾	Broughton Cross C.....	..	8 50	11 10	1 43	2 33	..	..
36¼	Camerton	7 36	8 55	11 15	1 48	2 38	6 26	8 23
38¼	Workington Bridge	7 43	9 2	11 22	1 55	2 45	6 33	8 30
39¼	Workingt'n, Main arr.	7 48	9 7	11 27	2 0	2 50	6 38	8 35
	624 dep.	8 6	11 5	12 17	..	3 0	..	8 40
41¾	Harrington	8 11	11 10	12 22	..	3 5	..	8 45
45	Parton.	8 21	11 20	12 32	..	3 15	..	8 55
46½	Whitehaven G 622 arr.	8 26	11 25	12 37	..	3 20	..	9 0

Miles	Up	Week Days only. mrn	mrn	mrn	mrn S	aft	aft E	aft	aft
	Bransty Station, Whitehaven ....dep.	6 9	7 44	9 7	1055	1 20	4 5	5 40	9 30
1½	Parton	6 12	7 47	9 10	1058	1 24	4 8	5 44	9 33
4¾	Harrington	6 22	7 57	9 20	11 8	1 34	4 18	5 54	9 43
7	Workingt'n, Main arr.	6 28	8 3	9 26	1114	1 40	4 24	6 0	9 50
	624 dep.	6 45	8 25	9 55	1150	2 10	4 35	6 4	10 0
8¼	Workington Bridge.....	6 48	8 28	9 58	1153	2 13	4 38	6 7	10 3
10¼	Camerton	6 55	8 35	10 5	12 0	2 20	4 45	6 14	1010
12¾	Broughton Cross C.....	..	8 41	1011	..	2 26	4 51	6 20	1016
13½	Brigham	7 3	8 45	1015	12 8	2 30	4 55	6 24	1020
15¾	Cockermouth D arr.	7 10	8 52	1022	1215	2 37	5 2	6 31	1027
	624 dep.	7 11	..	1030	1217	2 38	5 5	6 32	..
18½	Embleton	7 17	..	1036	1223	2 44	5 11	6 38	..
21	Bassenthwaite Lake....	7 25	..	1050	1229	2 50	5 17	6 46	..
26	Braithwaite...........	7 34	..	1059	1239	3 0	5 27	6 55	..
28½	Keswick, for Derwentwater arr.	7 40	..	11 5	1245	3 6	5 33	7 1	..
	dep.	7 43	..	1145	..	3 15	..	7 10	..
31¾	Threlkeld	7 53	..	1154	..	3 24	..	7 19	..
36½	Troutbeck B..........	8 7	..	12 9	..	3 38	..	7 33	..
38¾	Penruddock A.........	8 12	..	1214	..	3 43	..	7 38	..
42¾	Blencow A........[992	8 19	..	1221	..	3 50	..	7 45	..
46½	Penrith F436, 442arr	8 27	..	1229	..	3 58	..	7 53	..
281½	442London(Euston) arr.	4 40	..	1041	..	6L15	..	..	..

A Station for Greystoke (2 miles) **B** Station for Ullswater Lake (5¼ miles) **C** Station for Greysouthen (¼ mile)
D Station for Buttermere **E** Except Sats **F** Station for Ullswater Lake (Pooley Bridge) (5¼ miles) **G** Bransty
K Sunday night only **L** Morning time **N** Night time **S** Saturdays only.

OTHER TRAINS between Cockermouth and Brigham, page 624—Workington and Whitehaven, page 625.

'LMS Emergency Passenger Services'. September 1939 - until further notice.

of the cliffs on the South Coast at Brighton). By the end of the year it was agreed, however, that with the safety of the girls the paramount consideration, a move should be made. The problem was where to go. The prime sites had already been taken. Together with a number of the senior staff, the headmistress pored over a large map of England which had been spread out on the floor. Someone suggested the Lake District and in no time at all, Miss Tanner was visiting Mr and Mrs Wivall, the owners of the Keswick Hotel. A deal was provisionally agreed although on her way home the headmistress had second thoughts and felt the School was going to be overcharged for the use of the hotel. After further negotiations a settlement was finalised and Roedean moved to Keswick. Equipment and other items were moved up during the summer holidays (1940) ready for the arrival of the girls in September. Special trains were needed at the beginning and end of each term. Pupils travelling from the London area originally joined at Euston but later, as hostilities intensified, the point of departure became Addison Road (Kensington). After 1942 departures (and returns) were usually at Victoria. A West Country contingent joined the train at Crewe. Pupils coming from the North of England travelled to school in Keswick on normal service trains. The train at the end of term is remembered, not least for the departure time. Everyone had to be on the platform at 5.00 am and the train left shortly afterwards. Motive power was usually a class '5MT'.

The school remained in Keswick for five years and one term, using the hotel as the main base for the senior school (there were no other 'guests'!) and two smaller hotels for the junior school. Parts of the station and other buildings were used as classrooms. Classes were even taught in the waiting rooms. Apparently during the Latin lessons, in the waiting room on platform 1, the travelling public would wander in, much to the amusement of the pupils. At other times dancing lessons were given on platform 1 and on these occasions it was the turn of the travelling public to be bemused. On the whole School and hotel management got on well together, with the hotel staff providing stalwart service in these unusual circumstances. There were, perhaps inevitably, misgivings from time to time. For example, in the colder weather, some of the girls found their coal ration (one small tin full per day) inadequate and had the bright idea of asking the engine crews if they would supplement this rather meagre amount. The drivers and firemen were only happy to oblige but the coal provided made a dreadful mess when burned in a domestic grate - and the situation was not helped when, instead, logs (often large, wet and dirty) were carted into the hotel by the girls. Station master Pickthall and, in particular, porter Rigg (who had only one arm) both went out of their way to help the School feel at home. The hotel porter, Mr Dixon (described by some of the girls as 'particularly handsome'), also found himself fully involved and it fell to his lot to ring the bell on the station platform at 40 minute intervals during the day, to signify change of lessons.

The school building in Brighton, meanwhile, was taken over by the military and used initially by a Canadian contingent although later HMS *Vernon* moved in after its buildings had been bombed. Many pupils and staff left Keswick with happy memories. On the morning of the final departure in November 1945, an impromptu farewell party was held on the platform with the hotel and station

Penrith Shed, taken around 1930. A 'Cauliflower' is on shed.   *R.S. Carpenter*

A rare view of the inside of Penrith Shed, taken in the late 1940s. The 'Cauliflower' is unidentified.   *R.S. Carpenter*

staffs present. There was singing and dancing before the train left and when it did, the departure certainly went with a bang because some of the railway staff had placed fog detonators on the line. Keswick, the hotel and the railway must have seemed rather empty and quiet after the school had gone.

Train Control

The CK&PR was, initially a single line and so a train-staff system was in operation from the outset. At either end of the line there were signal boxes installed by the railways to which the CK&PR became linked. At Penrith, after the replacement of earlier boxes, the box controlling Keswick Junction was a LNWR type and dated from the 1879-80. This was on Wood's instigation, following a Board of Trade recommendation. It was referred to as Penrith No 1. At Cockermouth the box for Cockermouth Junction was installed in 1864 and this also was replaced by an LNWR type with a frame of 36 levers. As far as other boxes were concerned, it has already been mentioned that John Wood reported to the Directors in 1873 that Board of Trade requirements led him to the conclusion a number of improvements would have to be made with signalling and associated procedures and the Directors agreed, rather reluctantly, in view of the cost, to a series of improvements which included the signal boxes at Bassenthwaite, Penruddock, Keswick and Cockermouth. This work was started by Saxby & Farmer in 1874. In December of that year, it will be recalled, it was agreed to erect a block telegraph wire throughout the whole line and to introduce absolute block in addition to the train staff system. As a result of these various decisions, Cockermouth station acquired a Saxby & Farmer box with a frame of 40 levers although later, under the LMS, a replacement box was installed with 45 levers. Penruddock also acquired a Saxby & Farmer box under these improvements. It was sited at the down end of the up platform and was replaced in 1896 with a Tweedy frame consisting of 18 levers.Troutbeck also had a Saxby & Farmer box installed in 1874 although it eventually had a Tweedy frame with 16 levers. Bassenthwaite was the fourth place to be included in the 1874 scheme for a Saxby & Farmer box and the railway replaced this with one of its own boxes in 1911.This had a Tweedy frame. Blencow had a box installed in 1901 which had a Tweedy frame with 22 levers and this was replaced in LMS days with a frame having 35 levers. Threlkeld had a CK&PR box with a Tweedy frame of 18 levers which was installed in 1893.There were two boxes at Keswick; A and B. Box A was the one named under John Wood's scheme of 1873 and was a Saxby & Farmer box, erected in 1874. In the early 1930s it was replaced by a LNWR type with a 25-lever frame. Box B was located on the down platform and dated from about 1890. It was replaced by an LMS box with 24 levers in 1932. In spite of the decision, in 1873, to introduce the absolute block system throughout, the permissive block system was still in use between Troutbeck and Threlkeld at times when traffic was heavy. This was contrary to Board of Trade regulations and when the Board intervened in 1892 the company made the decision to install a box at Highgate, between the two. This box had a Tweedy frame with 4 levers. Redhills Junction was an important box as far as the CK&PR was concerned.

A view from the CK&PR line towards Penrith, showing the LNWR bracket junction signals.
Cumbrian Railways Association

Originally the box was a NER one but this was replaced by a CK&PR version in the late 19th century. This had a Tweedy frame. Following a decision in August 1883, the CK&PR was one of the first railways to introduce the Tyer's system of electric tablet working when this was devised and the installation was done on a one year trial basis between Cockermouth Junction and Cockermouth station. The cost of this, on a rental basis, was £5 per year with £150 to be paid if the equipment was retained. The trial, to which the Board of Trade gave a cautious blessing, was a success and in 1889 the system was extended to include Cockermouth station, Bassenthwaite Lake, and Keswick. Later still in the early 1890s Troutbeck, Penruddock, Penrith and Redhills wore added as well. The last two stations to be included were Embleton and Braithwaite in 1893. Blencow box had the system installed when it opened in 1901. By 1921, there were block posts at Cockermouth Junction, Cockermouth Station, Embleton, Bassenthwaite Lake, Braithwaite, Keswick A, Keswick B, Threlkeld, Highgate,Troutbeck, Penruddock, Blencow, Redhills, Penrith (Keswick Junction) and Penrith station. All were train tablet stations with the exceptions of Highgate, Troutbeck and Penrith station, with the train tablet system in operation from Cockermouth Junction to Threlkeld, Penruddock to Blencow and Redhills to Penrith (Keswick Jn). The LMS replaced the Tyer's electric train-tablet system with the Tyer's key token system.

Transition Looms

Following the end of the war in 1945 and towards the end of 1940s the Labour Government of the day decided to nationalise Britain's railways. The LMSR found itself in a rather similar position to the CK&PR in the early 1920s as 'take-over' loomed. Possibly the Directors had seen the writing on the wall when the plan to install a new turntable at Penrith was cancelled in December 1944.

One innovation which did give a lot of pleasure was the introduction of camping coaches. Two were sited at Bassenthwaite Lake and were painted green and white. They continued in service after the demise of the LMSR.

There is a final entry in the LMSR Directors' minute book which is hand written and reads 'On 23rd December, 1949 a notice appeared in *The London Gazette* formally dissolving the LMSR with effect from that date'. Another era in the history of Britain's railways had come to an end. Yet the 'little railway' between Penrith and Cockermouth in many ways hardly noticed any difference. It was, for those who were in control, no doubt seen as a low key operation and, as a result, for the moment, less likely to be significantly affected by the stirrings in the great world outside. Its fortunes, though, were soon to change.

The routine on the railway changed very little during this period and, initially, this was true for the motive power as well. Under the LMSR some Midland 2-4-0 locomotives appeared but these were just as ancient as the ex-LNWR locomotives being used. The strengthening of the bridges east of Keswick did eventually bring heavier locomotives from Penrith onto this section and the installation of a new 60 ft turntable at Keswick also facilitated the managing of these larger engines. By 1939, Stanier class '5MT' 4-6-0 ('Black Fives') started to appear and there were also appearances by Fowler class '4F' 0-6-0 engines working goods trains.

BR days. This local train, headed by 'Cauliflower' No. 58936 leaves Penruddock.

Millbrook House Ltd

A local freight headed by 0-6-0 No. 58412, in BR days. Notice the variety of wagons.

P. Ransome-Wallis/National Railway Museum

Chapter Nine

The British Railways' Period: 1948 to 1972

In 1948 the CK&PR became part of the London Midland Region of the nationalised railway network, British Railways. In many ways, the 1923 transition saw few significant changes and the same can be said for that of 1948. Locomotive numbers changed - although in some cases the process took quite a time - but to begin with, many aspects remained very much the same! The passenger timetable for September 1948 consisted of six down trains from Penrith to Whitehaven (the first at 7.25 am; the last at 8.10 pm) with a 'Saturdays Only' train from Penrith to Keswick and six up trains from Whitehaven to Penrith (the first ex-Cockermouth at 7.14 am; the last at 6.44 pm) with a reciprocal Keswick to Penrith on Saturdays only.

The only reigning monarch to use the railway in conjunction with an official visit to Cumberland was Queen Elizabeth II. On 17th October, 1956 she opened Calder Hall at Sellafield (acclaimed as being the first nuclear power station to make a significant contribution to the National Grid). After that engagement, the Queen moved on to Whitehaven and Workington and then travelled by road to visit the Lairthwaite School at Keswick. In the town itself she received what was described as a 'joyous welcome' as she drove to the station to join the Royal Train. In the station yard, the Queen inspected a guard of honour made up of members of the Cumberland and Westmorland Constabulary and this inspection had been preceded by a grand parade headed by the Pipe Band of the City of Edinburgh Police. Following this, and very much behind schedule, the Queen entered the station where she met the station master, Mr J. Armstrong. The train left to the sound of three cheers and travelled to Penrith, although it did not enter the station there. It used one of the lines running into the station and a locomotive was attached to what had been the rear of the train which then left for the South at 6.32 pm. At one point the Queen had made the remark, 'What a lovely trip it has been'.

Motive Power: A Radical Change

The 'Cauliflowers' were still in evidence after Nationalisation, hauling local passenger trains, with some additional workings. In 1951, Penrith Shed (12C) was home to two 'Cauliflowers', Nos. 58409 and 58412, whilst Workington (12D) had one, No. 58396. In addition, Workington had three ex-Furness '3F' 0-6-0s (52499, 52501, and 52509) two '3F' 0-6-0Ts (47290 and 47292) two '4F' 0-6-0s (44449 and 44505) five '4F' 2-6-0s (43004, 43006, 43007, 43008 and 43009) and two '2P' 4-4-0s (40694 and 40695). The '4F' 0-6-0s worked on the CK&PR, together with representatives from Carlisle's (12A) members of this class. By October 1964, as the proverbial storm clouds started to gather, Penrith Shed had gone and so had the LNWR locomotives. Workington boasted two '4F' 0-6-0s, one ex-Midland '4F' 0-6-0, 10 ex-LMSR '4F' 0-6-0s, four '3F' 0-6-0Ts and three

Two Ivatt class '2MTs' Nos. 46458 and 46455 work the up 'Keswick Convention Special' at Troutbeck on 17th July, 1965.
Derek Cross

New meets old as class '2MT' No. 46455 heading an excursion encounters one of the ubiquitous 'Cauliflowers' (No. 28589) on a local train in August 1950.   *Millbrook House Ltd*

The Keswick portion of the up 'Lakes Express' leaves Keswick and is about to cross the River Greta. Motive power is provided by class '2MT' No. 46432.   *Peter W. Robinson*

The station frontage at Cockermouth.   *D. Jenkinson*

A general view of Cockermouth, looking east, taken in 1966.   *Pendon Museum Trust*

'2F' 2-6-0s (46432, 46488 and 46491). It was this last group which was seen frequently on the CK&PR often hauling 'The Lakes Express', on the Workington to Penrith section, or goods trains. Locomotives from Carlisle (Kingmoor and Upperby) also appeared regularly. Class '5MTs' continued to visit and there were occasions when 'Scots' and 'Jubilees' worked trains on visiting excursions - in particular the Sunday 'Newcastle Trains'. In the late 1950s and early 1960s 'The Lakes Express' was sometimes hauled by a Fowler 2-6-4T.

It was in January 1955 that diesel multiple units appeared; a radical change. How welcome they were! Passengers found them clean, comfortable and efficient; they seemed to breathe new life into the line. The decision to introduce these units was seen by some as a sign that the prospects were good. Three years later, similar units were brought into use on the EVR with the publicity speaking of a 'faster diesel service'.

By the British Railways' era, the Keswick Convention had grown to become a very popular international event with some 5,000 Christians attending each year. The so called Budd Specials (named after their inaugurator, J.T.Budd, who first organised them in the late 19th century) ran from Euston to Keswick. These were usually double-headed down to Keswick, sometimes with two class '2s' or a '5MT' and a 2-6-4T but latterly they were diesel hauled and motive power included English Electric type '4s' (later BR class '40') and, on occasions, a class '50' (when this class of locomotive was still operating services on the West Coast Main Line). The practice, when run-round facilities were no longer available, was to run the train down to Keswick with a diesel engine at each end.

And yet . . .

Against all this activity, by the middle of the 1950s there was much deliberation about the possible need for the rationalisation of Britain's railway system. Once World War II was over the development of road transport moved on apace with its flexibility in carrying people and goods having an obvious appeal. These were hard times for some of the less busy minor railway lines. Some were losing money at a rate which was increasing annually and without local or, indeed, nationally based private ownership they became more vulnerable to possible closure. In May 1959 the region in which the CK&PR was located came under close scrutiny. (Blencow station had been closed in 1952 but reopened again in 1956; Embleton closed in September 1958.) The proposals coming out from a review for this area focused particularly on the line over Stainmore and included the EVR, the latter still having some associations with the CK&PR, being one link to the North East. Even so there was a great deal of uneasiness about the intentions of BR west of Penrith, in spite of a denial issued in Barrow (the Divisional headquarters) on 6th May to the effect that 'As for the Cockermouth Keswick and Penrith line, a great deal of the present publicity [about closure] is based on guesswork. We have not made any definite proposals concerning that line and we know nothing about any visit to Keswick connected with any such proposals . . .' The reference to 'a visit to Keswick' involves something of mystery. It had been reported in the Press only a few

The subway at Cockermouth, looking east, taken in 1966.   *D. Jenkinson*

Above left: Cockermouth station signal box.   *D. Jenkinson*
Above right: The water tank at Cockermouth.   *D. Jenkinson*

The 'Lakes and Fells Railtour' prepares to leave Cockermouth in April 1966.

W.J.V.A. Anderson

Embleton station.

Lens of Sutton

Embleton station in 1966.

J. Alsop

Bassenthwaite Lake station. Note the cattle vans in the siding beyond the platform.

Bassenthwaite Lake station. The picture was taken about 10 years before closure. Notice the well kept flower beds.   *BR/OPC Joint Venture*

Braithwaite station viewed from the train.   *BR/OPC Joint Venture*

Braithwaite station in 1966.   *John Alsop*

days previously that a 'stranger' had appeared in Keswick purporting to be a British Railways' investigator. He had 'upset' local people, it was alleged, by informing them he was there to find out whether the line was paying. 'As people went for their trains they saw a quiet stranger counting tickets and taking a census' stated one report. 'Quiet stranger' seems an unusual description but it was possibly intended to have a sinister nuance!

In January 1960 (the then) Mr William Whitelaw, MP for Penrith and the Borders, put in a plea for the retention of the line from Penrith to Cockermouth, during a speech to the Penrith Rotary Club at the George Hotel. 'Locally we have the line from Penrith to Keswick - the gateway to the northern end of the Lake District. I should have thought it would be a disastrous mistake to close that gateway [although he did go on to say] at least until every possible effort has been made to advertise travel to Keswick and the Lake District to the full. I cannot feel satisfied that has been done up to now'. He expressed the hope that more would be done by British Railways to attract additional tourist traffic. In other quarters there were more misgivings. The hotel industry would be adversely affected and how would the 5,000 visitors to the Keswick Convention arrive? It turned out that the CK&PR was not, in fact, the target of the review but a long and hard fought battle which centred on the EVR ensued, with move and counter-move being made by the various groups involved. (These events are described in detail in *The Eden Valley Railway*, by the author, published by The Oakwood Press (LP201).) Relief enough that at this stage the line from Penrith to Cockermouth was excluded from the threat of closure. However, in spite of this, a number of groups continued to express concern that the passing of the EVR would seriously damage the passenger traffic on the CK&PR. To a large extent such observations went unheeded and in January 1962, in spite of immense opposition and even questions being asked in the House, the EVR was closed, along with the route over Stainmore. It was reckoned, and not without good evidence, that the move had been taken in the face of one of the largest bodies of opposition ever mounted - and this was pre-Beeching!

When the dust had settled over the closure to the east of Penrith (and the track had for the most part been quickly removed) the CK&PR was still intact, running services very much as before. There were even Sunday services again. In spite of what might have appeared a measure of security as far as the future of the line was concerned there was uneasiness again in the early months of 1965. As a result, William Whitelaw decided to write, on 23rd June, to the Minister of Transport asking what plans there were for the railway. He did not receive a reply to his enquiry and in November decided to write to the Parliamentary Secretary. In his letter he pointed out that the uncertainty about the future was unsatisfactory, not least for those who worked on the line and those anticipating carrying out work on it. A reply was received in December and the news did not seem encouraging. The Minister, he was told, was considering this closure proposal in the light of the advice he had received about its possible implications for regional planning. Mr Stephen Swingler, the Parliamentary Secretary, assured Mr Whitelaw that the decision would be made 'as soon as possible'. He further acknowledged the fact that deliberations had been protracted but said this was because the matter had needed careful

The Workington portion of 'The Lakes Express' is seen here at Keswick in August 1960. A variety of motive power worked the train over the years. On this occasion Fowler 2-6-4T No. 42314 is in charge.   *John Marshall*

Class '2MT' No. 46432 heads a Workington to Manchester train at Keswick in August 1963.   *W.G. Sumner*

Keswick station, 1950.   *R.S. Carpenter*

Keswick station booking office and parcels office in BR days.   *D. Jenkinson*

The water tank and crane at Keswick.   *D. Jenkinson*

The Ivatt class '2MT' engines latterly did much of the work of hauling trains. No. 46488 is just coming off the turntable at Keswick in April 1964.   *G.N.G. Tingey*

The platform of the Halt at Briery Bobbin Mill. The site of this platform can still be easily seen today.   *Cumbrian Railways Association*

All that remains of the platform of Briery Bobbin Mill in the Summer of 1999.   *Author*

A view of Threlkeld showing the track layout.

The striking signal box at Threlkeld which formed an appendage to the station building. This view was taken in 1966. *J. Alsop*

The wharf used at the Threlkeld Granite Company.   *Cumbrian Railways Association*

A wagon used by the Threlkeld Granite Company.   *Cumbrian Railways Association*

Troutbeck (for Ullswater) in 1950, looking towards Penrith.   *H.C. Casserley*

Troutbeck , now with its new sign, in 1965.   *E. Wilmshurst*

Penruddock. This view shows the 'staggered' platforms.   *Lens of Sutton*

Penruddock signal box.   *D. Jenkinson*

Blencow station in 1966.   *J. Alsop*

The signal box at Blencow.   *Lens of Sutton*

consideration in order that the right decision should be made. All this was happening in a climate where road transport seemed very much on the way up. In October, the final humiliation for the former SD&LUR seemed imminent when it was decided the trackbed from Newbiggin to Tebay should be used to make a road. The Penrith by-pass was in the news and the prospect of a motorway in the region was in the air.

In the first week of January 1966 the whole of the old Board of Directors of the CK&PR must have turned in their graves. Yet again, the line was blocked by snow! The interruption in the service lasted for a period covering five days, starting on Monday at around noon and continuing until Friday morning. Nevertheless a sense of euphoria was generated later in the month when Barbara Castle, the Minister of Transport, announced that the line would not be closed - at least between Penrith and Keswick. Passenger services would, however, be withdrawn west of Keswick. Mrs Castle pointed out that in coming to a decision, she had listened carefully to the various bodies involved including the Consultative Committee and The Economic Planning Council for the Northern Region. She accepted the arguments put forward relating to the hardship which would be caused if the railway closed; the longer journey times, for example, if buses were to replace trains. Similar problems which would arise by closing the line west of Keswick were not seen to be as severe. There were caveats, albeit implied. The first came in the statement granting the continuance of the line. 'In so far as the proposed discontinuance relates to the section of the line between Keswick and Penrith and stations on that section, it may be that on a review of the situation in connection with a future proposal the matter might appear differently. But howsoever this may be and without in any way prejudging any future proposal the Minister does not feel justified in consenting to this discontinuance at the present time . . .' The second came in the statement that 'The Minister hopes that the Board [BR] will consider what further economies they can achieve in operating the service . . .' One man who was particularly pleased with the outcome was Sir Percy Hope who had been very active in opposing closure. Sir Percy had been dismayed some years earlier, in 1960, when, at a meeting of the Lake District Planning Board, his amendment that the Board should oppose the closure of the EVR had been defeated and the Board had decided to take no action. This time his efforts had achieved something positive.

Although to some 'pessimists' this truncating of the line seemed an ominous move, it was perceived by others as a realistic development and one which made sense in that what was reckoned to be the key section of the line (Penrith to Keswick) had been safeguarded. There was, it seemed, no reason to believe this section would go, linking, as it did, the heartland of the Lakes to the main line at Penrith. After all, it was reasoned, the line from Oxenholme to Windermere was holding up. Why not, then, the line from Penrith to Keswick?

Hold up it did - but, sadly, only figuratively. In fact the line continued to lose money, a factor which meant the whole situation was, as Barbara Castle had inferred, reviewed yet again in the late 1960s and early 1970s. It is worth bearing in mind that the railways were not alone in experiencing problems with dwindling numbers of passengers. At the same time as the railway was trying

Looking south from Penrith. The West Coast Main Line is on the left, CK&PR is the single track on the right.   *Cumbrian Railways Association*

The outside view of Penrith Shed as seen in 1953. Class '4F' 0-6-0 No 44084 is on shed.

R.S. Carpenter

to come to terms with this situation, the Ribble Bus Company attracted criticism when it made an application to increase fares on its routes in Westmorland, Cumberland and Furness. The reason given by the company and accepted by the Northern Transport Commission (NTC) in granting the application, was falling receipts resulting from loss of passengers.

Again, coincident with these events, more debate ensued about the problems becoming apparent as more and more visitors came to the Lakes and a 'Report on Tourism' went so far as to state that 'the time has probably come when day visitors to the Lake District must be positively controlled'. This was adopted in principle by the Lake District Planning Board although reservations were expressed. With better rail facilities these problems might have been eased, even if they were not solved but the process of significantly down-grading the line moved relentlessly forward in June 1965, when goods services were withdrawn. At the beginning of March 1966 the former engine shed at Penrith was demolished; an act which was perhaps symbolic rather than significant!

Services in the period just before the closure west of Keswick were

Weekdays

Down (ex-Penrith)	*Up* (from Whitehaven/Workington
am	*am* Times ex-Cockermouth unless stated)
7.18	7.23 through service to Carlisle
9.43 through service from Carlisle	9.32
11.02 to Keswick - through service	*pm*
from Carlisle	12.40 ex-Keswick to Penrith
pm	12.41 through service to Carlisle (SX)
1.35	3.38 through service to Carlisle
5.00 (SX)	5.38 to Keswick
5.05 (SO)	6.55 ex Keswick to Penrith
6.10 through service from Carlisle	7.32 through service to Carlisle
7.45	

Sundays (June to September)

Down	*Up*
am	*pm*
11.21 to Keswick: through service from Carlisle	12.45 ex-Keswick: through service to Carlisle
pm	2.35 ex-Cockermouth (Whitehaven) to Keswick
12.25 to Keswick: through service from Newcastle	4.15 ex-Keswick to Penrith
2.29 to Workington: through service from Carlisle	4.18 ex-Cockermouth to Keswick
4.50 ex-Keswick to Workington	6.35 ex-Keswick: through service to Carlisle
5.55 to Keswick	6.50 ex-Keswick: through service to Newcastle
7.00 ex-Keswick to Whitehaven	6.32 ex-Cockermouth to Keswick
8.11 to Keswick: through service from Carlisle	9.00 ex Keswick: through service to Carlisle

The charm of this line is seen in this photograph. The views could be observed much better from a dmu than from the old coaching stock.   *BR/OPC Joint Venture*

A scene at Keswick in the late 1950s. Local people and holidaymakers mingle.
BR/OPC Joint Venture

Some of the splendour of the line in winter is captured in this April 1966 photograph taken near Keswick.   *Derek Cross*

A bleak prospect at Cockermouth in April 1966 as the 7.18 am Penrith to Workington prepares to depart.   *Ian S. Carr*

Exciting views such as the one seen here were possible on many sections of the line. A Keswick to Penrith train is approaching Troutbeck in October 1970.   *G.J. Jackson*

The dmu on the Keswick service in the final week of operations in 1972. The former CK&PR route had been realigned during the construction of the M6 motorway extension. The West Coast Main Line can be seen to the right.   *Percy Duff*

The through Sunday workings from and returning to Newcastle operated from 10th July to 26th August. As mentioned earlier, it was this Newcastle service which gave rise to the visiting 'Scots' and 'Jubilees'. (*The Border Regiment* and *Samson* were two examples.)

Before the line was closed west of Keswick, a special train, which was steam hauled, ran along the line as part of 'The Lakes and Fells Railtour'. This was organised by the SLS and MLS for 2nd April and the motive power consisted of two Ivatt class '2' 2-6-0s, Nos. 46426 and 46458. This was the last steam-hauled train to use the entire length of the line. On 16th April the section west of Keswick was closed. Three months later, on 22nd July, No. 46458 was on special duty again. In immaculate condition it hauled the Royal Train to Keswick for a visit by HRH The Duke of Edinburgh. The previous year, on 17th July, it had (along with No. 46455) hauled the special which formed the return train of the Keswick Convention.

After closure west of Keswick, the pattern of services became:

Weekdays

Down		*Up*	
am		*am*	
6.50	through service from Carlisle	7.40	through service to Carlisle
10.06	through service from Carlisle	10.45	
11.25		*pm*	
pm		12.25	through service to Carlisle
1.05	through service to Carlisle		(15th June-7th September)
	(15th June-7th September)	2.05	through service to Carlisle
4.57	through service from Carlisle	5.35	through service to Carlisle
6.16	through service from Carlisle	7.20	through service to Carlisle

Once again, there was no Sunday service. Whilst the service could hardly be described as 'frequent' it was, nevertheless, adequate and met the needs of shoppers, for example.

The following year (May 1969 to May 1970) there was no significant change and the year after (May 1970 to May 1971) although the timings changed somewhat, the number of trains remained the same; six up and six down. The table was modified so that Carlisle timings appeared on the schedule, where appropriate. All this might have suggested a settled and secure situation. Not so, however. In late 1971 the line was under threat again. In November the talk of possible closure was challenged as being 'a move in the wrong direction'. There had continued to be numerous meetings over the preceding months involving different organisations to discuss the role of tourism in the Lakes and the ramifications of this growing industry. Possible traffic congestion remained the main fear - and now there was talk of closing the railway which many considered served the heartland. In January 1972 an imaginative scheme for a Keswick by-pass was unveiled; another sign of the times in the shift of emphasis to road transport. Then again, although there were certainly protestations from the tradespeople of Keswick, in particular, not surprisingly, the hoteliers, there seems to have been little other opposition. Road transport, it might be concluded, was king! If you chose to leave your car at home when you went on

A Keswick-bound dmu entering Penruddock station, passing the closed signal box on 29th February, 1972.   *C.A. Allenby*

A view looking west in 1972, showing the trackbed of the route to Cockermouth which had closed in 1966. The remains of 1874-built Keswick 'A' signal box, and the adjoining building behind the signal box, which had been the CK&PR's joiners' and plumbers' workshop, are in evidence.   *C.A. Allenby*

holiday to the Lake District then you could take a super-luxury coach which would not only whisk you from one hotel to the next (door to door) but in between would take you to all sorts of interesting places where you could stop off and spend some time. On the other hand, if you lived in Keswick and wanted to visit Penrith (or vice versa or, indeed, any other place *en route*) then you could take the car; why bother to walk to the station when you only need walk to the garage?

The end seemed to come very quickly. An announcement was made in the middle of January that the line would close on Saturday 4th March, 1972. The last train was the 8.00 pm from Penrith and, with the approval of British Railways, the Penrith and Keswick Round Tables decided to 'take over' this last run and make the journey a memorable one. Tickets for the trip were £1.

A large number of people turned out for the final train, some travelling long distances to witness the event, such was the affection for the line. The driver for the occasion was Mr J.H. Fordham. There were people wearing funeral attire and one traveller wore clogs because he said he recalled from his early journeys on the line that all the porters had worn them! The departure from Penrith had been to the strains of 'Auld Lang Syne' and there were some 450 passengers, according to a local report. Keswick station was decorated with flags and bunting and a special bar was provided where (it was suggested) people could drown their sorrows. A special raffle was organised and the prizes were two station signs. The winners received their prizes from Miss Cumberland (Miss Leonie Hartley). Before the train left Keswick for the return to Penrith, the chairman of Keswick Council, Mr Beanland, thanked the Penrith and Keswick Round Table members for their efforts. He went on to express the hope that a preservation society might be formed and that items of interest associated with the line might be placed in local museums. There was, perhaps, a sting in the tail of this event for Mr Beanland and his colleagues who travelled on the train; they had to return from Penrith to Keswick by minibus!

After all this, diesels did remain in evidence for a short while, hauling trains to and from Flusco Quarry to take away limestone. However, in the middle of June these, too, were withdrawn. Quite simply, with that, the railway had gone. There were still those, however, who felt it need not be the end. In May of the same year, the Carlisle Junior Chamber of Trade came up with a proposal to reopen the line from Threlkeld to Keswick and possibly to Bassenthwaite Lake as a narrow gauge railway. It was felt such a railway would be a major tourist attraction. British Railways noted the proposal but pointed out that the local planning authority would be given first option. Financial backing was sought, but even by June it had to be conceded that the response had been so poor (there had been nine replies with six coming from outside the area) that there seemed little future for the scheme and it was recommended it should be abandoned.

Once the track had been removed, some sections of the old trackbed were used to widen and generally improve roads. Other sections, particularly along the River Greta, near Keswick have been turned into tracks for walkers, cyclists and horse-riders. Many of the bridges remain, crossing and re-crossing the River Greta. Much additional evidence of the line still exists for those who wish to explore this delightful area.

Two of the bowstring bridges which were a feature of the line in the Greta Gorge, east of Keswick. These bridges are still in place. Will they carry trains again, one day?   *(Both) Author*

In Conclusion

During the last 25 years and as the new millennium opens, attitudes to, and views on, public transport have changed considerably; even dramatically. In this new climate, reintroduction of a passenger service from Penrith to Keswick has been (and is being) seriously debated. Not just by 'enthusiastic amateurs' but, we are led to believe, possibly at Government levels as well. Perhaps, after all, this line could once again have a role in a public transport strategy which, more and more, is urgently needed in the region. Perhaps . . .
    ' Now it is high time to awaken out of sleep . . .'

Postscript

After 1972, The Long Sleep, and Future Plans

For 28 years the railway has lain dormant; dormant, some would say (rather than 'dead') being the operative word. There have always been those who hoped that in some way and at some time in the not too distant future the railway would be reinstated. For others there seemed to be no doubt that the line would never reopen. The trackbed in the vicinity of Keswick has become a much valued and well established route for walkers and cyclists who would no doubt vigorously oppose any steps to remove this amenity and replace it with a railway. Yet through the years and especially during the 1990s, there have been signs and glimmers of hope that events might take what many people would see as an unexpected turn. Things seemed to come to something of a head in 1995. In May of that year Cedric Martindale, an engineer from Carlisle, wrote to Keswick Town Council pointing out that much of the trackbed of the former railway remained intact and in sections where this was not so, replacing it was not beyond possibility. He further proposed that landowners and construction firms could unite to open the line and in so doing be remunerated when the line became operational again. The immediate response from the town council was to defer discussion. At the same time, as if to make a statement, the Lake District planners were asked to investigate the possibility of using the old trackbed as part of a national cycle route. The spectre that seemed to be dogging so many schemes to reopen railways was raising its head here, as Sustrans, the co-ordinator of the National cycle network showed an interest in the scheme. Only a month later, Keswick station was in the news when a referendum was successfully called to consider future plans for the site; the issue was whether the station should become a retail outlet and many traders in the town seemed to be opposed to this. In some ways more significant was a move during the following month (July) to persuade the British Rail Property Board not to proceed with the possible demolition of Penruddock and Mosedale viaducts. Eden District Council (EDC) and the Lake District Planning Board (LDPB) both opposed the removal of the viaducts on the grounds that it would make any proposed reopening of the line virtually impossible as replacement

A selection artefacts now kept at the Keswick Hotel in 1999.

Author

Detail of Keswick Hotel entrance in 1999.

Author

Keswick Hotel in 1999, much as it was when built.   *Author*

Between the lobby and the ante-room in the Keswick Hotel, on a screen and double doors, there are four artists represented in stained glass. This 1994 view shows the image of Paul Veronese (1528-1588). The other artists to be seen are Sir Godfrey Kneller, Sir Peter Lely and Raphael Sanzio.   *Paul O'Callaghan*

might prove to be prohibitively expensive. The structures had both been pronounced sound and involvement by the EDC and LDPB clearly added momentum to the appeal. The petition was successful and the viaducts were retained (although there is a possible threat looming again in the millennium year when the situation will be reconsidered). The scheme to reinstate the railway has certainly gained momentum and the intention here is not to create a 'heritage line' but a fully operational system. In 1997 Cedric Martindale founded Iceni Enterprises Ltd which would manage the project to rebuild the line and also with this in view, CKP Railways Ltd has been formed and on 20th December, 1999 Companies House gave the go-ahead for it to become a public limited company. The public will be given the opportunity to buy bonds. These bonds, which it is planned will be repayable after 10 years, will provide a return for the purchasers. It is reckoned that the cost of reinstating the railway will be in the order of £25 million. However, the promoters are convinced, from their researches, that there is a great deal of support for re-opening a rail link between Penrith and Keswick and suggest that between 250,000 and 450,000 passengers, or even more, could well use the line annually. Railtrack plc and the train operator Northern Spirit are showing interest in the plans which, it is argued, if realised, will result in a profit making railway.

So the 'sleep', if such it is, may one day be over . . .

[Details of the project to reopen the line can be obtained from Cedric Martindale, Director, Iceni Enterprises, 1 Solway Park, Carlisle, Cumbria, CA2 6TH.]

The outlook from Keswick station in 1999, looking towards Penrith.   *Author*

Appendix One

Distance Table for each stage from Penrith to Cockermouth Junction

From Penrith station	Miles	Chains
to Penrith Junction	0	29
to Redhills	1	11
to Blencow	2	13
to Penruddock	4	1
to Troutbeck	2	21
to Threlkeld	4	59
to Keswick	3	38
to Braithwaite	2	36
to Bassenthwaite Lake	4	77
to Embleton	2	25
to Cockermouth station	2	62
to Cockermouth Junction	0	42
Total Distance	31	14

Passing the token at Cockermouth station box. *G.H.A. Townley*

Timetable, July 1869

Up Trains

Weekdays

Cockermouth dep.	Penrith arr.	
7.00 am	8.25 am	1, 2, and Parliamentary
9.00	10.10	1, 2, 3 and Mail
11.50	1.20 pm	1 and 2
3.40 pm	5.00	1, 2, and Mail
6.32	7.57	1 and 2

Sundays

9.35 am		1, 2, and Parliamentary
7.00 pm		1, 2 and 3

Down Trains

Weekdays

Penrith dep.	Cockermouth arr.	
6.15 am	7.35 am	1, 2, and Parliamentary
8.40	10.05	1 and 2
10.25	11.47	1 and 2
1.55 pm	3.20 pm	1, 2 and Mail
5.40	7.05	1 and 2

Sundays

7.00 am		1, 2, and Parliamentary
6.00 pm		1, 2 and 3

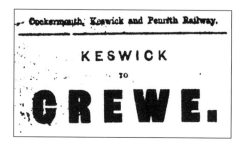

Cockermouth, Keswick and Penrith Railway.

KESWICK
TO
CREWE.

Appendix Three

Working Timetables for 1903 (July-September) and 1921 (October)

1903

Up Trains, ex-Cockermouth - unless stated

No.			am	
1	Workmen's	Keswick to Threlkeld	6.55	
2	Passenger		6.56	
3	Ballast	Threlkeld to Troutbeck.		
	Mondays Wednesdays and Fridays		8.10	(ex-Threlkeld)
4	NER Empties	Mondays only	7.30	
5	Express Passenger		8.15	
6	Ballast	Threlkeld to Flusco Sidings.		
	Mondays Wednesdays & Fridays		9.20	(ex-Threlkeld)
7	Passenger	to Keswick	9.00	
8	NER Empties		9.05	
9	Goods	Mondays	9.25	
10	Passenger		11.07	
11	Goods	not Mondays	11.10	
12	NER Empties		11.45	
			pm	
13	Excursion	Fortnightly - half-day*	1.05	(ex-Keswick)
14	Express Passenger		1.12	
15	Goods	Mondays, Keswick to Troutbeck	2.20	
16	Goods	not Mondays	1.20	
17	NER Coal		1.25	
18	NER Coal		1.35	
19	Passenger	Thursdays and Saturdays, to Keswick	2.24	
20	Goods and Cattle	Mondays	2.15	
21	Passenger		3.15	
22	Goods	Conditional. Run when required.		
	Threlkeld to Troutbeck		4.20	
23	Goods	Saturdays, from Threlkeld	5.25	
24	NER Empties	not Saturdays	4.30	
25	Light Engine	not Saturdays, Keswick to Threlkeld	5.55	(ex-Keswick)
26	NER Empties	Saturdays	4.45	
27	Goods	not Saturdays, from Threlkeld	6.20	
28	Passenger		6.02	
29	Excursion	Thursdays and Saturdays	8.00	(ex-Keswick)
30	Passenger		7.37	

Sundays

			am
1	Passenger	to Keswick	9.30
			pm
2	Passenger		6.00

---

* Wednesdays, 1st, 15th, 29th July, 12th, 26th August, 9th, 23rd September.

Down Trains, ex-Penrith - unless stated

No.			am	
1	NER Coke	Mondays	4.50	(ex-Redhills)
2	Mails	Mondays	5.30	
3	Goods/Mails		5.30	
4	NER Coke		6.15	(ex-Redhills)
5	Light Engine	not Mondays, Threlkeld to Keswick	7.15	(ex-Threlkeld)
6	LNWR Ballast	to Threlkeld	7.00	
7	Passenger		7.30	
8	Light Engine	Mondays, Wednesdays & Fridays Troutbeck to Threlkeld	8.35	
9	NER Coke/ Coal		7.50	(ex-Redhills)
10	Passenger		9.31	
11	NER Coke		10.25	(ex-Redhills)
12	Goods	to Keswick	10.45	
13	Empty Coaches	to Keswick*	11.45	
			pm	
14	Passenger	from Keswick	12.45	
15	Workmen's	Saturdays, Threlkeld to Keswick	1.05	
16	Light Engine	not Mondays Embleton to Cockermouth Jn	2.00	
17	Passenger		1.05	
18A	NER Coke	Mondays	1.20	(ex-Redhills)
18B	NER Coke	Thursdays and Saturdays	1.20	(ex-Redhills)
18C	NER Coke	Tuesdays Wednesdays and Fridays	1.50	(ex-Redhills)
19	Excursion	Thursdays and Saturdays	1.50	
20	Engine and van	Troutbeck to Threlkeld	3.10	
21	Passenger		3.00	
22	Light Engine	not Mondays Troutbeck to Threlkeld	3.38	
23	Light Engine	Mondays, Troutbeck to Threlkeld†	4.38	
24	Engine and van	Troutbeck to Threlkeld	4.50	
25	Passenger	Saturdays, from Keswick	5.00	
26	Workmens	not Saturdays Keswick to Briery Siding	5.38	
27	Passenger		5.10	
28	Goods	not Mondays	5.20	
29	Express Passenger		5.45	
30	Goods	Mondays	6.10	
31	Excursion	Thursdays, from Keswick	8.45	
32	Passenger		8.30	

Sundays

			am	
1	Passenger		7.20	
			pm	
2	Passenger	from Keswick	6.45	

* Wednesdays, 1st, 15th, 29th July, 12th, 26th August, 9th, 23rd September.
† Conditional on assistance being needed

1921

Up Trains, ex-Cockermouth - unless stated

There were 31 trains designated 'up trains', although 11 of these were workings into Cockermouth only (that is, from the West). The rest used the CK&PR in full or in part.

No.			*am*
1	M&CR Mails		6.06
2	M&CR Mails		6.38
3	Workmen's	Keswick to Threlkeld	7.05 (ex-Keswick)
4	Passenger		7.07
5	M&CR Passenger	to Keswick	8.20
6	M&CR Cattle	into Cockermouth	8.25
7	Passenger		8.54
8	Goods		9.20
9	M&CR Passenger	into Cockermouth	10.11
10	LNWR Passenger	into Cockermouth. Mondays	10.40
11	Passenger		11.15
12	NER Mineral	Conditional. Run when required	11.50
			pm
13	M&CR Passenger	into Cockermouth	12.17
14	Light Engine	Keswick to Threlkeld. Saturdays	1.00 (ex-Keswick)
15	LNWR Passenger	into Cockermouth. Saturdays	1.32
16	Goods	Keswick to Troutbeck	2.15 (ex-Keswick)
17	NER Mineral		1.40 (ex-Cockermouth Junction)
18	Excursion	Thursdays and Saturdays	1.55
19	Passenger		2.34
20	M&CR Passenger	into Cockermouth	3.33
21	Goods	Threlkeld to Troutbeck. Conditional. Run when required	3.38 (ex-Threlkeld)
22	Goods	Not Saturdays	4.15
23	Goods	Threlkeld to Penruddock	4.40 (ex-Threlkeld)
24	Light Engine	Keswick to Threlkeld	5.00 (ex-Keswick)
25	M&CR Passenger	into Cockermouth	5.30
26	Passenger		5.57
27	Passenger	to Keswick	6.00
28	Passenger		7.06
29	Excursion	from Keswick Thursday and Saturday	8.20 (ex-Keswick)
30	M&CR Passenger	into Cockermouth	8.14
31	LNWR Workmen's	into Cockermouth	8.44

Notes

No. 3 was made up of the engine and guard of No. 6 down and then this in turn became No. 7 down.

No. 5 was worked by M&CR men.

No. 7. Horse boxes, carriage trucks and empty vehicles were not to be conveyed by this train.

No. 8. When there was traffic from Harrisons Lime Works this would be taken on working No. 8. Information on how many wagons there were to be picked up was wired to Troutbeck. This train was also used to bring coal for the CK&PR stations, with the coal for Threlkeld and Troutbeck being put off at Keswick and then worked forward on working No. 16.

No 17. This train did not leave Bassenthwaite Lake until 2.25 pm and shunted at Keswick to allow No. 19 up to pass on Thursdays and Saturdays (during October).

No. 19 This train called daily (but not on Saturdays) at Highgate to set down school children

No. 26. Horse boxes, carriage trucks and empty vehicles were not to be conveyed by this train.

Down Trains, ex-Penrith - unless stated

No.			am
1	M&CR		
	Engine and van	from Cockermouth	6.15
			(4.15 if mails conveyed)
2	LNWR Passenger	from Cockermouth	6.45
3	M&CR		
	Engine and van	from Cockermouth	6.50
			(5.30 if mails conveyed)
4	LNWR Passenger	from Cockermouth	7.25
5	M&CR Passenger	from Cockermouth	8.05
6	Goods [Mails]		5.45
7	Light Engine	Threlkeld to Keswick	7.16 (ex-Threlkeld)
8	Passenger		7.30
9	M&CR		
	Engine and van	from Cockermouth	9.01
10	NER Mineral	Conditional. Run when required	8.40 (ex-Redhills Jn)
11	M&CR Passenger	from Keswick	9.45
12	M&CR Passenger	from Cockermouth	10.30
13	Passenger		9.55
14	NER Mineral		10.25 (ex-Redhills Jn)
15	Goods		11.00
			pm
16	Workmen's	Threlkeld to Keswick. Saturdays	12.25 (ex-Threlkeld)
17	M&CR Passenger	from Cockermouth. Mondays	1.50
18	Passenger		1.10
19	Excursion	Thursdays and Saturdays	2.20
20	Engine and van	Troutbeck to Threlkeld	3.18 (ex-Threlkeld)
21	Joint Line		
	Passenger	from Cockermouth	3.25
22	Passenger		3.00
23	M&CR Passenger	from Cockermouth	4.25
24	M&CR Cattle	from Cockermouth. Mondays	4.35
25	Engine and van	Troutbeck to Threlkeld	4.05 (ex-Troutbeck)
26	Goods	to Keswick	3.15
		Conditional. Run when required	
27	Workmens	Threlkeld to Keswick	4.45 (ex-Threlkeld)
28	M&CR Passenger	from Cockermouth	6.58
29	Passenger		6.25
30	Goods	from Keswick	6.40
31	M&CR Passenger	from Cockermouth	8.25
32	Excursion	from Keswick.	
		Thursdays and Saturdays	8.00
33	Passenger		8.31

Notes

The excursion trains were run until 29th October.

No. 8. This train called at Highgate Platform to pick up school children (Monday to Friday).

No. 16. This train was worked by the engine and guard of No. 15 down to return from Keswick to Threlkeld as No. 14 up.

No 22. Horse boxes, carriage trucks and empty vehicles were not to be conveyed on this train.

No. 27. This was worked by the engine and guard of No. 26 up, returning as 24 up.

No. 30. Coal for stations west of Keswick and empty coal waggons were on this train. However empty wagons for Embleton were to be sent only on Saturdays.

Passing Arrangements for the October 1921 Working Timetable

No. 4 up to pass No. 6 down at Keswick.
No. 5 up to pass No. 6 down at Embleton and No. 8 down at Bassenthwaite Lake.
No. 6 down shunted at Embleton for No. 5 up to pass, and to pass No. 7 up at
  Cockermouth station.
No. 7 up to pass Nos. 6 & 8 down at Cockermouth station, and to pass No. 10 down at
  Threlkeld, and to pass No. 13 down at Blencow.
No. 8 up shunted at Embleton for No. 11 down to pass, and to pass No. 13 down at
  Bassenthwaite Lake, and to pass No. 14 down at Keswick.
No. 11 up to pass No. 13 down at Cockermouth station and to pass No. 14 down at
  Keswick.
No. 12 up to pass No. 14 down at Bassenthwaite Lake and to pass No. 18 down at
  Penruddock.
No. 17 up to pass No. 18 down at Bassenthwaite Lake, shunted at Troutbeck for No. 19
  up to pass, and to pass No. 26 down at Penruddock.
No. 18 up to pass No. 18 down at Bassenthwaite Lake.
No. 19 up to pass No. 18 down.at Cockermouth station, to pass No. 26 down at
  Blencow.
No. 22 up to pass No. 22 down at Cockermouth station.
No. 27 up shunted at Penruddock for No. 26 up to pass.
No. 28 up to pass No. 29 down at Bassenthwaite Lake.
No. 29 up to pass No. 32 down at Penruddock.
No. 30 down shunted at Bassenthwaite Lake for No. 28 up and No. 29 down to pass.

COCKERMOUTH, KESWICK, AND PENRITH RAILWAY.

Cumberland Lakes and Mountains.

LAKES DERWENTWATER, BUTTERMERE,
CRUMMOCK,   ULLSWATER,
THIRLMERE & BASSENTHWAITE.

MOUNTAINS SKIDDAW, HELVELLYN,
SCAFELL, &c., &c.

GOLF LINKS EMBLETON,   KESWICK,
18 holes.   9 holes.

This Railway affords the readiest access to the heart of the Lake District, and
is in immediate connection with trains to all parts. Through arrangements with the
London and North Western, North Eastern, Midland, Furness, and other Railways.

Through bookings from Bassenthwaite Lake, Cockermouth and Keswick Stations to Patterdale (Ullswater),
by Rail, Motor and Boats.

COACHES leave Keswick Station daily for Borrowdale and Buttermere over Honister Pass, passing on the
way Barrow and Lodore Waterfalls, and allowing visitors the opportunity of visiting Scale Force
Waterfall.

COACH MOTOR TOURS round Derwentwater, Bassenthwaite Lake, and Thirlmere, daily during
Summer Season.

Particulars of Arrangements and Bookings, see Company's Announcements.

Keswick Station, June, 1921.   *J. CLARK, Secretary and Manager.*

Appendix Four

Freight Working Timetable September 1930

Up Trains

			dep.	arr.	
681	Freight	from Threlkeld	8.15 am	9.17 am	QTO
682	Stopping Freight	from Penruddock	12.00	12.55 pm	QTO
684	Stopping Freight	suspended			
685	Stopping freight	from Threlkeld	11.40 am	1.39 pm	
687	Light engine	from Keswick	12.29 pm	12.40 pm	SO
689	Stopping freight	from Cockermouth Jn	10.50 am	3.11 pm	
694	Freight	from Keswick (suspended)			
695	Freight	from Keswick	2.30 pm	3.16 pm	SX
697	LNER				
	mineral empties	(Keswick at 2.50 pm)			Q
698	Freight	from Cockermouth Jn	2.59 pm	4.29 pm	
702	Freight	from Threlkeld	4.40 pm	5.54 pm	SO
703	Freight	from Keswick	5.50 pm	7.45 pm	

Down Trains

705	Stopping Freight	from Penrith	5.35 am	9.45 am	[2]
706	Stopping freight	from Penrith	5.35 am	10.15 am	[2] MO
707	Stopping freight	from Threlkeld to Keswick	7.17 am	7.28 am	
708	Stopping freight	from Threlkeld (to Keswick)	6.55 am	7.39 am	[1] [3]
709	Stopping freight	from Penrith to Threlkeld	7.40 am	9.32 am	[3]
710	Stopping freight	from Penrith to Penruddock	10.30 am	11.19 am	QTO
712	LNER mineral	Redhills at	10.18 am		Q
713	LNER mineral	Redhills at	10.18 am		QSO
715	Stopping freight	to Keswick	10.30 am	1.10 pm	SO
716	Stopping freight	to Keswick	11.00 am	1.00 pm	SX
719	Engine and brake	from Troutbeck to Threlkeld	3.40 pm	3.48 pm	
721	Freight	from Keswick			
		(to Marron Junction)	3.08 pm	5.37 pm	
727	Freight	from Keswick			
		(to Cockermouth)	7.46 pm	9.05 pm	
728	Freight	from Keswick (suspended)			

Notes

Q	Runs when needed.
SX	except Saturdays.
MO	Mondays only.
TO	Tuesdays only.
SO	Saturdays only.
[1]	708 conveys cattle. Does not run when H&C Cockermouth to Penrith runs.
[2]	705/6 convey mails.
[3]	709 does not run when 708 runs and vice versa.

Sources

Deposited Plans &c
Acts of Parliament - various
Minutes of the Meetings of the Directors of the CK&PR
Minutes of the Meetings of the Shareholders of the CK&PR
Minutes of the Meetings of the Directors of the LMSR
Minutes of the Works Committee LMSR
Letters - various
Newspapers
 Cumberland and Westmorland Herald
 Westmorland Gazette
 Penrith Observer
 Timetables - various

Personal recollections

For information about Roedean School at Keswick, the author is indebted to Miss Nina Woodcock who was a housemistress at the school during its stay in the Lake District.

Locations

The Public Record Office, Kew
House of Lords Library
House of Lords Record Office
Cumbria Archives Offices:
 Carlisle
 Kendal
Kendal Library
Penrith Library
Keswick Museum

The author thanks all those who helped during the preparation of this history of the CK&PR; the various staffs of the 'Locations' listed above and the many others who gave information and advice.

Index